A world to win
Life of a revolutionary

Tony Cliff

BOOKMARKS

London, Chicago and Sydney

A World to Win: Life of a Revolutionary – Tony Cliff
First published 2000
Bookmarks Publications Ltd, c/o 1 Bloomsbury Street, London WC1B 3QE,
England
Bookmarks, PO Box 16085, Chicago, Illinois 60616, USA
Bookmarks, PO Box A338, Sydney South, NSW 2000, Australia
Copyright © Bookmarks Publications Ltd

ISBN 1 898876 63 0 (Hardback)
ISBN 1 898876 62 2 (Paperback)

Printed by Larkham Printing and Publishing
Cover by Sherborne Design

Bookmarks Publications Ltd is linked to an international grouping of socialist
organisations:
- **Australia:** International Socialist Organisation, PO Box A338, Sydney South
- **Britain:** Socialist Workers Party, PO Box 82, London E3 3LH
- **Canada:** International Socialists, PO Box 339, Station E, Toronto, Ontario M6H
  4E3
- **Cyprus:** Ergatiki Demokratia, PO Box 7280, Nicosia
- **Denmark:** Internationale Socialister, PO Box 5113, 8100 Aarhus C
- **Germany:** Linksruck, Postfach 304 183, 20359 Hamburg
- **Greece:** Socialistiko Ergatiko Komma, c/o Workers Solidarity, PO Box 8161,
  Athens 100 10
- **Holland:** Internationale Socialisten, PO Box 92025, 1090AA Amsterdam
- **Ireland:** Socialist Workers Party, PO Box 1648, Dublin 8
- **New Zealand:** Socialist Workers Organisation, PO Box 8851, Auckland
- **Norway:** Internasjonale Socialisterr, Postboks 9226 Grønland, 0134 Oslo
- **Poland:** Workers' Democracy, PO Box 12, 01-900 Warszawa 118
- **Spain:** Socialismo Internacional, Apartado 563, 08080 Barcelona
- **United States:** International Socialist Organization, PO Box 16085, Chicago,
  Illinois 60616
- **Zimbabwe:** International Socialist Organisation, PO Box 6758, Harare

Contents

Acknowledgements

Many people have helped me in the preparation of this book. Worried that my memory may play tricks on me, I checked details of the story with a number of comrades: Roger Cox, Claire Dissington, Paul Foot, Phil Marfleet and Jim Nichol. I have a particularly great debt to Ian Birchall, whose memory is phenomenal—while the ancestors of human beings are generally apes, his ancestors were elephants. Many thanks are due to Chris Bambery, Alex Callinicos, Lindsey German, Chris Harman, Dave Hayes, John Rees, Pat Stack, Sean Vernell and Julie Waterson for advice and suggestions. Chanie Rosenberg deserves a special thanks for participating in the editing of the manuscript and typing it. Thanks are also due to Donny Gluckstein for expert critical comments and many valuable stylistic suggestions, to Dave Renton for compiling the index, and to Rob Hoveman for very efficiently seeing the book through to publication.

Chronology

1956	October-November: Hungarian Revolution.
1957	*Mao's China*.
1958	4-7 April: First CND march—London to Aldermaston.
1959	January: Cuban Revolution.
1959	*Rosa Luxemburg*.
1960	Founding of journal *International Socialism*.
1960	February: Labour Party launches Young Socialists.
1961	Launching of *Industrial Worker*, subsequently *Labour Worker*.
1962	December: Socialist Review Group becomes International Socialists.
1964	15 October: Election of Wilson's Labour government.
1966	16 January: Founding of London Industrial Shop Stewards' Defence Committee.
1966	*Incomes Policy, Legislation and Shop Stewards* (with Colin Barker).
1967	13 March onwards: Student occupation at London School of Economics.
1968	30 January: Tet Offensive in Vietnam begins.
1968	May-June: General strike in France.
1968	June: *Labour Worker* becomes *Socialist Worker*.
1968	20 August: Russian invasion of Czechoslovakia.
1968	7 September: *Socialist Worker* becomes weekly.
1968	December: International Socialists adopt democratic centralist constitution.
1969	August: British troops take responsibility for 'law and order' in Northern Ireland.
1970	*The Employers' Offensive*.
1970	18 June: Heath's Tory government elected.
1972	21-26 July: Jailing of five dockers in Pentonville.
1974	5 March: Labour government formed following miners' strike.
1974	30 March: First Rank and File conference.
1974	25 April: Portugal—army overthrows Caetano.
1975-79	*Lenin* (4 volumes).
1975	1 July: Labour government introduces wage controls.
1975	September: *Portugal at the Crossroads*
1976	28 February-20 March: Right to Work March from Manchester to London.

1976	4 November: Walsall by-election.
1977	1 January: International Socialists become Socialist Workers Party.
1977	13 August: Lewisham anti National Front demonstration.
1978	30 April: First Anti Nazi League Carnival.
1979	23 April: Blair Peach killed by police at Southall.
1979	3 May: Tory election victory—Thatcher prime minister.
1979	10-14 November: SWP conference accepts analysis of 'downturn'.
1981	Benn campaign for deputy leadership of Labour Party.
1982	17 July: Closing of *Women's Voice*.
1984	April: *Class Struggle and Women's Liberation*.
1984-85	The Great Miners' Strike.
1986	April: *Marxism and Trade Union Struggle* (with Donny Gluckstein).
1988	October: *The Labour Party: A Marxist History* (with Donny Gluckstein).
1989-93	*Trotsky* (4 volumes).
1989	10 November: Fall of Berlin Wall.
1990	31 March: Riot against poll tax.
1997	1 May: Election of Labour government under Blair.
1999	*Trotskyism After Trotsky*.

Introduction

Paul Foot

When I went to Glasgow as a young reporter in the autumn of 1961 I carried the good wishes of the socialists who were grouped around the *New Left Review*. 'Be careful,' warned Stuart Hall, *NLR* editor of the time, 'there are a lot of Trots in the Glasgow Young Socialists.' I replied that I was quite confident I could deal with the Trots, even though I hadn't the slightest idea what a Trot was. I conjured up a vision of social misfits, slightly deranged and hysterical, against whom the masses could easily be converted by a dose of standard Oxford Union rhetoric. I had been President of the Union that previous golden summer at Oxford, and had only recently come into contact with socialists of any description.

As predicted, I met the Glasgow Trots very quickly. Most of them were in the Govan and Gorbals Young Socialists on the south of the River Clyde. Their mentor at that time was a lively barber called Harry Selby, who toured Young Socialist branches in the city. If he thought you were remotely interested in his ideas, he would reach for his bag and produce tracts from Marx, Engels, Lenin and Trotsky which he would lend you on payment of a small deposit. Selby was a member of the Labour Party. He believed passionately that revolutionary socialists should be members of workers' political organisations until those organisations became revolutionary. So steadfastly did Harry believe in this concept of 'deep entrism' that he eventually became a rather ineffectual Labour Member of Parliament for Govan. He was treated with suspicion by the Labour Party, and with something approaching hatred by the Communist Party which in those days controlled the Glasgow Trades Council. To the young workers who flocked to join the newly-established Young Socialists—the youth organisation of the Labour Party—he brought enthusiasm, humour and some electrifying ideas about how the ugly and cruel capitalist society could swiftly be changed by a revolution. When asked about Russia, he would reply that Russia was a 'degenerated workers' state' whose socialism had been corrupted by a Stalinist clique. The clique could quite easily be re-moved by a political revolution, though not a social revolution. The distinction was a little difficult to understand but, it seemed to me, would have to be accepted for the time being. My general approach was that the Oxford Union had little or nothing to contribute to these young firebrands, and my most sensible course was to keep quiet. Thus did I fulfil my promise to 'deal with the Trots' by effectively accepting everything they said. If I had any doubts, I quickly relegated them. The building of the Berlin Wall, I explained at one Young Socialist open air meeting just off Sauchiehall Street, had a clear purpose: to stop 'bourgeois elements' so vital to economic growth from leaving the country. When a rude fellow shouted, 'Nonsense, man—it's to keep the workers in,' I conveniently (and accurately) wrote him off as a drunk.

Some time during the winter of 1961-62 Gus MacDonald, the most able and engaging of the Govan and Gorbals Young Socialists, decided that the movement needed a theoretical shot in the arm somewhat stronger than that provided by Harry Selby. He told me he had heard of a Trotskyist sect based in London called the Socialist Review Group, and that its two leaders, Tony Cliff and Michael Kidron, were outstanding speakers. He duly set up a weekend school addressed by the two men. Their subjects covered the entire face of the earth, including Russia.

I went down with Gus to the British European Airways terminal in St Enoch Square to meet the mysterious duo. They arrived late on a flight from London. As they walked into the terminal I was struck by the differences between them. Mike Kidron was impeccably dressed, urbane and charming. His companion Cliff, short and scruffy, was plainly terrified of being bored. The usual chatter about the times of the plane and the journey to the place where they were staying noticeably irritated and embarrassed him. As we climbed into a taxi I spotted a newspaper poster about the war in the Congo. 'The Congo,' I sighed. 'I just haven't a clue what I think about that.' Quick as a flash, the dishevelled mess in the corner of the taxi sprang into life and, without pausing for even a moment's dialogue, let loose a volley of sentences impossible to decipher but equally impossible not to understand. I can't remember exactly what he said over the next ten minutes or so, but I do know that I never again had any doubts about the role of European and US imperialism in the Congo, and the subservience to that imperialism of the United Nations. I found to my surprise that

I was laughing, not because anything said had been especially funny but just because the political explanation was so obvious.

Over and over again in the 40 years or so since that first conversation I have had to stop myself bursting out laughing at something Cliff said. This is not only because he was a public speaker of natural and exceptional wit, but chiefly because of his ability to explain an issue with such clarity and force that I could not help laughing at my own inability previously to understand it. Another point struck me during that momentous weekend. The contributions from the platform seemed to be completely free of the self regard or self interest which I had come to expect as standard qualities in political speakers. There were no votes to be won, no careers at stake. There was only one driving force, one reason for what was being said: conviction.

The first bombshell dropped by Cliff was that Russia was not a degenerated workers' state, indeed not a workers' state at all. The forms of political organisation in Russia—no stock exchange or private profit—might appear socialistic but the content of that organisation, exploitation of the working class by a new ruling class, was capitalist. If Russia was state capitalist, moreover, so were the Russian satellites in Eastern Europe, so was China, so (this was far too much for me to take at the time, so soon after the Cuban Revolution) was Cuba.

In this little life story Cliff reveals how he puzzled over this issue for years before bouncing out of bed one morning and declaring to his long-suffering wife, Chanie, 'Russia is state capitalist.'

This issue may seem arcane, almost irrelevant in the 1990s, but to a young socialist at the beginning of the 1960s it was utterly crucial. The entire politics of the left were dominated by Russia and its supporters in the British Communist Party. My very first recollection of a difficult political argument was the alleged difference between the British and French invasion of Egypt in 1956 and the Russian invasion of Hungary a few weeks later. The first was plainly an act of blatant imperialism; the second (since Russia was a degenerated workers' state) a skilful device to protect the workers' states from reactionaries elsewhere, including the right wing fifth column in Budapest. Another consequence of supporting Russia against the West was a scepticism about democracy. Indeed, the very word 'democracy' was suspect, since it appeared to exist only in the capitalist West and hardly at all in the workers' states in the East.

Cliff laid waste to all this. Russia was state capitalist, he asserted, and therefore imperialist. The Russian invasion of Hungary was every bit as outrageous as that of Britain and France at Suez. The essence of socialism was the social control of society from below; and there was none of that in Russia, even less in any of what he called Stalin's satellites in Eastern Europe. Indeed, he observed, although he was down to speak about the Soviet Union, he could not even begin to do so since 'soviet' was the Russian word for workers' council and there were no proper soviets in any of the Russian Empire.

It is hard, after so long a period, to convey the effect of such opinions in the political atmosphere of the early 1960s. In this book Cliff tells the story of his conversion to the theory that Russia was state capitalist almost in passing. For those of us young socialists of the time to whom the theory was entirely new, the effect was the very opposite of transitory. It was devastating. It threatened not only a residual sympathy for what seemed at least like state planning in Russia, but also a whole view of politics, including, crucially, the notion that socialist change could come from the top of society, planned and executed by enlightened people, educated ministers and bureaucrats. The whole purpose of the Oxford Union was threatened by this message. For if Russia was state capitalist, what was the point of working politically with other enlightened people, for instance for more state control of British industry?

I resolved on no account to be hijacked by this new heresy. I got hold of a moth-eaten paperback edition of Cliff's book on the subject, then entitled *Stalinist Russia: A Marxist Analysis*, and read it so carefully that it fell to pieces. The broad brush of the theory fascinated me almost as much as it horrified me. But the broad brush did not matter. Cliff's writing style was hopeless—he had not the slightest idea how to use the English language to make his point. What finally convinced me was the relentless detail of the argument. It was in the chapter on the separation of the Russian Communist Party from the rank and file of the Russian working class, in the pages in which Cliff traced the removal from all political office of any trace either of the Russian Revolution or of the working class rank and file, that my resistance finally snapped. There was no way in which such a rigid and brutal bureaucratic society could be described either as socialist or as a workers' state, or indeed as even marginally democratic. 'State capitalist' exactly fitted the bill.

Not much later, when I was still in Glasgow in 1963, the third volume of Isaac Deutscher's majestic biography of Trotsky was published.

I read all three volumes in quick succession, utterly overcome by the depth of analysis and the grandeur of the language. When I exulted over the book to Cliff, he was not at all impressed. In an article in the 1963 winter edition of the quarterly magazine *International Socialism*, each issue of which, incidentally, I looked forward to with my first-ever intellectual passion, he wrote a ferocious attack on Deutscher, entitled 'The End of the Road: Deutscher's Capitulation to Stalinism'. With hardly a word of appreciation for the magnificent biography, Cliff honed in on a passage in a separate Deutscher article in a collection of essays entitled *Heretics and Renegades* in which the sage set out this advice to an 'ex-Communist man of letters' like himself. 'He cannot join the Stalinist camp or the anti-Stalinist holy alliance without doing violence to his better self. So let him overcome the cheap ambition to have a finger in the political pie. He may withdraw into the watchtower instead—to watch with detachment and alertness this heaving chaos of a world.' This conclusion sent Cliff into paroxysms of rage. Anyone who ever said a word in support of Isaac Deutscher was screeched at interminably: 'To the watchtower! To the watchtower!' Of all the awful crimes of the left, none infuriated Cliff like passivity. For people who knew the world was rotten, to sit back and do nothing about it was for him the ultimate aberration.

So it was for Trotsky. Many years later Cliff himself wrote a four-volume biography of Trotsky. I would still recommend the Deutscher but, like his equally long biography of Lenin, Cliff's *Trotsky* is indispensable to modern socialists. Throughout all his books the theme is action. The key question surpassing all others is Lenin's—what is to be done? At every twist and turn in the tussle between the classes, some action needs to be taken by the exploited majority. This is why the most fundamental issue of all is the building of a socialist organisation which takes its cue from the workers' battles against their rulers, and can unite in disciplined action the resources not just of those who want to change the world but of those prepared to do something about it.

This story starts in Cliff's childhood in Palestine. He often said that the case for socialism takes less than two minutes to understand—a mere glance at the world and the way it is divided into rich and poor makes that case immediately. A mere glance at the way Arab children were treated in Palestine in the 1930s was enough to make Cliff a socialist. Disillusionment with the compromising Communist Party soon followed. And so Cliff's youth was devoted unswervingly to a most fantastic aim: the building of a Trotskyist organisation in poor old impoverished, looted and divided Palestine. When he had little or no success at that, he duly devoted almost all the rest of his life to an even more fantastic aim: building a revolutionary socialist organisation in comfortable bourgeois post-war Britain. Everything round him militated against his objective. A Labour government was in office with a huge majority, supported by the vast mass of the working class. Any activity to the left of Labour was entirely monopolised by the Communist Party. For good measure, Cliff's early efforts were frustrated by his expulsion from Britain and five years enforced, isolated and utterly impoverished exile in Dublin. Reading this book's breezy account, you can't help wondering—where did he get the resolve to continue? Even when he was allowed to return to his wife and family in London, membership of his Socialist Review Group seldom exceeded 20. This book tells the rather fitful story of how, against impossible odds, the Socialist Review Group grew into the International Socialists which in turn (for reasons which are still not entirely clear) became the Socialist Workers Party. Since the comparatively huge edifice of the Communist Party vanished in a puff of smoke in 1989, the (still tiny) SWP became by far the largest socialist grouping in the country. Indeed, the only socialists who have survived the fall of Stalinism of 1989 with some confidence are those who consistently denounced it.

Tony Cliff was not a humble man and his account (which he started only because he was afraid he was about to die under the surgeon's knife) seldom errs on the side of modesty. Nor should it. For the characteristic which emerges from his life more than any other is single-mindedness. In spite of his wide-ranging intellect, his mastery of at least four languages and his extensive reading, he never allowed himself for a single moment of his 82 years to be deflected from his purpose. Such indomitable resolve is rare indeed among people who set out to change the world. When Cliff was accused, as he often was, of lionising the greats in socialist history—Marx, Engels, Lenin, Trotsky, Luxemburg—he replied that, if we want to see what is happening beyond the crowd, we have to stand on the shoulders of giants.

He would have been embarrassed, though I think quite happy, to be bracketed with the greats, but there are quite a few of us socialists in Britain over the past 40 years or so who thank our lucky stars that we had the chance to stand on his shoulders.

Preface

A preliminary remark: why am I engaged in writing this biography? In 1998, having been politically active for some 65 years, and in recent times speaking on average at three meetings a week (quite often travelling away from London and staying for a night or two away from home), I was instructed by my doctors to slow down due to a heart condition. I shouldn't complain. When I was 18 years old my doctor told me I would never reach the age of 30 because of my heart. However, he had not asked me when I had had my last meal. He did not know that as an activist I subsisted on a meagre diet of bread and of oranges 'that fell off the back of an orchard'.

But now I have no alternative but to obey orders. To do much original research is too much for me. I did manage in the four weeks prior to the heart operation to write a short book, *Trotskyism After Trotsky: The Origins of the International Socialists*. This was an easy task as it relied on my writings over the years since 1946. I lifted whole chunks from previous works.

However, the thought of doing nothing filled me with horror. My daughters Elana and Anna suggested that the most useful thing I could do while waiting for the operation was to write my autobiography.

If in the end the essay is not worthwhile, the wastepaper basket is there to be filled. However, I hope it can be a useful companion to *Trotskyism After Trotsky*. Where that book dealt with theories developed to adapt to changes in the capitalist world, the first part of this book concentrates on the genesis of those theories from a milieu of isolation and imposed independence of thinking that was my situation in Palestine. The latter part of the book looks at the effort to implement strategies and tactics which relate these theories and the wider aspects of Marxism to the practice of building a revolutionary socialist party.

There are difficulties in writing a political biography. The personal story must be entwined with the social and political history. Human beings act in a social and political environment that shapes them while they affect and change it. How much space has to be given to one element as against others depends on how much the reader is expected to know of the history of the period. I was politically active in Palestine for some 14 years (1932-46); then I was in Britain for a year; then four and a half years in Dublin (1947-52); and finally in Britain for the last 47 years. Readers probably know very little about the history of Palestine in the above period. Yet even when it comes to Britain the difficulties do not cease.

In a political biography of someone active in the revolutionary movement in Russia over four decades, the peaks of its history will be well known. It could be the 1905 revolution, the 1917 revolution, the civil war, or Stalin's liquidation of all the old Bolsheviks and establishment of the gulag. It is true that British working class history also has impressive peaks over the last four decades. For example, in 1972 the five dockers jailed in Pentonville prison for union activities were freed as the result of an all-out strike in the docks, solidarity action by printers (who stopped Fleet Street), and widespread strikes in the engineering industry which prompted the TUC to call for a one-day general strike. Alas, the peaks in Russia look like the heights of the Himalayas, in Britain like Ben Nevis. Many people know about the Himalayas; far fewer about Ben Nevis. This forces me, in the twin story of history and biography, to devote a lot of space to the former.

Added to these difficulties is my longevity. Lenin was both delighted and proud that his party was a party of youth:

> We are the party of the future, and the future belongs to the youth. We are a party of innovators, and it is always the youth that most eagerly follows the innovators. We are a party that is waging a self-sacrificing struggle against the old rottenness, and youth is always the first to undertake a self-sacrificing struggle.
>
> No, let us leave it to the [liberal bourgeois] Cadets to collect the 'tired' old men of 30, revolutionaries who have 'grown wise', and renegades from [revolutionary Marxist] Social Democracy. We shall always be a party of the youth of the advanced class![1]

Of course Lenin was right: the revolutionary party is overwhelmingly an organisation made up of young people. In Tsarist Russia, under the very harsh conditions of illegality, many revolutionaries drifted away in their 30s. In Britain possibly the threshold comes a little later, let us say, around the 40s. Of course many of the Bolsheviks who dropped out of activity in the period of reaction following the 1905 revolution returned to the fold in 1917. I am sure that 99 percent of the comrades who have left the International Socialists or the Socialist Workers Party have not changed their basic political beliefs. But still my longevity demands more space being given to the historical element in the biography than had I died at, say, the age of 40. I apologise.

Readers may be shocked by the narrowness of my own life story outside politics, and they will be absolutely right. I so concentrated on the political side of life that I neglected wider emotional and cultural elements. Division of labour increases productivity. This was demonstrated brilliantly by Adam Smith in his *Wealth of Nations*, when he showed how, if one worker previously only producing pins, was replaced by a group of workers with a division of labour doing different tasks, productivity rose enormously. But there is another side to the coin. Division of labour raises productivity but, alas, it makes a person half-human. There is a round hole for a round peg, and a square hole for a square peg. However, there is no hole in the image of man. Scarcity of resources, belonging for a long time to tiny groups of revolutionaries, forced me to concentrate every sinew of my being on the task ahead. For 65 years I found the going hard, with very little leeway for relaxation, for avoiding the extreme specialisation I chose.

I remember in Palestine one member of the group said to me, 'You fuck for world revolution.' I thought that was a compliment. At the age of 16 I met my first girlfriend. She was five months younger than me and we stayed together for six years. After being together for a few months she asked me one day, 'Do you remember what you said to me the first time we kissed?' I said I did not. She reminded me: 'You asked me, "If I gave you a hand grenade, would you throw it into a police station?" ' I asked her for her reaction. 'I was simply petrified,' she said. (I was never inclined to individual terrorism; it was simply a test of her revolutionary fervour.)

The way I met Chanie Rosenberg, my wife, is not a story of watching the full moon together, although in Palestine it is really beautiful in summer. Our getting together was far more prosaic. A few weeks after we first met in her kibbutz I contacted Chanie and asked her to come to Tel Aviv to translate into English and then type a leaflet for the British troops still in the country. I don't know if personality traits are inherited but only one of my children seems to have inherited my obsessive nature, and with curious results. My son Danny has the same attitude to music as I have to politics, which is probably why he is the only one of my four kids who has not joined the SWP. He is too busy composing and performing at the keyboard as the only white member of a well-known black band.

I was not always so narrow-minded. Until the age of 17 I devoured literary classics unceasingly. Decades later I still carried on a great love of the theatre. In Dublin, when I was financially hard up, I still managed to go to the theatre at least once a fortnight. But the priorities of revolutionary politics extinguished these aspects of my life.

My narrowness is not a demonstration of humanity under socialism. Thank heaven for the Chanies of this world whose interests are far more universal and who follow artistic and cultural pursuits with enthusiasm. Chanie and I are like chalk and cheese. She is very interested in the arts, goes to concerts, art exhibitions, and is herself a sculptress (and I think a talented one, if the sculptures that fill our house are anything to go by). With such a big difference between us, how can it be explained that we have been together for 55 years, and are at present closer to one another than ever? Basically we have something in common far more important than character traits: both of us are dedicated revolutionaries. Of Chanie I can say without exaggeration that she has devotion to the cause, energy, purity of character and unsurpassed steadfastness.

One incident demonstrates very well Chanie's single-mindedness. Being not a very good driver, she knocked down a dustman in Hackney. She visited him in hospital and recruited him to our organisation. Since then I have repeatedly asked her why she does not run over other dustmen, as we have too few of them in the organisation. Alas, she does not listen to me.

I always look at myself as a means to an end, not as an end in itself. To sculpt a beautiful David, Michelangelo did not use a beautiful hammer and chisel.

If I had to live my life again I would not change it radically. Of course I would like to have committed fewer mistakes, and besides the commissions, also made less omissions.

This book is about my life, about the past, but I hope it will also be a weapon in the long struggle for the future.

Chapter 1

Palestine

My childhood

I was born in Palestine on 20 May 1917, at the end of the Ottoman occupation of Palestine and the beginning of the British takeover that lasted for 31 years. At the time of my birth some 95 percent of the country's people were Arabs, and they continued to be the overwhelming majority for many years to come; in 1945 Arabs made up 68 percent of the population.

I was born to a middle class family. My parents, uncles and aunts were dedicated Zionists. My father and mother came to Palestine from the Russian part of Poland in 1902; one of my uncles came as early as 1888. The political background of my parents was very right wing. I remember seeing a photograph of Tsar Nikolai II meeting a delegation of the Jewish community in Russia led by Banker Gluckstein, blessing the Tsar to overcome his enemies. Banker Gluckstein was my father's elder brother. Thank heaven I do not believe in predestination, and I do not believe there is a gene for right wing ideas.

My father was a big contractor who built sections of the Hedjaz Railway. His building partner was Chaim Weitzman, the first president of Israel. Friends of my family were among the leading Zionists. Moshe Sharet (later foreign minister), a frequent visitor at our home, was a kind of political teacher to me. When I stayed with my uncle Kalvarisky in Rehavia, David Ben Gurion would sometimes come to ask him for something, or to Paula (his wife) to ask for a folding bed. Dr Hillel Yoffe (a leading Zionist) was another uncle of mine. My family was implanted at the core of the Zionist community. This probably made it more difficult for me to break from Zionism.

The fact that my parents, as well as my uncles and aunts, came from Tsarist Russia, where anti-Semitism was rampant, of course slowed my move away from Zionism. My family, like all families from Europe, in later years suffered the horrors of the Holocaust. I met only a few family members who were exterminated by Hitler, although I heard of many others. One was an aunt who came to visit us in Palestine from Danzig (later called Gdansk) in the mid-1930s. Then there was a daughter of my uncle Kalvarisky, whom I knew very well—she was the same age as my older brother. She married a Dutch Jew with whom she had a child aged five when we met. All three of them were victims of the Holocaust.

Chanie's family suffered no less, but as she lived in South Africa she had no opportunity to meet them. As a matter of fact there is probably not one Jewish family in Europe or the US which did not have many of its members fall victim to the Holocaust. Oriental, Sephardic and Yemenite Jews were largely not trapped in this way.

It took me a few years to make the transition from being an orthodox Zionist to being a semi-Zionist with a pro-Palestinian position and then to making a complete break with Zionism.

My parents were very hurt when it was recorded in the local paper that my elder brother and I were arrested for distributing anti-Zionist leaflets in 1937. My mother was in tears, but I heard my father reassuring her: 'He will grow out of it'. It was especially painful to them, as I was the baby of the family, and also had been sickly for many years, so that great attention had been paid to me. I only managed to stand at the age of two and at the age of five I was taken to Vienna to see a rheumatism specialist. After this my health improved a lot.

Different circumstances and events trigger socialist ideas in individuals. A specific issue of oppression can lead an individual to become a critic of existing society. Nobody becomes a socialist because he or she read Marx—the reading of Marx is the result of looking for an explanation for the injustices of society. Similarly the Utopian Socialism of Charles Fourier and Robert Owen—the criticism of class exploitation and oppression, and the aspiration for a classless society —preceded the scientific socialism of Marx and Engels. Every individual goes through a similar experience by first becoming a critic of society and then looking for ways to change it.

The specific spur that pushed me to become a socialist was the wretched conditions of Arab kids that I witnessed. While I was always shod, I saw Arab kids running barefoot all the time. Another issue was that there were no Arab kids in my class at school. It seemed unnatural to me that it should be like that. After all, my own kids, born and educated in England, never came home to tell us there were no English kids in the school (though I would not have been surprised if they said there were no Dutch, Danish or French kids). After all, we live in England. At the age of 13 or 14 I wrote a school essay, as all the kids were asked to do, but the subject of my essay was: 'It is so sad there are no Arab kids in the school'. The teacher's comment was short and clear: she wrote, 'Communist'. I had never dreamt of considering myself a communist until then. For the rest of my life I have felt very grateful to this teacher. I wish I could hug and kiss her.

There was another factor which focused my attention on the issue of the exclusion of Arab kids from the school. There was one small school in the country where Arab and Jewish kids were together. This school came into being and was financed by an uncle of mine, Chaim Margalit-Kalvarisky. He was very well off, being head of Rothschild's organisation in Palestine. He also founded a minuscule group of liberal Jews and Arabs called Brit Shalom (Peace League). This uncle was the butt of my father's and mother's derision as they thought he was mad. He was so single minded that he hardly talked about anything else except peace with the Arabs. When he met Chanie for the first time he did not ask her about anything but barged straight into the subject of peace with the Arabs. Chanie thought there was a great similarity between him and me—both a bit deranged. She said to me, 'There must be a blood relationship explaining it.' I told her Kalvarisky was not related by blood but through marriage: he married my father's sister. His actions probably concentrated my attention on the issue of the exclusion of Arabs from my school even more. I identified myself with the underdogs.

The exclusion of Arabs was not confined to education. They were also excluded from Jewish-owned houses. This segregation meant that throughout the 29 years I lived in Palestine I never lived in a house with Arabs. As a matter of fact the first time I lived with a Palestinian Arab in the same house was in 1947 when I stayed in a small boarding house in Dublin.

Another factor that spurred me to identify with the Palestinians was the name my parents gave me—Ygael (Gluckstein). This was taken from a John Wayne type Zionist hero who murdered a number of Arabs. At the age of 13 I changed my name from Ygael to Ygal. Seeing that in Hebrew there are no vowels but only consonants the two names are spelt in exactly the same way, so it was easy to do. The root of the name Ygal is this: Moses sent 12 spies from the 12 tribes of Israel to go to Canaan to spy out the land. Two said they would like to settle there; ten said they would not. The first of those who did not want to settle was called Ygal.

Closed Zionist economy

The Zionists who emigrated to Palestine at the end of the 19th century wanted its whole population to be Jewish. In South Africa, by contrast, the whites were the capitalists and their hangers-on while the blacks were the workers. In Palestine, with the very low standard of living of the Arabs compared to Europeans, and with widespread open and hidden unemployment, the means of excluding the Arabs was by closing the Jewish labour market to them. There were a number of methods used to achieve this. First, the Jewish National Fund, owner of a big proportion of the land owned by Jews, including a large chunk of Tel Aviv, had a statute that insisted only Jews could be employed on this land.

I remember in 1945 a cafe in Tel Aviv was attacked and almost entirely broken up because of a rumour that there was an Arab working in the kitchen washing the dishes. I also remember, when I was in the Hebrew University in Jerusalem between 1936 and 1939, repeated demonstrations against the vice-chancellor of the university, Dr Magnes. He was a rich American Jew and a liberal, and his crime was that he was the tenant of an Arab landlord. Probably no student of, let us say, the London School of Economics knows or cares whether the vice-chancellor owns his own house or rents it from a Catholic, Protestant or Jewish landlord.

In March 1932 David Ben Gurion, the leader of Mapai, the Party of the Workers of Eretz Israel, and a future prime minister of Israel, made it clear that he was vehemently against the employment of Arab workers by Jews. He said, 'Nobody must think that we have become reconciled to the existence of non-Jewish labour in the villages. We will not forgo, I say we will not forgo, one place of work in the country. I say to you with full responsibility that it is less shameful to establish a brothel than to evict the Jews from their work on the land of Palestine.' Do not think that these were mere idle words. Tel Aviv's numerous brothels could hold their own with the best of them, but there was not a single Arab worker in the town.

In this attitude there was no real distinction between right or left Zionists. The left Zionist socialists of Hashomer Hatzair did not lag behind and there is no doubt that Bentov, one of their leaders, was right in saying, 'Mapai hasn't the monopoly over the demand for Jewish labour. We are for maximal expansion of Jewish labour and for its control in the Jewish economy'.[2] Indeed in all the many instances of picketing against

Arab labour there is not a single instance when Hashomer Hatzair did not participate in or at least support the pickets.

The Zionist trade union federation, the Histadrut (General Federation of Hebrew Labour), imposed on all its members two levies: one for the defence of Hebrew labour and one for the defence of the Hebrew product. The Histadrut organised pickets against orchard owners who employed Arab workers, forcing the owners to sack them.

I remember the following incident. It was when Chanie was quite new to the country and she joined me to live just next to the Jewish market in Tel Aviv. One day she saw a young Jewish man walking among the women selling vegetables and eggs, and from time to time he smashed the eggs with his boot or poured paraffin on the vegetables. She asked, 'What is he doing?' I explained that he was checking whether the women were Jewish or Arab. If the former, it was alright; if the latter, he used force. Chanie reacted, 'That's just like South Africa', from where she had just come. I replied, 'It's worse. In South Africa the blacks are at least employed.'

Chanie arrived in Palestine in June 1945, and we started living together in October of the same year. We were desperately poor and our only income was the pittance earned by Chanie as a part-time English teacher. We rented a room in a huge squalid suburb on the outskirts of Tel Aviv, built on sand dunes with no roads or amenities—something never mentioned in Zionist propaganda. The landlord was a Yemenite from a community known as 'black Jews'. His wife, aged 25, already had a number of children, had lost all her teeth and was as thin as a rake. On our request for a room to rent the landlord pointed to an empty sand dune. 'Where's the room?' we asked. 'It'll be there tomorrow', he said, and amazingly it was—a tiny room with walls of single brick thickness and floor tiles laid out directly on the sand. When it rained the water flowed underneath the tiles, creating a damp fog which turned our shoes, books and everything else in the room green. Our books were further devoured by mice. Our kitchen was a primus stove, our lighting an Aladdin lamp. The toilet was a communal flush-toilet, considered superior to the traditional floor toilet which was on another dune and did not flush. Our bed was a two and a half foot metal structure donated by the Zionist authorities to all immigrants that sagged right down the middle. It regularly became infested with lice and every week we conducted a louse-burning ceremony with our primus stove 'to welcome the Sabbath!'

A friend visiting us once leaned on the window and the whole frame came out. This same friend worked in a restaurant and sometimes brought us Wiener schnitzels which were beginning to rot and could not be used for customers. For us this was a treat which we added to our potato, spaghetti and orange diet. Once a month we treated ourselves to a restaurant meal of camel meat, the cheapest type on the menu. In this room I worked on my 400-page book on the Middle East which Chanie translated into English and then typed on an old, almost broken, typwriter. She did this no less than eight times over till it reached its final form.

Chanie's parents decided to move to Israel from South Africa and we could not possibly let them see our conditions. So we succeeded, at great expense for our limited means, in finding a room consisting of half the boiler room in a tall block of flats. It was six feet wide, enough to accommodate a bed and wardrobe which we were donated. At the foot of the bed was a small table with a side that dropped down to enable the door to open and close. We considered this room luxurious compared to our previous one. However, Chanie's father nearly fainted when he saw it, and remarked, 'But my garage is three times the size.'

When mass arrests by the British took place prior to the establishment of the state of Israel, we had to stuff all our illegal papers down the toilet, which refused, in the end, to accommodate our wishes. By good fortune the British soldiers making the arrests did not go into the toilet, and we were released after many hours and Chanie sweet-talking the soldiers in English. This persuaded them to forgo investigation into my status as a wanted person with a summons over by head.

All the comrades lived in this poverty, yet we still made collections to assist our comrades internationally—like for our Italian group fighting their elections. The members' subscription to the group was a day's wages a week. This, and the extra collections we made meant members went without meals in order to pay.

While Zionism dug a wide and deep trench to separate Jews from Arabs, imperialism colluded. When the British administration in Palestine did employ both Arabs and Jews to do the same jobs, they paid the Arab workers about a third of what they paid Jewish workers. The policy of 'divide and rule' dominated everything, even prison. When I was arrested in September 1939 I was taken to a prison in which there were only Jewish prisoners. The conditions there were not different to those prevailing in Arab prisons. We had to sleep on the floor—43 of us packed together like sardines—so that at night it was not possible to turn over. At six in the evening we were locked in for 12 hours. A bucket served as a communal lavatory. The place stank. Early in the morning our first job was to delouse ourselves and our blankets. Food came in a large cauldron, and each prisoner had to put his hand in the broth and fish out a piece of meat to eat; after this the broth was poured into each tin bowl. But the conditions improved radically when I was transferred to a new prison. It still contained only Jews, but this time it was within sight of nearby Arab prisoners so that they could compare conditions. Suddenly we got beds, and a lavatory separate from the room we slept in.

The policy of the Labour Zionists towards the Arabs sat awkwardly with their constantly repeated statements of sympathy towards them in the early years of Zionist colonization. Thus in 1915 Ben Gurion wrote:

> Under no circumstances must the rights of these inhabitants (ie, the Arabs) be touched. Only 'Ghetto-dreamers' like Zangwill could imagine that Palestine can be given to the Jews in addition to the right to drive the non-Jews out of the country. No state will agree to this. Even if it seemed that this right might be given to us…the Jews have no justification and no possibility of exercising it. It is not the task of Zionism to drive the present inhabitants out of Palestine; if it had this aim it would merely be a dangerous Utopia, a harmful and reactionary Fata Morgana.[3]

In 1920 Ben Gurion wrote about the fellah, the Arab farmer, and his land as follows, 'Under no circumstances must the land be touched which belongs to the fellah and which he tills. Those who live from their hands' toil must not be torn away from their soil, not even for financial compensation'.[4] 'The fate of the Jewish worker is tied up with that of the Arab one. They will rise together and fall together,' he said in 1924.[5] Later on, in 1926, he said, 'The Arab population is an organic insoluble part of Palestine. It is rooted here, it works here and will stay here. Though it is not impossible at the present time to expel great masses of people from a country with the aid of physical force, only lunatics or political quacks could accuse the Jewish people of harbouring such a desire'.[6] Dr Weitzman, president of the World Zionist Organisation and future first president of Israel, said in a speech in London on 11 December 1929, 'Up till now there has been no case—and I hope there will be none in the future—where an Arab has been ousted from his land, either directly or indirectly.'

If such declarations are of any value, we could even cite Jabotinsky, the representative of the most extreme and greedy Zionist wing, the Revisionists (now the Likud Party), who once declared some of his fundamental principles to be:

Equality of all citizens.

Equal rights must be maintained for all citizens regardless of race, religion, language and class, in all walks of the public life of the country.

In every cabinet where a Jew is prime minister, an Arab will be his deputy and vice versa...[7]

However, these were merely lullabies that Zionists sang to the Arab population of the country to put them to sleep. The logic of the development of Zionism led to changes over time in the attitude toward the Arabs. The greater the Zionist advance, the more it fed Arab resentment and resistance. This fed back into a deeper and deeper fear of the Arabs among the Jews.

Jewish workers trapped by Zionism

The working class of Palestine was deeply divided between Arabs and Jews. Arabs and Jews used different languages—only a tiny minority of Jewish workers understood Arabic, and an even smaller minority of Arabs understood Hebrew. In a few workplaces there were both Jews and Arabs. Thus of the 5,000 or so railway workers in the early 1940s some four fifths were Arabs and a fifth Jews. The oil refinery in Acre employed both Arabs and Jews, again the majority Arabs. The lowest echelon of the civil service also employed workers from the two communities. But these were exceptions. Some nine tenths of all workers were in segregated workplaces.

One incident warmed my heart, seeing Arab and Jewish workers together. It was one evening at the beginning of the 1940s when I was travelling on a bus from Acre to Haifa. It was full of Arab and Jewish workers from the Acre oil refinery. Among them were two members of our group. They started singing socialist songs in Arabic. One of them followed this by saying, 'Let us sing in Hebrew for our Jewish brethren.' And so they did. This was marvellous but, alas, it was like a meteor only briefly lighting up a very dark night.

Ideologically, 'Zionist socialism' trapped its supporters, preventing them from making a clear break from chauvinism and imperialism, although some of them very often condemned both.

An illustration of the complexity of Zionist socialism and of the contradictions tearing it apart is the following. When Chanie came to Palestine from South Africa she was a member of the most left wing trend in the Zionist socialist movement—Hashomer Hatzair. They considered themselves Marxists and some described themselves as Trotskyist. She joined a kibbutz (collective farm) belonging to the Hashomer Hatzair movement. In the kibbutz there is no private ownership of wealth or private property. Production is collective. Consumption is collective. The rearing of children is done collectively. There is no individual kitchen, etc. The members of the kibbutz saw it as an embryo of a future socialist society. And here there is a paradox. A short while before Chanie arrived the members of the kibbutz faced a nasty test. There were four kibbutzim and four Arab villages in this particular valley, surrounding a stony hill. The kibbutzim all decided to oust the Arabs from their villages which were on land the Jewish National Fund had bought from Arab landlords. They therefore formed a long phalanx at the foot of the hill, picked up stones as they climbed up and threw them at the Arabs on the other side. These Arab tenants had cultivated this land for generations, and they had received nothing at all from their landlords for their land. They fled in fear and the Zionists took over the whole hill. Chanie then decided to find out what the 'Trotskyists' in the Hashomer Hatzair kibbutzim were doing politically, and went round the country to visit them. She found them—mostly, oddly enough, cowherds—fully immersed in the economy and life of their particular kibbutz, and not relating to the Arab workers or peasants at all, or to the political crimes of the Zionists.

A little story shows how enthusiastic but naive I was about my politics at this time. A short while after the ousting of the Arab tenants I was invited to come and speak at this kibbutz. Our group was contacted and asked for a speaker. I arrived at the kibbutz on Friday afternoon, after the end of the working day. A dozen comrades, all from South Africa, came to listen to me. I started speaking at 2pm and went on speaking until 1am. After asking for questions (but allowing no time for them) I then went on speaking till 4am. A few days later

Chanie told me the following, 'I understood Hebrew better than the other comrades but still I couldn't follow you. You spoke so fast that I only managed to pick out key words like "capitalism", "socialism", "Zionism", "internationalism" and "revolution". The others didn't understand anything.' Disillusioned with the prospects of revolutionary progress through the Kibbutz movement Chanie then left the kibbutz, came to Tel Aviv and we started living together. Probably one of the spurs for her to join me was the wish to understand what I had said at the time! We have been together now for 55 years and she probably still doesn't know what I said. I certainly don't remember.

The Zionist socialists were trapped ideologically. They believed that the future belonged to socialism, that in the kibbutz we could see the embryo of a future socialist society (rather than a collective unit of colonists). But in the meantime Arab resistance to Zionist colonisation had to be overcome so they collaborated with Zionist moneybags and rich institutions as well as the British army and police. The Zionist socialists held the *Communist Manifesto* in one hand and a coloniser's gun in the other.

Of course there was class conflict within the Jewish community in Palestine. Workers and capitalists did fight round wages and conditions. But the Zionist colonial expansion blunted the class struggle and prevented it from taking the political form of opposition to Zionism and imperialism, and solidarity with the Arab exploited and oppressed.

The contradiction in consciousness of Jewish workers in Palestine arose from the fact that while they were in conflict with the Arabs, at the same time they came from the background of a community with a socialist consciousness. Thus in Poland, where the biggest community of Jews in Europe existed at the time, council elections took place in December 1938 and January 1939 in Warsaw, Lodz, Cracow, Lvov, Vilna and other cities. The Bund, the Jewish socialist workers' anti-Zionist organisation, received 70 percent of the votes in the Jewish districts. The Bund won 17 out of 20 seats in Warsaw while the Zionists took only one.

Dependence on imperialism

Knowing that they would face resistance from the Palestinians the Zionists were always clear that they needed the help of the imperialist power that had the major influence in Palestine at the time.

On 19 October 1898 Theodore Herzl, the founder of Zionism, went to Constantinople to have an audience with Kaiser Wilhelm. At that time Palestine was in the Ottoman Empire which was a junior partner of Germany. Herzl told the Kaiser that a Zionist settlement in Israel would increase German influence as the centre of Zionism was in Austria, another partner of the German Empire. Herzl also dangled another carrot: 'I explained that we were taking the Jews away from the revolutionary parties.'

Towards the end of the First World War, when it was clear Britain was going to take over Palestine, the leader of the Zionists at the time, Chaim Weitzmann, contacted the British foreign secretary, Arthur Balfour, getting from him on 2 November 1917 a declaration promising the Jews a homeland in Palestine. Sir Ronald Storrs, the first British military governor of Jerusalem, explained that the Zionist 'enterprise was one that blessed him that gave as well as him that took, by forming for England "a little loyal Jewish Ulster" in a sea of potentially hostile Arabism.' The Zionists would be the Orangemen of Palestine.

With the Second World War it became clear that the main power in the Middle East would cease to be Britain and would be the US. Ben Gurion, the Zionist leader at the time, therefore rushed to Washington to cement deals with the US. Israel is now the most reliable satellite of the US. It is not for nothing that Israel gets more economic aid from the US than any other country, even though it is so tiny. It also gets more military aid than any other country in the world.

Zionism is not for sale; it is for hire.

From Zionist socialism to Trotskyism

At the age of 14 I joined the youth of the Zionist social democratic party, Mapai. The party was a very contradictory phenomenon. It dominated the trade unions as well as practically all local councils. The members sincerely believed they were socialists. The left wing of the Zionist socialist movement went as far as publishing in Hebrew many of Marx and Engels' works. It also published a translation of Trotsky's *History of the Russian Revolution* and *My Life*.

At the age of 16 I joined the left wing Zionist organisation called Mifleget Poale Zion Vehachugim Hamarksistim b'Eretz Israel—The Party of the Workers of Zion and the Marxist Circles of the Land of Israel (MPZVCMEI).

But the tensions and contradictions in the policy of the organisation put my ideas and beliefs to a very serious test. I shall refer only to one significant event.

In February 1934 a magnificent fight took place in Vienna where workers rose against fascism. Although the workers were defeated Vienna became a torch inspiring the whole international working class movement. The year before, in 1933, the German workers' movement—the strongest and best organised in the world—had capitulated to the Nazis with hardly a struggle. Throughout the world, I remember, socialists, communists and anti-fascists repeated the slogan 'Rather Vienna than Berlin'. During those days a meeting was organised by Mapai in Haifa which I attended. The secretary of the Haifa trade union council spoke. He started his speech with the words, 'Only once in history was there such heroism—the Paris Commune.' What a brilliant left wing statement. He finished his speech with the words, 'What we need is workers' unity.' When he ended, I heckled and added one word: 'international'. In Hebrew the adjective comes after the noun, hence my heckling meant 'international workers' unity'. Had I shouted 'Long live the British working class,' or, 'Long live the Chinese working class', I am sure the speaker would not have minded. But in the context of Palestine my words signified unity with Arabs. Three stewards then approached me, two held my arms while the third held fast to my fourth finger and twisted it round and round until he broke it. The Paris Commune is alright, but Arab workers are not.

Being more and more disappointed with the MPZVCMEI a few of us started calling ourselves Trotskyists and acting as a faction inside this organisation. The brilliant writings of Trotsky on Germany facing the Nazi menace came into our hands only after the victory of Hitler. They were crucial in turning us into Trotskyists.

In 1938 we were expelled from MPZVCMEI. The background to the expulsion is quite interesting, throwing a light on the contradictory nature of left centrist organisations. MPZVCMEI was affiliated to the centrist International Bureau of Revolutionary Socialist Unity. As its secretariat was located in London it was known as the London Bureau. Among its members were the Independent Labour Party in Britain, POUM in Spain, the SAP in Germany, and other organisations.

In late 1938 two MPs representing the Independent Labour Party,

Campbell Stephen and John McGovern, came to Palestine. Our party organised a couple of public meetings for them. At the first, in Jerusalem, a very large crowd turned up, probably nearly 1,000. The attraction was the MPs and not our party, which had only a few dozen members in the town. At the end of the meeting the audience stood up to sing the Zionist national anthem, Hatikvah. Our party always refused to rise for this anthem but this time the leaders of the organisation did stand up, probably to hide the fact that the majority of the audience were to the right of us. Everybody on the platform stood up except for me. I represented the youth of the organisation. I was really surprised that neither of the ILP MPs asked me why I did not stand up. At the next public meeting with the ILP MPs, in Haifa, a young member of our faction got up and read a short statement in English against imperialism and Zionism. We thought that now the differences would be clarified. Alas, the leaders of the party were very clever and underhanded, and after the statement was read they stood up and applauded. Probably the British visitors thought that the young man with his poor English simply expressed himself poorly. A few days after the ILP MPs left Palestine to return to Britain our group was expelled for making the above statement.

By the way, eight years later, in 1946, my path crossed that of Campbell Stephen again. I was in Britain, threatened with expulsion from the country. Chanie and I went to the House of Commons to ask him for help. He probably remembered me. Anyhow, practically at the beginning of the discussion he asked me, 'What do you think is the solution to the situation in Palestine?' I started speaking of the need to oppose imperialism and Zionism. But he must have been in another stratosphere because he said, 'Return to the Lord, you the Jews, the martyrs of humanity.' I though I must have misunderstood as my grasp of the English language was not 100 percent. I asked Chanie in Hebrew, 'What is he saying?' She explained the meaning of his words—what a centrist muddle! But he did help me.

In a very short time—over a couple of years—I moved from being a left wing Zionist to becoming a supporter of the Communist Party, ie a Stalinist, and then moving on to become a Trotskyist. I did not belong to the Palestine Communist Party as it was an underground party and I found no opportunity to join it.

The events in Germany were crucial to my becoming a Trotskyist.

Prior to Hitler coming to power I accepted the Comintern character-isation of the social democratic parties as 'social fascists'. When Rem-mele, leader of the German Communist Party MPs, declared that the coming to power of Hitler would be a transitory event—'After Hitler, us!'—I accepted it. I remember the day after Hitler came to power. Walking in Jerusalem I met youngsters, members of the Zionist social democratic party, Mapai, and I said to them with glee, 'Hitler finished you. Now it's the turn of us Communists.' After a few weeks it became clear to me that the Stalinist theory of 'social fascism' was disastrous. It was during this time that I got a few articles written by Trotsky before the rise of Hitler that analysed brilliantly the nature of Nazism and the catastrophe that would ensue if Hitler were victorious. Trotsky called for a united front of all workers' organisations to stop the Nazis' advance.

I became a Trotskyist. I never regretted this. But it would be a mis-take to underestimate the agony of the break with Stalinism. Stal-inism had a huge attraction for people fearful of Hitler. Stalinism was not merely a political movement; it was also a fanatical religious movement. What Marx said about religion—'a heart in a heartless world, the sigh of the oppressed, the opium of the people'—applied to Stalinism at that time. The more defeats the working class move-ment suffered, the greater was the attachment to Stalinism as a force that could stand up to Hitler in the future. Alas, it was Stalin's policy that facilitated Hitler's victories: from 'social fascism' to the massive shift to the right with the Popular Front policy in France and Spain, to the Hitler-Stalin pact. Breaking from this power to become a Trotskyist was a very painful experience. To understand the religious aspect of Stalinism I shall mention one incident, when a member of the Palestinian Communist Party got a pair of boots from Russia. He kissed them; they were icons for him.

The short period of my youth—some few months—in which I be-longed to Stalinism helped me grasp the strength of the hold Stalin had over his adherents. A rationalist cannot understand the strength of religion with its absurd arguments. He cannot grasp the appeal of religion to the weak and vulnerable facing hostile nature and society. Only power, struggle, can free humanity from religions.

Having been a Trotskyist for the rest of my life I can say, with all honesty, that I have never wavered in my total support of Trotskyism and detestation of Stalinism that caused such catastrophes for humanity.

Arab workers trapped in the camp of feudal reaction

I have already referred to Zionism trapping the Jewish workers of Palestine. A strong and dynamic Arab working class in Palestine could have got rid of the cul-de-sac in which Zionism trapped the Jewish working class. Alas, it was the same Zionist expansion (threatening the Arabs with what was later called 'ethnic cleansing') that prevented Arab workers from separating themselves from the most reactionary Arab leaders.

The Zionist colonisation frightened the mass of Arabs. It put their opposition to Zionism at the top of their agenda, making them ready to unite with the feudal landlords and religious parties who preached accommodation with imperialism while aiming to stop Zionist expansion. Naturally the Arab masses had only a pale picture of the impact of the future of this expansion. The ethnic cleansing of the Arabs following the founding of the state of Israel was still to come.

'The catastrophe' is the term used by the Palestinians to refer to the establishment of the state of Israel in 1948. Since then, in the three wars between Israel and the Arabs (in 1948, 1967 and 1973), there has been a massive ethnic cleansing of the Palestinians. Today there are 3.4 million Palestinian refugees, far more than the number of Palestinians remaining in the areas they lived in before. Figures of land ownership testify to their elimination: in 1917 the Jews owned 2.5 percent of the land in the country. In 1948 it rose to 5.7 percent, and today it is about 95 percent in the pre-1967 borders. Now in Israel, where the Palestinians make up some 20 percent of the population (one million out of five), one prominent Palestinian reports, 'In the 22 universities there is not even one Arab employee, not even a secretary. The electricity company employs 25,000 people, of whom only six are Arabs. We are 20 percent of the population, we have 2.5 percent of the land.[8]

The mass of the Palestinian proletariat felt entrapped into facing the strong expansion of Zionist settlement aided and abetted by British imperialism. They were therefore prey to the influence of feudal reaction.

Heading this reactionary trend was the mufti of Jerusalem, Haj Emin el-Husseini, the top cleric among the Muslims, and head of a rich land-owning family. He was appointed to his position with the consent of the British authorities. In 1936-39 there was an uprising of the Arabs against the expansion of Jewish settlements. It was brutally repressed by the British army and Zionist volunteers. At the time of these riots *A Liwa*, the paper of Haj Emin el-Husseini, wrote in a leading article, 'It is the Jewish influence which has infiltrated into the very heart of British politics in Palestine, that does harm to the authorities and prevents them from doing the duty that human feeling puts upon them'.[9]

Proclamation No 3 of the leadership of the Arab revolt, made on 4 September 1936, says, 'It is regrettable that Britain suffers this number of casualties in a holy part of the Arab countries, their allies of yesterday and today, in order to serve Zionism and erect a national home for it in Arab Palestine. They were not fighting British interests, as the Arabs do not fight Britain, and do not wish to damage her interests, but fight against the Jewish settlement and Zionist policy alone. If not for these two, the Arabs would live in friendship and peace with the English'.[10]

On 13 December 1931 *Al-Jami'a Al-Arabiya*, the paper of the Muslim Council of the Husseinis, printed a section of the notorious forgery *Protocols of the Elders of Zion* which 'proved' the connections of the Jews with Communism. Similar documents were printed frequently by the same paper and the Arab press in Palestine generally.

This idea of the identity of Zionism and Bolshevism was created to encourage the imperialist ruler to disengage from Zionism. It was given clear expression in a book intended mainly for British readers, especially those connected with the Palestine administration. 'It is natural that the Arabs should have been irritated by the self-assertion and aggressiveness of these new arrivals and be influenced by the social and Bolshevik principles which they bring with them. A strong Bolshevik element has already established itself in the country and has produced an effect on the population'.[11]

Every reactionary deed done in the world was warmly applauded by the official Arab leaders and newspapers. Thus on 4 April 1935 *Al-Jami'a al-Arabiya* published an article by Shakib Arselan, a Druze leader in the pay of the Hitler-Mussolini Axis, in which he wrote, 'We do not forget the praiseworthy stand of the leader of Italy in support of the Arabs at the time he was editor of the paper *Popolo D'Italia...* We consider it an honour to meet a great man who today is almost the leading statesman in Europe.' He goes on to count the benefits

Mussolini accorded Tripoli. On another occasion, in connection with the Italian invasion of Abyssinia, he wrote, 'We do not need to feel sorry for the Abyssinian government as it has for hundreds of years suppressed the Muslims in its country.' Have the leaders of any other colonial national movement reached greater depths of degradation as to support an imperialist war against another colonial people?

In the same issue of *Al-Jami'a al-Arabiya* (4 April 1935) an article was published called 'Islam and the Jews' written by the English Muslim Dr Khaled Sheldrick, in which, *inter alia*, he says, 'Hitler saved Germany from the yoke of Jewish capitalists... Germany is today stepping on the path of progress... If the success of this movement continues, the other countries will follow in its footsteps...'

The same paper constantly printed anti-Semitic news from the English paper the *Fascist*, and the same ideas were clearly and unequivocally repeated on innumerable occasions by all the Arab national leaders in Palestine.[12] The Franco revolt was warmly praised by the paper *Al Liwa*.

The existence of Zionism and the support the Jewish masses gave it enabled the Arab feudal reaction to divert anger against Zionism away from imperialism and the minority of capitalists among the Jewish community. Instead it was diverted towards an anti-Jewish channel of racial hatred.

The class struggle of the Arab proletariat, which was yet in its swaddling clothes, did not advance or strengthen during the national uprisings of 1929 and 1936-39. On the contrary, it was paralysed. Whereas in popular uprisings in the colonies strikes against foreign capital play a progressively increasing role, in Palestine something very different happened. From 1933 to 1935 there were large-scale economic strikes of Arab workers, mainly in the enterprises of foreign capital: Iraq Petroleum Co, Shell, the railways, the port of Haifa, the large tobacco company Karaman, Dick i Salti, and so on. As against this, during the whole period of the riots from 1936 to 1939 not a single strike took place in the enterprises of foreign capital and the government.

For the Arab feudal lords and bourgeoisie Zionism was the sole source of discord with imperialism. The Arab leaders unceasingly strove to prove that they could be allies of imperialism which could therefore safely dispense with Zionism as a pillar in the East. Constantly they repeated the refrain: the British policy of support for Zionism is due to the influence of the Jews but is against the interests of the empire.

The impasse facing Arab workers and Jewish workers could have been broken only by a strong and dynamic Arab working class movement. Alas, the Palestinian working class was far too small and weak to deliver this.

Building a Trotskyist organisation in Palestine

From 1938 until September 1946 I was engaged in an effort to build a Trotskyist organisation in Palestine. It was very hard going. Throughout the world Trotskyism, the Fourth International, never managed to bring about a large-scale breakaway from the ranks of the traditional parties of the labour movement. In this its fate was very different to that of the First, Second and Third Internationals.

The First International was made up of relatively large organisations, and although there was a break of some two decades between the end of the First and establishment of the Second International, many thousands who were members of the First joined the Second. The Third International, the Communist International (or Comintern) came into being as the result of huge splits in the Second International. The Italian Socialist Party, at its conference in Bologna in September 1919, voted to join the Communist International, adding 300,000 members. In Germany the Independent Social Democratic Party, which split in 1917 from the Social Democratic Party, also decided to join the Communist International, adding another 300,000 members. In 1920 the French Socialist Party joined, adding 140,000 members. In June 1919 the Bulgarian Socialists voted to affiliate, bringing 35,478 members. The Yugoslav Socialist Party, also a mass party, joined. The Czechoslovak Social Democratic Party split in December 1920, the Communist left taking over half the membership and establishing a Communist Party of 350,000 members. A separate split in the Social Democratic Party of the German speaking minority added further forces, and after their unification the party claimed 400,000 members. The Norwegian Labour Party joined the Comintern in spring 1919. In Sweden the majority of the Socialist Party, after a split, joined the Comintern, adding another 17,000.[13]

Sadly, there was hardly any continuity in terms of individual revolutionaries between the Communist International of Lenin and Trotsky in the early 1920s and the Trotskyist movement of the 1930s onwards. Crushed between the overpowering influence of Stalin and fear of Hitler, Trotskyist organisation always consisted of tiny groups on the margins of the mass movements. Thus the number of Trotskyists in Berlin on the eve of Hitler's victory was 50! Despite the Spanish Revolution of 1936, in September 1938, according to the report of the Founding Conference of the Fourth International, the membership of the Spanish section was between ten and 30!

The First, Second and Third Internationals came into existence during periods of working class advance; the Trotskyist organisations were born during a dire period in working class history—the victory of Nazism and Stalinism.

Trotsky's criticism of Stalinism in the 1920s and 1930s was absolutely correct. But tragically this did not benefit Trotskyism. The disastrous errors of Stalinism contributed to Hitler's victory and to setbacks in Britain, Spain and China. In consequence a defeated working class looked for a strong organisation to save it from the Nazi catastrophe. Stalinism became a religion.

I had to use three languages in Palestine: for Jewish workers I wrote in Hebrew, signing my articles Y Tsur; for Arabs I used the pseudonym Yussuf el-Sakhry, and my English articles were signed L Rock. All the names mean rock or stone.

While trying to build a Trotskyist organisation in Palestine in 1938 we made contact with the US Trotskyist organisation, the Socialist Workers Party. It sent us a regular supply of Trotsky's writings. This was of fantastic importance for us. But the going was very hard. By 1946 our membership reached nearly 30, of whom seven were Arabs, the rest Jews. It was very difficult, if not impossible, for Jewish members to distribute the Arabic magazine or Arabic leaflets. It was extremely difficult for them to recruit Arabs into the organisation because very few of them worked with Arabs, as I have remarked above.

With perseverance we did manage to win precious Arab workers and intellectuals. They were human diamonds. At the beginning of 1940 I managed to win over the editor of *El Nur*, the legal Arab paper of the Palestine Communist Party, although the party as such was illegal. His name was Jabra Nicola, a really brilliant man. While editor of *El Nur*, Jabra earned his living as a journalist on a bourgeois Arabic daily. He worked during the night. Every day at the end of his shift I would meet him and discuss with him for three or four hours. After nearly a month I convinced him. Perhaps he was also motivated by the prospect of not being pestered any longer! This was a really great achievement. To grasp the harsh conditions under which Jabra lived, I shall relate one incident. Chanie had to go and visit him to get an article he wrote. I couldn't do this as I was on the run from the police. She went to his 'house'—one room. In this one room he lived with his wife and one year old child, his widowed sister and her young child, and his mother who was dying from cancer.

In 1942 we won the Arab secretary of the Communist Party in Jerusalem. The story is quite fascinating. From the Seventh Congress of the Comintern in 1935 until August 1939 the Stalinist parties throughout the world insisted that the coming war would be an anti-fascist crusade. With the Hitler-Stalin Pact of August 1939 the line changed completely: now the war was an imperialist war. When Nazi Germany invaded Russia in June 1941 a new sharp turn took place. Now Churchill was Stalin's pal and the policy of the British Communist Party, for example, was to call for an alliance with Churchill, to wave the Union Jack, and to sing 'God Save the King' with gusto. That was simple.

But what could be done in a country like Palestine in which two separate peoples lived, with separate national leaders, national anthems and national flags? With the Hitler-Stalin Pact in place the Palestine Communist Party argued that the whole East was the foe of imperialism and 'the masses of Indians and Arabs were on the eve of open revolts against imperialist rule'.[14] When the Nazis invaded Russia a decisive change of line occurred. Now, 'The government must understand that it has an important region of friends in the Middle East'.[15] Before, the 'British government in Palestine represented the regime of subjugation, exploitation, repression and black reaction. This regime is the same regime of Hitler and Mussolini with whom British-French imperialism struggle for monopoly over the exploitation of the proletariat of the capitalist countries and the oppressed nations of the colonies'.[16] Now the British high commissioner was the representative of democracy, and 'we keep in our hearts his good personal features...the manifestation of his true social characteristics'.[17]

With the 180 degree swing in the policy of the Stalinists in June 1941, becoming enthusiastic supporters of the 'war for democracy', the Jewish Stalinists began, with a few reservations, to be ambivalent about Zionism. Obviously the Arab Stalinists could not stomach this so the party split into two: the Jewish one (which had not a single

Arab member) continued to bear the name Palestine Communist Party (PCP); the Arab one, which according to its statutes might include only Arabs, was called National Freedom League. A patriotic race between the two began. On VE Day the PCP marched under the blue-white Zionist flag, their slogans being 'Free immigration', 'Extension of colonisation', 'Development of the Jewish National Home', and 'Down with the [British government's 1939] white paper' (restricting Jewish immigration). The National Freedom League participated in the Arab National Front, which included feudal and bourgeois parties, and called for a fight 'Against Zionist immigration', 'Against the transfer of land to Zionists', and 'For the white paper'.

We sent two comrades—one Arab and one Jew—to the National Freedom League to apply for membership. The comrades were told, 'The Arab can join, but the Jew cannot'. Our comrades replied, 'We want to join together. We will not accept leaving one of us out in the cold.' Then we sent the same couple to the PCP where the roles were reversed. Faced with this the Arab secretary of the NFL in Jerusalem joined us.

The most scandalous behaviour of the Stalinists occurred in the 1944 national railway strike. This opened the way to our recruiting a leading Arab railway worker. The Stalinists issued a leaflet, one side of which was written in Arabic, the other side in Hebrew. The first ended with the slogan: 'For a democratic strike committee without difference of religion or nationality'. The Hebrew side ended, 'Elect a strike committee on the basis of parity between Jews and Arabs'. As hardly any Arab worker could read Hebrew and very few Jews could read Arabic, the Stalinists were confident they could get away with it. One of our comrades approached a leading Arab militant and translated into Arabic the Hebrew side of the leaflet. The railwayman was really shocked, and after confirming the translation with someone else, he broke from the Stalinists and joined our group.

Alas, throughout the long months and years, in spite of really great efforts on our part, the group continued to be minuscule. Even more frustrating, it had no impact at all on the working class. As a matter of fact, the average branch of the Socialist Workers Party in Britain today has greater impact than we had in Palestine.

Our very meagre achievements were not the result of laziness, slovenliness or dilettantism; we worked very hard indeed. I personally lived as a professional revolutionary, engaged as a full-timer in building the group. In 1936, before we started the group, I worked for one year for my living. I became a building worker, believing that without the sweat of my brow I could not understand workers. So for a year I worked something like 12 hours a day six days a week. The result was that in practice I did no political activity to speak of, being too tired. This experience immunised me from the four-letter word: work. I spent hardly any time doing anything other than political activity. I managed to translate two books into Hebrew for money—one from English, the other from German. In passing, the first translation caused some fun. The book I translated was the massive volume *The Decline of American Capitalism* by Lewis Corey (a founding member of the US Communist party). After I finished the translation for the publishing house of Hashomer Hatzair, Lewis Corey was approached for permission to publish it. He refused because, as he stated, 'I stopped being a Marxist.' The second was a book of Fritz Sternberg, the German theoretician of the Socialist Workers Party (SAP).

The money from these two translations helped me along. In winter I picked oranges from the nearby orange grove. This was an important supplement to the bread, jam, one egg a day, tea and milk that I survived on.

Every step our group took met with great difficulty. To collect articles for our magazines, one of us, who was not known to the police or to the Zionist organisations, would have to travel to pick up the article, let us say from Haifa, to bring to Tel Aviv.

The printing was a very burdensome task. We could not go to a commercial printer as our publications were illegal. We did not have a printing press of our own; we did not even have a duplicator. What we had was a flatbed copier. To start with one had to type the magazine on a stencil. Then the stencil was put over a single sheet of paper, and a roller covered with ink passed over it to bring up the print. One had to be very careful not to put one printed sheet over another. They had to be carefully spread until they dried—a very time-consuming process.

For a couple of months our printing became even more burdensome. A comrade who was a printing worker got hold of a small hand activated printing machine. It was kept in my room. I had to set the type by hand, letter by letter. It took ages. One day, on returning home, a young girl who lived in the same house, rushed to tell me, 'The police are in your room.' Naturally I scarpered. But what a relief to get rid of this printing machine. For a time I used to wake up in the middle of the night with a nightmare, thinking that perhaps I had informed the police myself to get rid of the burden.

Then came the difficulty of the delivery of the paper to different towns—one could not use the post. A comrade had to go by coach, let us say from Tel Aviv to Jerusalem, and put a package on the rack, pretending that it had nothing to do with him in case the police searched the coach—a very common event. The individual copies of the magazine then had to be distributed directly among contacts of our members.

The burden on a small group of less than 30 members of publishing two separate magazines—one in Arabic, the other in Hebrew—plus from time to time leaflets in English for the British troops occupying Palestine, was really massive.

When it came to the distribution of leaflets we had to be very innovative. One could not stand in the street and distribute leaflets. I invented a couple of mechanisms for accomplishing this. I had to find a tall building, let us say of two or three storeys, by the town's main road. I would then climb up to the roof and tie a string to the leaflets. The string would go through a candle, and its end would then be tied to something on the roof. The candle was inside a tin to protect it from the wind. After being lit and melting the candle away the fire would reach the string and burn through it, thus releasing the leaflets which floated down to the street below, hopefully to be caught and read by passers by. What a joy it was to stand in the street and see the leaflets dispersed.

Another contraption consisted of a string to which on one end the leaflets were tied, on the other a tin of water with holes in the bottom. The resultant loss of water would cause the leaflets to tip over, then drop, float down and thus get distributed.

We faced danger not only from the police, but also from the Zionist organisations. I shall illustrate this with a couple of incidents.

One day I and my girlfriend were walking towards my home in Jerusalem. When I was just opposite it I saw two tall young men at the gate of the house. I guessed who they were, but it was too late. My friend had already gone through the gate, and I could not leave her on her own, so I followed her. The two young men beat me up. We eventually got away. On later returning I found a notice on my door threatening me with dire consequences if I did not leave Jerusalem.

I had no alternative but to follow the instruction of Etzel, the fascist paramilitary organisation.

The second incident I shall relate occurred at an assembly of students at the Hebrew University in which there was an extreme right wing speaker from the Revisionists, now called the Likud Party. The Revisionists used to use the same salute as the Italian Fascists and German Nazis—an outstretched arm. Their headquarters in Tel Aviv was called the Brown House in imitation of the Nazi HQ in Munich. This particular speaker made a fierce attack on Marxism, calling it a 'gentile ideology poisoning our Jewish spirit'. This was a mirror image of Nazi propaganda about Marxism being Jewish. After he spoke I got up and said, 'I agree with the speaker, Marxism is gentile, but the Hitler salute and the brown shirts are not.' I paid for it by being beaten.

The final threat, of course, was from the police. A few days after the beginning of the Second World War on 1 September 1939, two plainclothes policemen knocked on the door of the house I lived in in Haifa. They came to search the place. They found nothing incriminating, but while carrying out the search they spoke to one another with the obvious aim of intimidating me. One of them described quite accurately the looks of my girlfriend; the other added, 'When shall we rape her?' Although I was convinced it was merely psychological warfare against me I was still scared.

A few days later the same two detectives returned. In the meantime I wrote an anti-war leaflet, the main theme of which was that it was an imperialist war and that workers should unite to fight capitalism; to use Lenin's words, 'Turn the imperialist war into civil war', and carry out an international revolution. One sentence in the leaflet sticks in my memory: '52 states in the League of Nations recognise the right of Zionism to build a Jewish National Home in Palestine, but the village of Qaqoon does not.'

Just before we started distributing the leaflet I asked my brother, who was also a member of our Trotskyist group, to be sure that our room was clean. A day later the two detectives turned up again. A few seconds after they entered the room one of them lifted a newspaper and found underneath it the draft of the leaflet in my own handwriting. Had it been a printed leaflet I could have claimed that I simply found it in the street, but now the evidence was incontrovertible.

I and my brother, who was two years older than me, were taken and put in a cell in a police station. After three days and nights of complete isolation, some time after midnight we were woken up, handcuffed together and taken for a walk. Behind us the two detectives were talking to one another: 'Where should we dump the bodies?' I whispered to my brother, 'Don't worry! They are simply preparing us for interrogation.' Alas, when we arrived at the headquarters of the CID, my brother's face was white as a sheet.

An officer had barely interrogated me when he put on the table a printed form with my name filled in and a sentence of '12 months detention'. (My brother was sentenced to six months of early evening curfew. He left our group.)

Arriving in prison I met the general secretary of the Palestine Communist Party, Meir Slonim, who had been detained for a number of years. When the war broke out he applied to join the British army—after all, since the Seventh Congress of the Comintern in August 1935 the Stalinists had argued strongly that the coming war would be a war against fascism. It took a few weeks until the Colonial Office in London answered Slonim's request to leave prison and join the army. Alas, in the meantime he learnt that the war was not an anti-fascist war, but an imperialist one, so he refused to leave prison. There were five Trotskyists in the same prison. So we went around saying, 'We are prisoners, but Slonim is a volunteer here.'

The background of the four other Trotskyists was interesting. They were emigrants from Germany. Having come to Palestine they had enquired about us and came to the conclusion that nothing could be done in Palestine. They made a collection of our literature with the intention of producing an article for Trotsky explaining why activity was pointless in Palestine. When they were arrested the police found this considerable quantity of material with them and concluded that they had uncovered the HQ of Trotskyism. These unfortunate individuals got 30 month jail sentences. When I met them I said, 'You see, if you are active you get 12 months, but if you are passive you get 30.'

In the same prison I met Avraham Stern, of the extreme right wing Zionist terrorist group the Stern Gang, that organised some sensational attacks on British installations. Stern was later assassinated by British agents. He explained the adoption of fascist symbols to me, saying that Britain needed Zionism to face the Arab world. Italian imperialism is much weaker than British and therefore it would need Zionism even more. Therefore, in the expectation that

Italy and Germany would win the war, he was orientating on wooing the fascists. Of course, this position was developed before the Holocaust was known of.

Also there was Moshe Dayan, the future defence secretary of the first Israeli government, detained for illegally smuggling arms into the country.

There was a funny aspect to the prison. In its library one could find a book called *Capital* in the geography section. But when one of the prisoners received by post the novel by Stendhal called *Red and Black*, he was not allowed to have it because political books were banned. Facing the paucity of literature I did two things: first I decided to learn French, so I took Jules Verne's *Around the World in Eighty Days* in French, together with its translation into English, and read them sentence by sentence. That was a useful way of learning the language.

But that was not enough to fill the many hours of the day. One book was in abundance in the prison—the Bible. I became intrigued with the possibility of using Engels' *The Origin of the Family, Private Property and the State* to interpret events described in the bible.

Engels describes the disintegration of primitive communism as a result of the development of the productive forces and man's advance of knowledge. The result was the move from hunter-gatherer society to land cultivation. This was associated with the rise of private property and the monogamous family.

I wrote in the thick notebook that I filled on the subject that the same process is described in the fable of Adam and Eve being pushed from the Garden of Eden for eating an apple from the Tree of Knowledge. God told Adam, 'In the sweat of thy face shall thou eat bread.'

Even the names Adam and Eve reflect the process. The name Eve comes from the Hebrew word chava, which derives from the word chaim meaning 'life', because 'she was the mother of all living'. And where does the name Adam come from? I argued that it comes from the word adama, the Hebrew for earth. It was women who first nurtured animals; it was men who cultivated the land.

A similar development is described by Cain's murder of his brother, Abel. In Hebrew the names are Cain and Hevel. The word Cain, I believed, was derived from the word cinian, property, while Hevel means something like vapour. And so the murder of Hevel by Cain was the victory of the private ownership of the land fighting the nomadic tribes.

A similar story is told by the conflict between Jacob and Esau. Esau was a hunter. He sold his birthright to his brother Jacob, which made him so angry that he wanted to kill his brother.

Engels' *The Origin of the Family, Private Property and the State* owed a lot to Lewis H Morgan's *Ancient Society*, which I also read. Morgan argues that at the beginning of society and for a long period afterwards unrestricted sexual relations prevailed within the tribes, every women belonged equally to every man, and every man to every woman. Between this state that Engels denoted as primitive communism and the stage of the rise of the family there was a transition period in which the tribe was divided into gentes.

After the exclusion of parents and children from sexual intimacy with one another, a second stage was the exclusion of sisters and brothers. This led to the division of the tribe into separate gentes. The gens denoted the lineage of descent and was associated with a certain social and cultural structure.

> With the increase in population, each of these original gentes splits up into several daughter gentes… The tribe itself breaks up into several tribes, in each of which we find again, for the most part, the old gentes.[18]

In prison I decided to investigate whether, and to what extent, the rise of the gens reflected itself in the Bible. I remember finding dozens of examples to demonstrate this. Alas, my knowledge of the Bible has become very rusty, as has my knowledge of Hebrew. The result is that when, while working on the present biography, I spent a couple of hours rereading the Bible I found I could not dig out once again the evidence for these ideas.

I also analysed the changes in religious ceremonies in terms of reflecting changes in class structure. For example, in one part of the Bible all Israelites were entitled to participate in eating from the altar after the sacrifice. In another only the priests (Cohenim) were entitled to do so. Elsewhere there was differentiation among the priests, between Cohenim and Levis.

So one could decide which part of the Bible was written earlier and which later according to the religious customs described. And this gave an opening to look at other aspects of the time. The standard practice among Bible experts was to look at the style of language as the key to decide the order in which the different parts of the Bible were written.

I did a lot of work and sent my conclusions to a Bible expert who was very impressed. I do not know if my contribution was of any value at all but it helped me to grasp the Marxist method of analysis, not as a dogma but a weapon of research.

Alas, the manuscript has been lost and will probably never be found.

An urge to leave Palestine and go to Egypt

The fact that we were getting nowhere was becoming more and more frustrating. Formally we said the right things: Arab workers should fight Zionism and imperialism and break with the reactionary Arab leadership; Jewish workers should join the Arab masses in the struggle. We repeated the word 'should' again and again. One expression of this was a series of three articles I wrote for the American Trotskyist monthly *New International*: 'British Policy in Palestine' (October 1938), 'The Jewish-Arab Conflict' (November 1938), and 'Class Politics in Palestine'(June 1939). I used the pseudonym L Rock.

Formally we stuck with Trotsky's theory of permanent revolution. But this theory did not limit itself to using the subjunctive 'should'. Trotsky did not confine himself to arguing that the proletariat of Petrograd should lead the mass of the peasantry in fighting Tsarism and capitalism, or should carry out the tasks of the bourgeois-democratic revolution (solving the land question, achieving national self determination of the oppressed nationalities, etc). As a matter of fact the revolutionary action of the Petrograd proletariat in 1905 did have just such an impact on the whole of Russia, and in 1917 it went even further and was able to encourage international revolution.

The workers of a provincial Palestinian town or a few provincial towns could not have the same impact. We were right in saying that the Arab working class could have overthrown imperialism and Zionism and smashed the reactionary leadership of the Arab people. But the Palestinian working class was only a very small part of the Arab working class. It was a minnow compared to the Egyptian working class. Thus, in 1944 the total number of Palestinian wage earners was estimated at 160,000. As against this, the number of Egyptian wage earners, excluding agricultural workers who were very numerous, was more than two million.

The largest number of Palestinian workers working in one unit—

the railways—in 1944 was 4,000. As against this, in Egypt Mekhala el-Kubra textiles employed over 30,000; engineering and tyre repair factories in Tel el-Kabir employed 17,000 workers; Alexandria's weaving works, Filatule Nationale, employed 10,000.[19]

Working class struggle in Egypt was far ahead of anything happening in Palestine and has remained at a high level ever since.[20]

Comparing Palestine to Egypt I became more and more convinced that the former working class was far too weak to be a lever to move events in the Middle East. The Egyptian working class was the key factor in the Middle East.

The manuscript of a book on the Middle East

I decided to devote far more time to studying the Middle East. Long before I had been drawn to analysing the situation in Egypt. Already in 1935 I had written an article entitled 'The Present Agrarian Crisis in Egypt', and sent it to a serious economic journal published in Tel Aviv, *Hameshek Hashitufi*. I was surprised by the editor's letter accepting the article. He wrote that it was clear that I had spent years in studying the subject. As a matter of fact I spent about a fortnight. The article was a result of my enthusiasm for the subject, the study of a number of statistical reports and absorbing Lenin's writings on the agrarian question in Russia. (In passing, one day I came across the editor, and both of us were very embarrassed when he saw me as a young man aged 18 wearing shorts.)

After spending a couple of years in preparing the material, and then a further two years in writing, I produced a manuscript on the Middle East. The manuscript described and analysed the economic structure of the countries of the Middle East, the social and political forces struggling within them, the role of imperialism, the national movement and the workers' movement. The countries covered were Egypt, Palestine, Syria, Lebanon and Iraq. The rest of the Arab Peninsula (Jordan as well as Saudi Arabia, Kuwait, Yemen) were not dealt with because they were so backward that no national movement, or even less, a working class movement, existed there. They were not moved by the mighty rumblings shaking the Arab East as part of world history.

My English was very poor, so I wrote in Hebrew. The Hebrew version was completed in July 1945. It took another ten months for its translation into English. This was done by Chanie.

A summary of the book's contents shows how serious (and how ambitious) was the approach to the subject. It starts with a historical survey from the golden age of Arab feudalism (8th to 13th centuries), when the Arabs were at the peak of world culture. It goes on to describe and analyse the invasion of Europe into the area from the conquest of Egypt in 1798 by the French until the present time. The influence of Europe was contradictory: it undermined the foundations of the old order but at the same time preserved them. Five chapters were devoted to this.

Two chapters analyse the invasion of the Arab East by the imperialist powers in recent decades, followed by a long chapter on the development of industry and banking in Egypt. A further chapter is devoted to the agrarian question there. These are followed by chapters dealing with similar matters in Palestine, Syria and Iraq.

The manuscript then deals with the national question, with five separate chapters on Egypt, Palestine, Syria and Lebanon, and finally Iraq. This is followed by a chapter on Zionism. Then comes a section dealing with the working class movement in the Arab East: first a chapter on the trade unions, then a chapter on the Stalinist organisations and their attitude to the war, to unity with the leaderships of the capitalists and landlords, to the agrarian question, and to Zionism. This is followed by a chapter on the rise of independent proletarian power in Egypt.

The last chapter deals with the tasks of a revolutionary workers' movement in the Arab East.

The writing of this manuscript convinced me that I should make the effort to move to Egypt.

Making an effort to move to Egypt

In 1940 I had an opportunity to test the possibility of moving to Egypt. In our Trotskyist group there was a comrade whose sister was married to a British soldier stationed there. I had heard of a Trotskyist group in Egypt.

I asked her to look into the situation. Being a foreigner with a very poor command of Arabic, and an accent that stood out for miles, I knew I would face great difficulties. (The Egyptian dialect of Arabic is radically different to that of the Palestinians.) I needed comrades to support me, hide me and look after me. Sadly, the report I got from my friend after visiting Egypt was very disappointing indeed. According to her, the tiny Trotskyist group was made up of dilettantes. One person told her, 'If you want to find the Trotskyists in Cairo, look around until you find three or four Rolls Royce cars in the street together; you'll then know the Trotskyists are meeting.' (Of course this was a big exaggeration). She met a couple of Trotskyists. I remember the names of two of them—Ramses Yunan and Georges Heinan. They belonged to a group called Art et Liberté (Art and Freedom). Its name makes it clear that it was a literary group—in fact it was a Surrealist group. The language used was French, although the members were Arab-speaking indigenous Egyptians.

She disabused me of the thought of going to Egypt to work illegally. Even with solid support from revolutionaries, the enterprise would have been very risky.

When my efforts to get to Egypt collapsed I was very depressed. But revolutionaries cannot indulge in self pity. I continued to make great efforts to build the Palestinian group and to get our publications out.

Summary: the advantages of backwardness and isolation

Developing as a Marxist in backward and isolated Palestine had its advantages. The place provided a concentrated political education because it was a crossing point for so many currents—imperialism and nationalism, feudalism and capitalism, oppression and exploitation, plus the full range of political responses from far right through Stalinism to the left. Above all it encouraged self reliance, independence and daring in thought and action.

To refer to one incident: in August 1935 the Seventh congress of the Communist International took place. This was the one that launched the policy of the Popular Front. If I had lived in Britain, France or the United States I would have got Trotsky's comment on the Seventh Congress a few days after it took place and would not have had to write about it myself. Alas, in Palestine, Trotsky's writings on this subject reached us some two months later. In the meantime, a few days after the Congress, an editor of a centrist paper in Palestine asked me for an article on the subject.

I obliged. My article pointed out, quite correctly, that the move towards the Popular Front—an alliance of the workers' parties, the communists and socialists, with bourgeois liberal parties—was a massive move to the right. I did not see the other side of the coin: the contradictory nature of the Popular Front. It raised the expectations of millions of workers and led to mass actions and a big turn to the left. In May 1936, for example, the Popular Front won the general election in France. Workers said to themselves, 'We have the government, now let's take over the factories,' and a mass occupation of the factories took place. Backwardness and isolation do not guarantee you against errors, but they do spur you towards independent thought and action.

The situation I faced has certain parallels with the argument Marx made about German philosophy: the French made the revolution in 1789, the Germans thought about it. Thus the French bourgeoisie in 1789 was far more effective than the German revolutionary movement in 1848. But German philosophy, above all that of Hegel, far surpassed French philosophy. The self reliance imposed on me in Palestine would affect the rest of my life. This became especially so after the death of Trotsky when the alternatives were either repeating, parrot-like, his sayings, or facing up to new situations, new problems with independent thinking.

The urge for intellectual independence affected even my first steps in learning Marxist economics. After reading the three volumes of *Capital* I spent a year or so reading the books Marx was responding to—from William Petty to Adam Smith, David Ricardo, James Mill and John Stuart Mill. I did not indulge in this because I had any doubts about Marx's analysis. On the contrary I did it because I was not sure I could understand his criticism of classical political economy without reading the texts. I always knew that the best way to improve the working of the brain is to use it. President Hindenburg of Germany—the man who summoned Hitler to become Chancellor in 1933—is reported to have stated, 'To preserve my brain I never read books', but I knew he was wrong. Many a young man could knock out the boxer Mike Tyson if he was in constant training while Tyson lay in bed for a year or so. I do not know how good my brain is, but I am sure now and always that I am very single minded in keeping it at work.

The situation of backwardness and isolation was not inevitably favourable to political development. It could 'make or break' a person. As it turned out I was forced to rise to the occasion.

Out of the blue—an opportunity to go to London

A few months after completing and editing the manuscript on the Arab East, an opportunity to leave Palestine and go to London came out of the blue.

Chanie's parents emigrated from South Africa to settle in Palestine during 1945. Her father was a factory owner in Cape Town. He wanted to visit Britain to buy textiles for his factory. After getting a visa to travel to Britain he found out that he did not need this document as his South African passport was valid without it. Hearing of this, I jumped at the idea of going to Britain to be his representative. It was an incongruous situation for me to be carrying an order for textiles worth £40,000 when in my whole life I had never seen as much as £100.

Before travelling to England Chanie and I decided to get married, as her good South African passport could subsume my rotten British Protectorate of Palestine one, and make travel for me easier.

We were penniless and my total worldly possessions were a pair of short trousers, a pair of shoes, a shirt and books. We had to apply to the rabbis, as there was no civil marriage. The first hurdle of many was for me to get a divorce from the fictitious marriage I had entered into ten years earlier to save a Jewish woman from Hitler's Germany. This was a practice the rabbis were party to then. But now they demanded a proper legal divorce which took precious weeks to organise, and preyed on our nerves as the woman had disappeared. With the threat that we would 'live in sin' (as if we weren't already!) the rabbis delivered the divorce.

Chanie remembers what happened next:

My brother, who was in the diplomatic service, and his wife were to be witnesses to the wedding. So we decided to try to put on some show. Without any money this proved to be a problem. First of all the essential chupah (canopy) had to be out on the pavement for free, as it cost money to have the ceremony inside a building. Then we thought the 'groom' needed long trousers, and for religious purposes certainly had to acquire a hat. A ring, wine and a cloth to cover my face (as the 'bride' was not supposed to be seen till after the ceremony) were also required.

The trousers: we knew no one with long trousers except one South African member of our organisation who was considerably thinner than Cliff. So the groom had to wear his trousers unbuttoned.

The hat: the only person we knew with this article was a building worker who used a slouch cap covered with cement. This Cliff wore, perched ridiculously on his huge head.

The cloth and ring: my sister-in-law lent these—the first an attractive net cloth, which the rabbi immediately discarded, as my face could vaguely be seen, and was replaced with a handkerchief—the second, a ring made of platinum. In the middle of the ceremony the rabbi looked at this and asked, 'What's this? (As the husband buys the wife through the ring it needs to be of value and is thus nearly always gold.) Cliff replied, 'Platinum.' The rabbi did not know what platinum was, and thought it was tin, so he asked, 'How much does it cost?' Cliff mentioned some large sum of money. All this in the middle of the ceremony!

Finally, the wine we had spent the last of our borrowed money on, and intended to drink with my brother and sister-in-law: the rabbi put the glass to each of our lips as the ceremony requires, snatched it away—and kept the bottle.

Meanwhile beggars surrounded the pavement chupah, and as soon as the ceremony was over, moved forward in droves to beg. My brother emptied his pockets, and, fuming at the avaricious rabbis, we angrily stomped away—with a piece of paper to say we were married!

And I could now travel with peace of mind.

When I next washed my clothes the wind blew away my only shirt, and, having to pay back our debt for the marriage fees, we were poorer than ever.

The Palestinian immigration authorities did not want to antagonise the British trade commissioner in Palestine who needed to ratify my travel, so I was allowed to leave the country with a warning ringing in my ears, 'We will have you back in Palestine in less than three months' time.' After all, I had been on the run from the police for a couple of years.

When we arrived in Dover the immigration officer naturally asked me for the name of the company I represented. I did not know it! With my ridiculous showing at the port he stamped my passport with the minimum stay—three months.

Chapter 2

The crisis of Trotskyism

On our way from Palestine to Britain Chanie and I passed through Paris. We visited the headquarters of the Fourth International.

Until then I had concentrated my research on developments in the Arab East, above all Egypt and Palestine. I only glanced at developments elsewhere. We visited Paris just five months after the International Pre-Conference of the Fourth International, which took place in April 1946 (the founding conference was in 1938). I must say I read its resolutions with a feeling of unease. The description of the world in those resolutions jarred with reality. This could be recognised even at a glance.

For example, the Trotskyists in 1946 slavishly followed Trotsky's statement that the Stalinist regime in Russia could not, would not survive the war. Thus the Fourth International of April 1946 stated, 'Without any fear of exaggeration one can say that the Kremlin has never confronted a more critical situation at home and abroad than it does today'.[1]

In September 1946 I met Ernest Mandel in Paris. He was a leading member of the Fourth International and showed me an article he had written a few weeks earlier. In it he tried to demonstrate the profound instability of Stalin's regime by quoting a working class woman in a mass meeting telling Kalinin, president of the USSR, 'You have boots. I am barefoot.' This, he argued, was indicative of mass resentment at bureaucratic privileges simmering away. I told Mandel that I had read the story years before and it related to events a quarter of a century earlier! A few months ago, when researching my book *Trotskyism After Trotsky*, I asked Ian Birchall, who has been extremely helpful in my research, whether he could locate this article. A few days later Al Richardson of the Socialist Platform Archive located the article, and it was exactly as I had remembered it.

I was shocked to read Mandel's argument. As a matter of fact it was a hard blow to my trust in the leadership of the Fourth International. This reaction against a sloppy attitude to historical accuracy was not a matter of bourgeois morality, that by such deception one's immortal soul is damaged. No. Revolutionaries need to tell the truth, good and bad, not only because not to do so cheats the workers they are addressing, but because they deceive themselves. Without an honest accounting it is impossible to orientate properly on a situation. A too pessimistic analysis can lead to passivity, an over-optimistic one leads to adventurism and in the long run to disappointment, which also leads to passivity.*

Nevertheless the conference of the Fourth International in April 1946 continued to assert that 'behind the appearance of power never before attained, there lurks the reality that the USSR and the Soviet bureaucracy have entered the critical phase of their existence'.[2]

The highest form of sophistry was used by James P Cannon, leader of the Trotskyists in the US, when he stated that the fact that Stalin continued to rule Russia proved that the war had not ended! 'Trotsky predicted that the fate of the Soviet Union would be decided in

---

*A couple of incidents, quite tiny, happening at our meeting with the International Secretariat of the Fourth International, helped us become sceptical towards it. Incidents can play a general role when they throw light on the general issue, when one can 'see a world in a grain of sand'.

When Chanie and I met J Stuart (Sam Gordon), the American SWP member of the International Secretariat, he suggested to me that I stay in Paris so as to be able to help the subsequent congresses as they needed simultaneous translations. The fact that my linguistic prowess was not up to it was not the issue for me. What made me laugh was the clear picture I had of the last conference a few months earlier. At this conference a representative of our Palestinian group was present, and he wrote telling us that the total number of people present was just two dozen and that they all knew English except for one, who needed a French translator. Stuart had simply tried to impress us.

When we met Stuart he made us wait for him for nearly an hour, while he turned his back on us and went on typing. Had he asked us whether we minded, of course we would have said no. We were not in a terrible rush. But again, I believe he did this simply to impress.

Finally, he offered us cups of coffee with cream and sugar. At this time scarcity prevailed in France. A day earlier we had visited a relative of mine and his wife who had a young child, and they complained bitterly that they could not get hold of milk for the kid. And here we had cream and sugar. Was this also done to impress us?

the war. That remains our firm conviction. Only we disagree with some people who carelessly think the war is over. The war has only passed through one stage and is now in the process of regroupment and reorganisation for the second. The war is not over, and the revolution which we said would issue from the war in Europe is not taken off the agenda. It has only been delayed and postponed, primarily for lack of a sufficiently strong revolutionary party'.[3]

The position of the Fourth International leadership looked completely mistaken to me, although at the time I did not have an explanation of the developments in Russia and Eastern Europe.

The 1946 International Pre-Conference also took an absurd position when it used Trotsky's pre-war analysis to describe the current state of world capitalism. Trotsky thought that capitalism was in terminal crisis. As a result production could not expand and, associated with this, there could be no serious social reforms or a rise in the masses' living standards. In 1938, in *The Death Agony of Capitalism and the Tasks of the Fourth International*, he wrote that the Western world was 'in an epoch of decaying capitalism: when, in general, there can be no discussion of systematic social reforms and the raising of the masses' living standards...when every serious demand of the proletariat and even every serious demand of the petty bourgeoisie inevitably reaches beyond the limits of capitalist property relations and of the bourgeois state'.[4]

It was impossible in 1946 not to see that capitalism did not suffer from general stagnation and decay. Full employment, a speedy rise of production and improvements in living standards were to be seen everywhere. But the Fourth International leadership was completely blind to reality and so the International Pre-Conference declared that 'there is no reason whatsoever to assume that we are facing a new epoch of capitalist stabilisation and development...the war has aggravated the disorganisation of capitalist economy and has destroyed the last possibilities of a relatively stable equilibrium in social and international relations'.[5]

Furthermore, 'The revival of economic activity in capitalist countries weakened by the war, and in particular continental European countries, will be characterised by an especially slow tempo which will keep their economy at levels bordering on stagnation and decay'.[6]

Using his theory of permanent revolution Trotsky argued that in backward, underdeveloped countries the accomplishment of bourgeois democratic tasks—national liberation and agrarian reform—could be advanced only by working class power. This too was refuted by actual events. In China, the most populous country in the world, Mao led a Stalinist party entirely divorced from the working class to unify the country, win independence from imperialism and institute land reforms. Similar processes occurred elsewhere, such as in Cuba and Vietnam.

I did not yet have an answer to the question of why the world after the war was so different to Trotsky's prognoses. In the coming few years I devoted a lot of time and effort to developing three interlinked theories to deal with the three areas of the world: Russia and Eastern Europe, advanced capitalist countries, and the Third World. The three theories were: state capitalism, the permanent arms economy, and deflected permanent revolution.

The basic points are dealt with in *Trotskyism After Trotsky* so what follows is the briefest of sketches. Trotsky's theory of an insecure bureaucratic layer usurping power in what was basically a workers' state predicted the downfall of Stalinism when faced with a serious crisis like war. The fact that Stalinism emerged from the Second World War immeasurably strengthened and in command of vast territories in Eastern Europe meant that Trotsky must have been mistaken. A different theory was needed. State capitalism fitted the facts. Since 1929 the Stalinist state bureaucracy had, through collectivisation of the farms and forced industrialisation in the cities, massively accumulated capital. It behaved like any other capitalist ruling class by exploiting the workers and competing internationally, in the form of an arms race. It differed from other capitalisms only in that formally all the means of production were owned by a corporate group—the state bureaucracy—rather than private individuals.

My rejection of Trotsky's definition of Stalinist Russia as a 'degenerated workers' state' took place in 1947-48. For two months I was riven by doubts about this definition. I did practically nothing during the day or night but think about it. Poor Chanie suffered. We slept in a narrow bed, and she had to get up at six every morning to go and work far away in Kent—in the worst winter for a long time. One early morning I jumped out of bed and told her, 'Russia is not a workers' state but state capitalist.' It took me more than a year afterwards to put flesh on the skeleton. In Dublin I managed to research *The Class Nature of Stalinist Russia*. Completed in 1948, this was a very long duplicated document of 142 pages. *On the Class Nature of the*

People's Democracies followed in July 1950 (also in duplicated form), as did a book, *Stalin's Satellites in Europe* two years after that.

It is important to note that though a break from Trotsky, the theory of state capitalism built on the Trotskyist tradition. My criticism of Trotsky's position was intended as a return to classical Marxism. Historical development—especially after Trotsky's death—demonstrated that the 'degenerated workers' state' position was not compatible with the classical Marxist tradition which identified socialism as the self emancipation of the working class. To preserve the spirit of Trotsky's writing on the Stalinist regime the letter of his writing had to be sacrificed.

There were other groups, such as anarchists and sectarian Marxist groups, which described Russia as state capitalist, but they argued it had been so from the very beginning—from 1917. Locating the move to state capitalism in 1929 meant recognising the importance of the tradition of the October Revolution which created the first workers' state in history after the 1871 Paris Commune. It also meant defending the lessons of the struggle at home (of Trotsky against Stalin) and on the international scale (in particular the first four Congresses of the Communist International). The year 1929 is significant because it was the moment when Stalin transformed the programme of the dominant bureaucracy, making it one of deliberate accumulation of capital. It became a capitalist ruling class and simultaneously converted the mass of the population into an exploited proletariat through forced collectivisation and industrialisation.

The argument about state capitalism was confirmed and deepened by changes in Eastern Europe after the Second World War. If Trotsky had been right, the creation of governments identical to Russia by order of the Red Army, would have meant the creation of workers' states (without the destruction of the existing state machines) by order of Stalin and entirely without the intervention or involvement of the working classes in these countries.

The theory of state capitalism was not only important in explaining what was going on in one sixth of the world. It was an essential guide to future action of the international working class. This would be shown in a number of ways. It was not just useful in debates with Stalinists organised in the Communist Party (which was then a powerful force on the industrial front). It helped us in arguments with non-Stalinist workers who looked at Russia and said, 'If revolutionary socialism really equals labour camps and vicious repression of workers, then we don't want to have anything to do with it.' Finally, it avoided the difficulties and ambiguities that orthodox Trotskyists faced, which, in a sharply polarised situation of Cold War, often turned them into apologists for Stalinism.

Crucially, the theory of state capitalism put the concept of the emancipation of the workers as the act of the working class itself back at the centre of Marxism. Although it might have seemed miles away from issues such as struggle over wages and conditions in the factories, building a non-Stalinist tradition among workers meant there was an alternative to depending on trade union officials claiming to act on their behalf. This would be the workers acting in their own interests. The concept of rank and file action, of socialism from below, logically followed on from the definition of Russia as state capitalist.

A few years later I took the first step to deal with the theory of the deflected permanent revolution in my book *Mao's China* (1957) and developed it further in my article 'Deflected Permanent Revolution'.[7]

If the theory of state capitalism dealt with the 'Second World', then deflected permanent revolution covered the Third World. Once again the notion of workers' self activity was crucial. In the same way that it seemed to me impossible that a workers' state could be imposed by Russian army tanks in Warsaw, Berlin or Prague, so it was impossible that Mao's peasant army or Castro's rural guerrilla forces could bring socialism to the workers of China and Cuba. The explanation for what had happened did not involve rejecting Trotsky's theory of permanent revolution but reorienting it. Trotsky predicted the weakening of imperialism and social change here being driven by the working class struggling to complete the tasks of the bourgeois revolution and at the same time carrying on through to the struggle for socialism.

What happened in China and Cuba did not depend on working class action in any way. In both cases the conquering military forces came from outside the industrial cities and demanded that the workers remain passive. In a social crisis where the revolutionary subject, proletarian activity and leadership were absent, the result could be a different leadership (a political/military elite) and a different goal—state capitalism. Using what was of universal validity in Trotsky's theory (the conservative character of the bourgeoisie) and what was contingent (the subjective activity of the proletariat), I came to a variant that, for lack of a better name, was called 'deflected permanent revolution'. Reaching this idea actually helped preserve the central theme of Trotsky's theory—the proletariat must continue its revolutionary struggle until it is triumphant the world over. Short of this target it cannot achieve freedom.

While arguments about China and Cuba might have seemed rather abstract in the 1950s and early 1960s they were to be important later. If, as many Trotskyists and Maoists came to believe, socialism could be created by social forces other than the workers, and without workers' involvement, then, if the working class failed to respond to appeals, it could be dropped and forgotten about. Belief that Cuba and China were socialist therefore became a bridge leading away from working class politics. This could be a very strong pull. In 1968 it led Trotskyists in the International Marxist Group (the British section of the Fourth International) to the idea that students could bring about socialism. The International Socialists also recruited students, but we never believed that they could substitute for the working class and its activity. For the Maoists, who led the revolutionary movements in places like Italy and Portugal, confusion about the central role of the workers led to the idea that a determined minority could, through sheer will, bring about social transformation. Later on a variety of 'movements' of the oppressed—women, blacks and gays—and the environmental movement were substituted for the hard slog of winning over the working class, which alone has the power to fundamentally challenge capitalist society.

The theory of the permanent arms economy dealt with events in the 'First World'. It was evolved over a number of years. It first appeared as part of the theory of state capitalism in the duplicated document *The Class Nature of Stalinist Russia*. In 1957 the argument became more specific in an article entitled 'Perspectives for the Permanent War Economy', which moved from the effect of military expenditure on the dynamics of Stalinist Russia to its effect on capitalism in the West and in Japan.[8]

In this, military competition between Russia and the Western capitalist countries was identified as the chief mechanism enforcing the dynamic of capital accumulation in Russia. The converse was also true—on the other side of the Iron Curtain the Cold War ensured that arms spending remained at a high level. The massive cost of weaponry ensured that demand was kept high and employment maintained through the production of goods that were in effect pure waste. They were stockpiled and did not return to the economy for sale. As a result not only could there be full employment, but overproduction of goods for sale was avoided and the tendency of the rate of profit to fall (because investment in machinery grows faster than investment in surplus value making labour) was offset.

Another factor helped me to grasp the workings of the permanent arms economy. Coming to Britain from Palestine in 1946, and viewing the conditions here from the perspective of a colonial country, I was struck by the fact that:

> The standard of living for workers was high. When I first visited a worker's house—just an ordinary house—I asked his job and he said he was an engineer. My English wasn't very good so I thought he meant an engineer with a degree. But he was a semi-skilled engineering worker. It was a complete shock. Children were better off than in the 1930s. The only time I saw children without shoes in Europe was in Dublin. Children didn't get rickets any more. This helped me to realise that the final crisis wasn't just around the corner.[9]

The permanent arms economy predicted a quite different evolution to that expected by Trotsky's followers and proved useful in escaping dangerous political traps. For example, Gerry Healy insisted that Trotsky's reading of the late 1930s was valid for the 1950s and that capitalism was on the brink of catastrophe. So his Trotskyist organisation, the Socialist Labour League (SLL), which was the largest of the post-war groups, was always calling for general strikes and expecting imminent revolution. It also believed that a transitional programme of demands could provide a shortcut to influence over a mass of workers rapidly moving to the left. When none of this happened the members either became disillusioned and left, or gradually found it harder and harder to relate to the real (if limited) struggles of workers under a booming capitalism. This led the SLL ultimately into a sectarian dead end where it was isolated politically from the real debates and arguments in the movement. A practical example of this was the launching of a daily paper which ruined the organisation very quickly. Not only did the situation in the outside world mean that the circulation of such a paper was bound to be very limited, but the organisation itself was far too small to sustain the burden.

The permanent arms economy theory suggested there were no shortcuts like transitional programmes or calls for general strikes. Instead work would have to be adapted to the actual level of the struggle on both the ideological and industrial planes.

On the other hand there were those on the left who, consciously or unconsciously, understood that post-war capitalism was booming. However, without a Marxist theory to explain it, they took the surface appearance of things to be all there was. There were many former Marxists who were now prophets of an eternal capitalist boom, such as John Strachey. He argued that the system would thrive so long as Keynesian economic policies were followed. The right wing reformist Anthony Crosland also waxed lyrical about a capitalism reformed by Keynesian methods. His book *The Future of Socialism* published in 1956, argued that the anarchy of capitalism was withering away, and so also class conflicts. The system was becoming more and more rational and democratic. Capitalism itself would peacefully dissolve. Now that Keynesianism guaranteed uninhibited growth, said Crosland, the state could look forward to high tax revenues which could finance social reforms and social welfare plans. Instead of class struggle, we socialists would:

> …turn our attention increasingly to other, and in the long run more important spheres—of personal freedom, happiness, and cultural endeavour; the cultivation of leisure, beauty, grace, gaiety, excitement…more open-air cafes, brighter and gayer streets at night, later closing-hours for public houses, more local repertory theatres, better and more hospitable hoteliers and restauranteurs…more murals and pictures in public places, better designs for furniture and pottery and women's clothes, statues in the centre of new housing estates, better designed street lamps and telephone kiosks, and so on ad infinitum.[10]

The theory of permanent arms economy explained that capitalism had not changed its spots, and that the reprieve from declining profit rates and the boom/slump cycle was only temporary. The fundamental contradiction between capital and labour had not disappeared. The employment effects of arms spending would decline once weapons production moved from being concentrated in the metal-bashing industries (engineering factories turning out lorries and simple tanks) to sophisticated, expensive weapons plants which employed fewer workers. The cost of arms spending might lead to stability at first but, because it was unevenly shared, would lead to ever greater instability in the future. So it was that Germany and Japan, with small military budgets, grew very fast and posed problems for Britain and the US, while Russia and its Eastern Bloc were thrown into turmoil, which has brought war back to the continent of Europe. Without a long term perspective of the breakdown of capitalism it would have been easy to have been drawn into the reformist road of Labour politics or bureaucratic trade unionism.

The theory of permanent arms economy took it for granted that the irrationality of capitalism did not lessen with its ageing. Capitalism, which in Marx's words, was covered throughout its history in blood and mud, did not become more benevolent in old age. As a matter of fact the permanent arms economy is the most extreme expression of the horrors and barbarism of the system. The economic growth, a byproduct of the permanent arms economy, meant prosperity balancing on the cone of a nuclear warhead.

The troika—state capitalism, the permanent arms economy, and deflected permanent revolution—make a unity, a totality, grasping the changes in the situation of humanity after the Second World War. This is an affirmation of Trotskyism in general, while at the same time partially its negation. Marxism as a living theory must continue as it is, and change at the same time. However, the troika was not conceived as a unity and did not come into being in a flash. It was the result of several long explorations into economic, social and political developments in three portions of the globe: Russia and Eastern Europe, the advanced industrialised capitalist countries, and the Third World. The paths of research criss-crossed each other again and again. But it was only at the end of the process that the interrelationships between the different spheres of research became clear. Only at the top of a mountain can one see the relationship between the different footpaths designed to reach the summit and from the vantage point the analysis turns into a synthesis.

Once the old has been moved out of the way it is much easier to accept the new. The idea that the earth moves round the sun becomes quite convincing once the age-old common sense idea that the sun moves round the earth is rejected.

We have moved very much ahead with our story, for which the justification is that the critique of Trotsky's theory has to be taken as one whole. It was a radical change in the theory, and was advanced slowly, through many doubts and real soul searching. However, it was not true that I did nothing but engage in study, in theoretical work.

Parallel to this activity I spent a marvellous year in Britain, engaged in talking to real 'worker intellectuals', or what Gramsci called 'organic' intellectuals of the working class. I learnt such a lot from them about real workers and their struggle. I went through a learning curve, not sharp but continuously upward. I did not jump up shouting, 'Eureka!' as I was not faced with a sharp turn like in my theoretical work. But it was a most enjoyable, most inspiring experience.

Chapter 3

The Socialist Review Group

Coming to England

I was so excited. I had to learn Marxism afresh.

By force of circumstances, my Marxism, shaped in Palestine, was very one-sided. I hungrily read Marx's works. Before I reached the age of 18 I had read the three volumes of *Capital*. I also read a number of Marx's other writings, as well as the works of Engels, Lenin, Trotsky and Luxemburg. Alas, my Marxism was very abstract even though I repeated again and again that the heart of Marxism was the unity of theory and practice and that 'the philosophers have only interpreted the world in various ways; the point is to change it'.[1]

Until this point the restricted scope for activity in Palestine meant that Marxism had been for me very much a science. It is true that Marxism as a guide to action is of necessity a science, but it is also an art, a creative art. Newton's law of gravity is scientific. Using this science to throw a stone at a target, or even more, to direct an artillery bombardment, is an art which can be achieved only by the application of experience to the science. It was not an accident that Napoleon was a brilliant artillery officer: he was very good at mathematics, but also endowed with imagination, a realistic grasp of circumstances resulting from experience and practice.

London opened a new chapter in my political life. I felt like a pupil, having to learn the ABC of Marxism as an art, which is the foundation for turning knowledge into practice.

Straight after coming to London Chanie and I joined the Revolutionary Communist Party (RCP), British section of the Fourth International. It had 400 members, practically all of them workers, trade unionists and worker intellectuals.

From the moment I came to Britain I was invited to attend the weekly meetings of the Political Bureau of the party. I believe the main inducement for the leadership to invite me was that, they, like me, did not agree with the perspective of the International Secretariat regarding the state of world capitalism. With full employment in

Britain, rising production and rising wages, it was ridiculous to repeat the International Secretariat's dictum that 'the revival of economic activity in capitalist countries weakened by the war, and in particular continental European countries, will be characterised by an especially slow tempo which will keep their economy at levels bordering on stagnation and decay'. The leadership of the RCP welcomed my participation in debates on the subject in party meetings. They also welcomed my article criticising Mandel, entitled 'All that Glitters is not Gold,' published in the Internal Bulletin of the RCP in September 1947.

My article was a critique of an article by Mandel dealing with the perspectives for capitalism after the war. Mandel's statement was mechanical in the extreme. He did not grasp the dialectical relation between the destruction of capital during the war and the prospect of accelerated capital accumulation after the war. The one contributed to the other. He also forgot that so long as capitalism exists the rhythm of slump and boom cannot be avoided any more than a heartbeat can be avoided so long as a person is alive.

At that time I had very close, warm relations with Jock Haston, the general secretary of the RCP. He was a very impressive worker-intellectual, a few years older than me, and he referred to me as his 'young brother'. Also at the time, in 1947, Jock did toy with the idea that perhaps Stalin's Russia was not a workers' state. But a few months later he dropped this idea completely.

I had a marvellous time in Britain. Sadly, at the end of 1947 the British authorities threw me out of the country when a long struggle to renew my permit to stay was lost. The permit had been renewed repeatedly, but only for a month at a time.

Throughout this uncertain period we made great efforts to move to France. I was registered as a student at 17 French universities. Chanie went over to Paris to try to clinch the move. The French foreign office was still under wartime restrictions, so she had to use the telephone to speak to someone. The official she spoke to was delighted to practice his English and spent an hour talking to her, ending: 'Don't worry, just ring back in an hour and I'll have everything ready.' She rang back in an hour, and was bluntly told, 'Your husband will never come to France.'

I was very pessimistic about my prospects. I had already had a few rejections previously. In 1938 I was registered at Columbia University in the US, but I was refused entry by the American authorities; my police record did not cast me in a good light. In 1946 I tried, on my way to Britain, to pass through South Africa, where Chanie was born and where the majority of her family still lived, but I had been refused entry there too.

Finally, one day, towards the end of September 1947, I got a letter from the Home Office. I did not keep the letter, but I remember it very clearly. It said something like, 'Dear Sir, unless you leave the country within 24 hours, we shall have to use force against you. Your obedient servant, Chuter Ede, home secretary.' I thought, 'What hypocrisy. If he was my servant, he could not kick me out of the country; I could kick him out.' I was allowed back to Britain in 1952 which was, of course, a great relief. However, at that time I said, 'Until now there were two people who took my politics seriously—the home secretary and me. Now only I am left.'

Thirty one years later, in 1978, I applied to the Home Office to get British citizenship. I had already been 26 years resident in the country. My application was supported by Michael Foot, at the time deputy prime minister, and other prominent MPs. In due course my application came up to the office where it was to be dealt with but the *Daily Mail* somehow got wind of the story. It decided to make headline news of Michael Foot's sponsorship of 'this Trotskyist'. A worker in the *Daily Mail* notified us of this. Our house became surrounded by journalistic snoopers with cameras. Chanie warned her headmaster that her school might be invaded by them, and we went down to Fleet Street at 2am to see the first edition of the paper. To our amazement there was nothing. We learnt subsequently that Michael Foot had used a D notice to prevent the paper publishing the story.

Michael Foot could browbeat the *Daily Mail*, but he could not browbeat Special Branch into granting me British citizenship, which they refused. Special Branch had a grudge against me. After all, in 1939, the British authorities in Palestine had imposed a detention order on me for one year. It raises the question: who is more powerful, the elected MP and deputy prime minister, or the Special Branch?

Coming back to September 1947, the same post office delivery that brought me the letter from Chuter Ede telling me to get out of the country included a letter from the Irish authorities, allowing me to come to Dublin to be a student at Trinity College. It seems that the Irish authorities, not being on friendly terms with the British at the time, did not check with them whether I was an undesirable person. As a matter of fact, a few weeks after I went to Ireland, I got a letter from the authorities, asking to see me. When I arrived an official said to me, 'You came here on false pretences. You did not tell us you are a Trotskyist.' I answered, 'You did not ask me.' I stayed in Ireland for four and a half years.

Chanie came with me to Ireland. She tried to find a job that would provide for both of us. The best she could find was a teaching post in a Protestant school—living in—and offering the princely salary of £3 a week. Not even a single person could dream of living on that!

So Chanie returned to England, and for the next four and a half years we lived in separate countries. For nearly a year I was not allowed to visit Britain, but then the authorities relaxed and I was allowed to come to Britain during the university holidays. Chanie came to visit me in Dublin during many of her school holidays.

Life was very hard. Finances were a real headache. Chanie's income of £7 a week, in today's prices some £150 a week, had to provide for two separate rooms, one in London and one in Dublin, food for two people, and after the birth of our first child, Elana, in 1949, for three, and also for travelling to and from Dublin. After paying the rent I had the princely sum of £1 a week to spend on myself. That was enough to keep body and soul together—bread and jam and a cup of tea for breakfast, the same for dinner, and the same plus an egg for supper. I never used the bus or bought a newspaper. I went to the public library to read. My only luxury was the theatre. At that time a ticket to both Dublin theatres was very cheap. Chanie had it tougher. As a teacher she worked through the lunch hour to get a free meal during the week; the problem as regards food was the weekend. Incidentally, when Elana was born I related the glad tidings to my Palestinian Arab co-tenant. 'Oh,' he replied sympathetically, 'too bad. Better luck next time.'

Politically, life in Dublin was very tough. I felt even more isolated and lonely than in prison; I hardly knew anyone. When I moved to Ireland the *Quatrième Internationale* journal reported that Comrade Cliff moved to Ireland to work under the auspices of the Irish section. Alas, it was difficult to do so, as the total membership of the section was one—Johnny Byrne, a very fine, honest, tough council worker, tall and well-built with astonishing hands—as big as five hands, we always said. The report in *Quatrième Internationale* was probably written to encourage Trotskyist comrades elsewhere.

In this desert there was one oasis—the household of Owen Sheehy-Skeffington, his wife, Andree, and their lovely children. His father, Francis, had been executed by the British in 1916 because of his sympathy for the Easter Rising. It was a most welcoming and warm family. Every Friday I was invited to have supper with them, but more important, to enjoy their warm friendship.

Owen Sheehy-Skeffington (1909-70) was a radical socialist pacifist. He had a beautiful personality. He was very honest, morally courageous and had a fine sense of humour. I shall give a few examples.

There was a mass open-air meeting in Dublin, chaired by the Irish president, Éamon de Valera, dedicated to the resurrection of the Gaelic language. The Green Tories in the Irish Republic were using the Gaelic language as a figleaf to hide their capitulation to the partition of Ireland. After the main speech, Owen moved forward and asked to speak to the meeting. Being the son of a martyr he got a warm welcome. He said one sentence in Gaelic, to further applause. He then spoke in English, saying, 'For those who don't understand Gaelic, I'll translate what I just said. I said, "I hardly know a word of Gaelic, and the whole language is not worth a farthing".'

Another example. We both went to a meeting organised by the Stalinists in Dublin. In the discussion Owen said the following, 'In 1938 Chamberlain said we were not living in the medieval time of religious wars. If the Germans want to support the Nazis it is their business.' He then stopped a moment and went on to say, 'I'm terribly sorry. I made a mistake. It was not Chamberlain in 1938, but Molotov [the Russian foreign minister] in 1940 at the time of the Hitler-Stalin Pact.' You should have seen the face of the Stalinist speaker!

The third incident was this. Father O'Brian, a professor in Galway University, declared, 'Socialism believes in free love. Free love is prostitution.' Owen wrote a letter to the *Irish Times* saying, 'I know we have prostitution in Dublin. I did not know we had socialism.' For contradicting the priest Owen was expelled from the Labour Party.

Things became much tougher when a complete break took place between me and the leadership of the RCP. We had a common position regarding the economic perspectives of the West. But when I developed the theory that Stalinist Russia was state capitalist, our paths diverged completely.

The difference was sharpened by the reaction of the RCP leadership to the February 1948 Stalinist coup in Czechoslovakia, when a totalitarian regime was established. The *Socialist Appeal* of March 1948 had the following headline: 'Capitalists Routed In Czechoslovakia' by Jock Haston. Although the article had strong criticisms of the Stalinist regime's lack of democracy, it still hailed the February 1948 coup as a great triumph for the proletariat. We in Britain 'should be rejoicing at the victory over the capitalists'.

A comrade from Britain who visited me in Dublin brought me the paper. My reaction was clear and sharp. That was the end of the RCP. One cannot maintain a Trotskyist organisation while singing the praises of Stalinism. The RCP practically disintegrated a year later.

Jock Haston, general secretary of the RCP, by far the strongest member of the leadership, made astonishing zigzags. After kowtowing to Stalinism, he veered sharply rightwards, and in effect aligned himself with the Labour Party.

When Nye Bevan resigned from the Labour government in April 1951 in protest at the imposition of prescription, denture and spectacle charges, Jock Haston opposed Bevan's resignation from the right. When the debate raged in the Labour movement on the issue of German rearmament—the right Labour leaders following the Tories in supporting it, the left (including the Communist Party) opposing it—Haston supported German rearmament. The last time I came across Haston was when I read in the Confederation of British Industries journal a glowing report of his role as education officer of the Electrical Trade Union, at that time under the control of the McCarthyite right wing leadership of Frank Chapple and Les Cannon: 'Now some 1,000 trade unionists attend the courses given by Jock Haston and his staff. They include shop stewards, branch secretaries, and other full time officials.' Jock Haston told Ford management, 'I'm a socialist but we have a common interest to see the job is run efficiently'.[2]

My break with the RCP leadership crystallised around my document *The Class Nature of Stalinist Russia*, which saw the light of day in June 1948. For a year I worked on this essay. I finished a section at a time and posted it to Chanie in London. My English had improved since I left Palestine, but it was still very imperfect. I would write a couple of sentences in English, then a sentence in Hebrew, and then possibly a sentence partly in English and partly in Hebrew. Chanie had to translate. Every time I sent a section it was 'Found open or damaged and sealed by the Post Office'. As a matter of fact I was very careful to wrap it up well. When Chanie informed me about what happened to the manuscript I suggested she contact Special Branch, as probably they had already typed it, so that she could save time and effort!

The document was for the Internal Bulletin of the RCP. The normal size for articles in this publication was two to five pages. But mine grew and grew like topsy. When Chanie finished cutting the stencil the RCP leadership was aghast. But they found it difficult to reject publication of the document as I had been but a few weeks earlier the darling of the party. In addition, Chanie did all the typing and another comrade did all the duplicating. An editorial statement accompanied the document, saying, 'This long work of Comrade T Cliff has been published as a concession to the author. It cannot be regarded in any way as a precedent.'

The Socialist Review Group

The comrades who held the state capitalist position were either expelled by Gerry Healy, who took control of what was left of the RCP and formed the Socialist Labour League, or left it. To start with, we had eight members.[3] Among them were two very impressive worker-intellectuals, Duncan Hallas and Geoff Carlsson, both engineers. Duncan had a fantastically rich knowledge. He had read and absorbed wide areas of world history, history of the international labour movement, Marxian economics, historical materialism and philosophy. It was a pleasure to listen to him speak. Geoff Carlsson was also a very serious worker-intellectual. However, his knowledge was not as broad as that of Duncan. But still Geoff had a very great desire to learn. I remember him in 1954 writing an article on Guatemala for *Socialist Review*. He was, quite rightly, very proud of it.

Late in 1950 we began to publish a duplicated monthly paper, *Socialist Review*, the new group taking its name from the paper. It held its founding conference in summer 1951. At the first recorded meeting (September 1950) there were just 33 members present. Groups existed in London, Thames Valley, Crewe, Birmingham, Sheffield and Manchester. Nineteen of the 33 were in the Labour League of Youth. We were a minute force. We produced 350 copies of the first issue of the paper; sales were apparently sufficiently encouraging for the figure to be raised for the second issue…to 375![4] A little later the print order went up to 500. Half the sale of *Socialist Review* was done by three comrades: Chanie, her sister Mickey Kidron and her brother Mike Kidron. (Chanie, although one of the SWP's oldest members, is still one of its best paper sellers!) The Socialist Review Group was, throughout the 1950s, a purely propagandist group; it was not able to make any meaningful intervention in the class struggle. But even propaganda has to have an audience.[5]

Mike Kidron, Chanie's youngest brother, came to Britain in 1955. He joined us straight away. He became a leading member of our group, and very popular as a lecturer. He was, for five years, the editor of what became our monthly magazine, *Socialist Review*. In 1960, when we started a theoretical quarterly, *International Socialism*, Mike became the editor, and held this position for five years. In 1958 his book *Western Capitalism Since the War* was published. This made a significant contribution to the theory of the permanent arms economy. Sadly, in the late 1970s, he drifted away from revolutionary socialism. However, he never made any open criticism of our organisation.

I drew great encouragement in building the Socialist Review Group from two veteran revolutionaries I met in the early 1950s: Alfred Rosmer (1877-1964) and Heinrich Brandler (1881-1967). Rosmer was one of the few revolutionary socialists who opposed the First World War from its beginning, collaborating with Trotsky. He was a member of Trotsky's Left Opposition. He was so full of enthusiasm hearing about our tiny group, that it really gave me courage. He told me how small the anti-war grouping in France was at the beginning of the First World War, and so he did not pooh-pooh our tiny little group. It was inspiring to hear him arguing seriously and with respect with my daughter Elana, who at the time was five or six years old!

Another meeting which was important to me was with Heinrich Brandler, who was the leading member of the German Communist Party (KPD) after the deaths of Rosa Luxemburg and Karl Liebknecht. Brandler was the key leader of the party in 1923, when the revolutionary wave rose in Germany, and the Communist Party had the majority of workers behind it. I asked him why the KPD did not take power at the time. He replied, 'We were waiting for instructions from Moscow.' I said to him, 'I'm sure Lenin and Trotsky would not have dreamt of waiting for instructions from Rosa Luxemburg, however brilliant she was, on the eve of October.' He explained that the Communist Party of Germany was very inexperienced. At its foundation in December 1918 it had about

4,000 members who 'were really not Marxists, but pacifists'. The KPD was founded one month after the overthrow of the Kaiser. As against this the Bolshevik Party was founded some 14 years before the overthrow of Tsarism. This strengthened my conviction that time was needed to train cadres. One cannot wait for the revolution to do that. This spurred us on in building the Socialist Review Group.

Of course *Socialist Review* disseminated ideas. We followed Lenin in seeing a revolutionary paper as an organiser, as 'scaffolding' for building the party. And, of course, our puny magazine was nothing compared with Lenin's *Iskra*. In an article, 'Where to Begin', Lenin wrote that 'the role of a newspaper' should not be:

> …limited solely to the dissemination of ideas, to political education, and to the enlistment of political allies. A newspaper is not only a collective propagandist and a collective agitator, it is also a collective organiser. In this last respect it may be likened to the scaffolding round a building under construction, which marks the contours of the structure and facilitates communication between the builders, enabling them to distribute the work and to view the common results achieved by their organised labour. With the aid of a newspaper, and through it, a permanent organisation will naturally take shape that will engage, not only in local activities, but in regular general work, and will train its members to follow political events carefully, appraise their significance and their effect on the various strata of the population, and develop effective means for the revolutionary party to influence those events. The mere technical task of regularly supplying the newspaper with copy and of promoting regular distribution will necessitate a network of local agents of the united party, who will maintain constant contact with one another, know the general state of affairs, get accustomed to performing regularly their detailed functions in the all-Russian work, and test their strength in the organisation of various revolutionary actions.
>
> This network of agents will form the skeleton of precisely the kind of organisation we need—one that is sufficiently broad and many-sided to effect a strict and detailed division of labour; sufficiently well-tempered to be able to conduct steadily its own work under any circumstance, at all 'sudden turns', and in the face of all contingencies; sufficiently flexible to be able, on the one hand, to avoid the open battle against an overwhelming enemy, when the enemy has concentrated all its forces at one

point, and yet, on the other, to take advantage of his unwieldiness and to attack him when and where he least expects it.[6]

Writing articles for *Socialist Review*, selling it, and contributing to its financing, cemented the comrades together and created bridges to the periphery of the group, trying to win them over. We always looked at two key features: what was common between us and the people who did not belong to our group, but whom we talked to, and what differences there were between them and us. If there was nothing in common, there was no way we could influence them—it was like speaking Greek to English people. On the other hand, if we only confirmed what there was in common we would not teach them anything, and once they have one issue of the paper, there is no reason for them to buy another one. There must be a tension between members of the group and people outside. At one and the same time there must be tension inside the group—intellectual tension. It is neither only agreement or only arguments. Both are needed.

We were worried that a sectarian spirit would dominate our members if we had no regular contact with people in the Labour movement. Hence we decided to work in the Labour Party. Alas, there was also a danger of opportunism arising from this. This became clear in 1954 when the debate on German rearmament took place in the Labour movement and at least one of our members took an extremely opportunist position. In a way it was funny when he met me and bragged, 'You see I won my Labour Party General Management Committee to oppose German rearmament, unlike Jean who lost the vote in her GMC.' I then compared the two resolutions that were put forward. Jean Tait's resolution said more or less the following: 'We, who oppose all imperialist armament, also oppose German rearmament.' His successful resolution said something to this effect: 'Those Germans, who made two world wars, cannot be trusted.'

We, unlike many in the Trotskyist movement, had no illusions then or later, about transforming the Labour Party into a revolutionary party. In a speech to the Second Congress of the Communist International in 1920 Lenin defined the Labour Party as a 'capitalist workers' party'. He called it capitalist because the politics of the Labour Party do not break with capitalism. Why did he call it a workers' party? It is not because workers voted for it. At that time more workers voted for the Conservative Party; and the Conservative Party is, of course, a capitalist party. Lenin called the Labour Party a capitalist workers' party because it expressed the urge of workers to defend themselves against capitalism.

Compare this with the nature of the revolutionary party as set out in the *Communist Manifesto*:

> The Communists are distinguished from the other working class parties by this only: (1) In the national struggles of the proletarians of the different countries, they point out and bring to the front the common interests of the entire proletariat, independently of all nationality. (2) In the various stages of development which the struggle of the working class against the bourgeoisie has to pass through, they always and everywhere represent the interests of the movement as a whole.
>
> The Communists, therefore, are on the one hand, practically the most advanced and resolute section of the working class parties of every country, that section which pushes forward all others; on the other hand, theoretically, they have over the great mass of the proletariat the advantage of clearly understanding the line of march, the conditions, and the ultimate general results of the proletarian movement.[7]

So our stay inside the Labour Party had strictly limited aims—to recruit to the cause of revolutionary socialism. Recruitment was especially possible in the youth section of the party. A resolution carried by the Socialist Review Group in the 1950s, decided 'that we concentrate in the next period on recruiting, and direct our primary efforts towards the League of Youth, accepting all elements who will accept our theoretical position, even though their theoretical level is low.'

We also did our best not to limit our activities to the Labour Party or the League of Youth. Birchall wrote, quite rightly, that trade union intervention was necessarily very limited for a small group with few industrial workers. But priority was always given to the few opportunities that did exist. Minutes of the first few months of the group's existence record discussion of the coming USDAW shop workers' union conference, at which a comrade was to be a delegate, and the recommendation that a comrade should stand for the national executive committee of the NALGO local government union. There was also regular work on the Birmingham Trades Council.

And in 1959 Geoff Carlsson, a founder member of the group and now chair of shop stewards at the ENV factory in north west London, ran for the presidency of the engineers' AEU union. The number of

AEU members in the group could have been counted on the fingers of one hand, and there was no intervention other than the work of individuals. But candidates had the right to circulate an election address and Carlsson used this to put forward an alternative policy for the union. After criticising the right wing leadership of the union for failing to give a lead over wages or redundancies, he went on, 'In the elections over the past years, members have had to choose between candidates backed by right wing Labour or the Communist Party. The choice has not been easy. Although most members owe allegiance to the Labour Party, they cannot accept the policies pursued by the right wing of the trade unions and Labour Party when these have included wage freezing, class collaboration and "sell outs". Alternatively, although they respect the militant activities of the individual Communist Party member in the daily struggles on the shop floor, they cannot ignore the external loyalties of the Communist Party to Russia; nor forget the anti working class measures adopted by that country in East Berlin, Poznan, Hungary, etc.'

That there was some response to this position was shown by the voting; Carlsson, without any machine at his disposal, got 5,615 votes out of a total of 91,400, against 57,127 for right wing Carron and 19,799 for Communist Party member Birch.

One person who was quite removed from the pantheon of the 'greats' of Marxism for many years was Rosa Luxemburg. Stalinism was not compatible with her concept of the self-activity of workers, with the unity of economics and politics and her concept that in the mass strike there is to be found the heart of the socialist revolution.

In Stalinist theory the party replaces the class as the active force. However, for Marxists, the revolutionary party does not substitute for the class. The party does not relate to workers as the foreman relates to his subordinates in the factory, or the officer to the privates in the army—barking at them. The role of the revolutionary is to raise the self activity and confidence of the workers. We do not emulate hierarchical capitalist institutions; after all, the essence of Marxism is 'the emancipation of the working class is the act of the working class'.

However, the Trotskyist movement, being isolated, fell into the trap of substitutionism. This is the idea that the mass self activity of the working class is unnecessary and that other groups or forces can substitute for it. In the conditions of the 1950s the particular form that substitutionism took was the belief, common to all sects, that if it has the right position the problem is solved.

For the intellectual ideas are not a weapon for action, the ideas are themselves the action. This would be the approach of the New Left growing up in Britain at this time. For the New Left the concept of the unity of theory and practice was the following: Marx wrote a book—that was theory. I read the book and interpret it—that is practice. Actually, both of them remain in the realm of theory. The practice is when the theory relates to the class struggle.

To the rest of the far left, the Socialist Review Group were the 'state caps'. The far left emphasised that which was a point of distinction, that which separated them from others. Our standpoint was different. State capitalism as a theory was important, but only if it was a starting point for a correct orientation in practice, not a mark of difference.

One rule I have always followed is not to read sectarian literature. I never read Healy's newspaper, nor that of the International Marxist Group. Once I met Gerry Healy after his paper had carried a long series of articles attacking our tendency and me personally, and asked him, 'Why do you spend so much time on criticising me? I am not a commander of US troops in Vietnam; I am not the head of the CBI.' While I avoided sectarian literature I always read the wider left press avidly. This included *Tribune*, the left Labour paper which had a significant influence on the left in general and whose arguments, therefore, were important to know about.

That the Socialist Review Group was small and had very little influence in the conditions of the 1950s was inevitable, but that it should adopt the attitudes of a sect and fall into substitutionism was not. To fight against this danger I wrote two things. One was a summing up of Rosa Luxemburg's life, *Rosa Luxemburg* (1959), and an article called 'Trotsky on Substitutionism'.[8]

The monthly production of *Socialist Review* was quite an effort. Because our human resources were very limited, I had to be a Jack of all trades. I wrote about half of all the articles, using a number of pseudonyms: articles on Britain were signed R Tennant; on Russia, L Turov; on France, De Lacroix; on Spain and Latin America, L Miguel; there were another couple of pseudonyms I have forgotten. I remember a funny incident. Looking into the paper of the POUM, published in Paris, I saw an article by L Miguel, 'our correspondent in Puerto Rico'. The nearest

I came to that country was the reading room in the British Museum!

I was also the circulation manager of *Socialist Review* and acted as secretary of the group, though without a title. For many years I was also the treasurer of the group. I used to give an annual report. Sadly, practically every year the finances did not balance. Either the expenditure was larger than the income, or vice versa. In the first case, in drafting the financial report I added to the plus side an item called 'Miscellaneous Income'. If the income was larger than the expenditure, I added 'Miscellaneous Expenditure'. The difference was never more than a couple of pounds, and as I never managed to buy a Rolls Royce, I was never mired in sleaze. In addition to these multifarious roles, Chanie and I had quite often to act as psychotherapists. Individual members were often sunk in depression.

In 1960 the Socialist Review Group was still tiny, some 60 members in all. Its small size had prevented it benefiting, in a limited way, from the events of 1956—the radicalisation caused by the Tory invasion of Egypt and the split in the Communist Party following the Hungarian Revolution.

The Hungarian Revolution

My document *The Class Nature of Stalinist Russia*, written in 1947-48, ends with the following words:

> The struggle in Stalinist Russia must inevitably express itself in gigantic spontaneous outbursts of millions. Till then it will seem on the surface that the volcano is extinct. Till then the omnipotent sway of the secret police will make it impossible for a revolutionary party to penetrate the masses or organise any systematic action whatsoever. The spontaneous revolution, in smashing the iron heel of the Stalinist bureaucracy, will open the field for the free activity of all the parties, tendencies and groups in the working class. It will be the first chapter in the victorious proletarian revolution. The final chapter can be written only by the masses, self-mobilised, conscious of socialist aims and the methods of their achievement, and led by a revolutionary Marxist party.[9]

Eight years later, in 1956, this prognosis was confirmed by the Hungarian Revolution. On 24 October mass strikes broke out throughout Hungary, culminating in a general strike. On 26 October

Revolutionary Workers' Councils were established throughout the country—in every town and village, in factories and government offices and newspapers. Dual power came into being: side by side with the official Stalinist government a revolutionary workers' government was in place. Dual power, by definition, is unstable and cannot carry on for long. One side or the other must win. In Russia the February 1917 revolution created dual power: side by side with the bourgeois government was a new government, that of the soviets. In October the former was eliminated by the latter.

A crucial element for the victory of October 1917 was the existence of a revolutionary party in the Soviets since February. It is true there were only 40 Bolsheviks out of 1,600 delegates (or 2.5 percent) in the Petrograd soviet of February 1917. After a hard struggle, with Lenin arming the Bolshevik Party and guiding it, in September the Bolsheviks won the majority and took control of the Petrograd soviet as well as the Moscow soviet.

Tragically, in Hungary, as a result of eight years of the rule of totalitarian Stalinism, there did not exist a revolutionary party. In addition, there was no time granted for the development of such a revolutionary party. On 11 December 1956, 30 days after the birth of the Workers' Council of Greater Budapest, all members of the council were arrested.

Workers reacted to the arrests by a mass wave of strikes. On 15 December the death penalty was introduced for inciting strikes. And this did not remain a dead letter; immediately strike leaders were executed. The Hungarian Revolution was given no time to develop. The presence of some 200,000 Russian troops, with 3,000 tanks, guaranteed the victory of the counter-revolution.

During the first week of the Hungarian Revolution, I could hardly close my eyes. I stayed up practically throughout the night, every night, listening to the radio.

Now that the prognosis of 1947-48 was confirmed by the Hungarian Revolution, one could assume that this would bring many of the people in the Communist Party who were disgusted with the Russian butchery into our camp. But this did not happen. Some 10,000 left the British Communist Party in reaction to the events in Hungary. Of these the total number who joined our group could be counted on the fingers of one hand.

There were other political forces in the field that were much more attractive to disappointed Stalinists. First of all there was Isaac Deutscher; secondly, there was the Socialist Labour League led by Gerry Healy.

Isaac Deutscher, a founding member of the Trotskyist organisation in Poland, and the biographer of both Stalin and Trotsky, with his serious research and majestic style, was attractive to dissident Stalinists. Above all, he was less demanding than we were for a complete break from Stalinism.

Deutscher argued that the Stalinist regime was bound to reform itself and automatically bring forward socialism. Following Trotsky, he argued that scarcities caused the rise of the bureaucracy. Therefore a rise in production would bring abundance and with it equality:

> With the growth of productive forces, which makes possible an alleviation of the still existing poverty in consumer goods, a reduction of inequality becomes possible, desirable, and even necessary for the further development of the nation's wealth and civilisation. Such a reduction need not take place primarily or mainly through the lowering of the standards of living of the privileged minority, but through the raising of standards of the majority. In a stagnant society, living on a national income the size of which remains stationary over the years, the standard of living of the broad masses cannot be improved otherwise than at the expense of the privileged groups, who therefore resist any attempt at such improvement. But in a society living on a rapidly growing national income, the privileged groups need not pay, or need not pay heavily for the rise in the well-being of the working masses; and so they need not necessarily oppose the rise.
>
> The privileged minority in the USSR has no absolute interests—it may still have a relative and temporary one—in perpetuating the economic discrepancies and social antagonisms that were inevitable at a lower level of economic development. Nor need they cling to a political regime designed to suppress and conceal those antagonisms behind a 'monolithic' facade.[10]
>
> The reform of the most anachronistic features of the Stalinism regime could be undertaken only from above, by Stalin's former underlings and accomplices.[11]

What mechanical thinking! Scarcity led to the rise of the Stalinist bureaucracy; increased production would automatically lead to the withering away of bureaucracy. A fish gets gills because it lives in water; take it out of the water and it will grow lungs, run around and start barking!

Writing after the death of Stalin in 1953, Deutscher concluded that the locus of all reforms would be the Communist Party of the Soviet Union:

> The process by which the nation may relearn to form and express its opinions may at first be slow and difficult. It can start only from inside the Communist Party. The regime will, either from self-preservation or from inertia, continue as a single party system for years to come. This need not be an important obstacle to democratic evolution as long as party members are permitted to speak their minds on all matters of policy. All politically minded and active elements of the nation are, anyhow, in the ranks of the Communist Party, if only because there has been no other party to turn to.[12]

According to Deutscher Stalinism was revolutionary. It not only protected the achievements of the revolution, but also deepened and enlarged them:

> In 1929, five years after Lenin's death, Soviet Russia embarked upon her second revolution, which was directed solely and exclusively by Stalin. In its scope and immediate impact upon the life of some 160 million people the second revolution was even more sweeping and radical than the first.[13]

> Stalin…remained the guardian and trustee of the revolution. He consolidated its national gains and extended them. He 'built socialism'; and even his opponents, while denouncing his autocracy, admitted that most of his economic reforms were indeed essential for socialism.[14]

Deutscher opposed all the popular uprisings in Eastern Europe, from June 1953 in East Germany, to October 1956 in Poland and Hungary. He declared the latter to be a counter-revolution trying 'unwittingly to put the clock back'.[15] He cheered the Russian tanks which smashed the workers' uprisings:

> Eastern Europe, [Hungary, Poland, and East Germany]…found itself almost on the brink of bourgeois restoration at the end of the Stalin era, and only Soviet armed power (or its threat) stopped it there.[16]

The conclusion: one should keep detached and passive. The

ex-Communists should 'withdraw to the watchtower':

> To watch with detachment and alertness, this heaving chaos of a world, to be on sharp lookout for what is going to emerge from it, and to interpret it *sine ira et studie* [without anger but with attention]...this is now the only honourable service the ex-communist intellectual can render to a generation in which scrupulous observation and honest interpretation have become so sadly rare.[17]

For thousands of ex-Stalinists, Deutscher gave a very soft option. For many of them on the way out of active politics, the offer to sit in a 'watchtower' served as an intellectual justification for giving up all struggle. I remember going to lectures by Deutscher at which there were 1,000 or more present. Twice I spoke from the floor in the discussion, criticising Deutscher's position, but I hardly cut any ice with the audience. My criticisms of Deutscher were published later in an article in *International Socialism* entitled 'The End of the Road: Deutscher's Capitulation to Stalinism'.[18]

Our puny group, offering a tough approach to Stalinism, could not overcome Deutscher's soft soap. Gerry Healy and the Socialist Labour League were more attractive to ex-Stalinists who wanted to continue public activity. Deutscher himself was far more friendly to the SLL than to us. Defining Russia as a workers' state, even if a deformed one, was more attractive than defining it as state capitalism. Hundreds of members of the Communist Party joined the SLL. Among them were a number of prominent intellectuals (like Brian Pearce, John Daniels and Cliff Slaughter) and several prominent workers (among them Brian Behan, the popular building worker and a former member of the national executive of the Communist Party).

Formal logic cannot explain why we were not successful in attracting many to us when events proved we were so right in our analysis. Dialectical thinking makes things much clearer. Our group did not expand very much as a result of the Hungarian Revolution. Quantitatively the impact was minimal, but qualitatively it was significant. We became harder and more convinced in the rightness of our position. And that of course applied to me also.

The state capitalist regime survived the 1956 revolution in Hungary. While surviving in the whole of Eastern Europe and Russia, it withered on the vine; 1989 was not far away.

CND and beyond

At the end of the 1950s new possibilities beckoned. These came with the Campaign for Nuclear Disarmament (CND) calling for unconditional, unilateral abandonment of nuclear weapons by all powers.

The movement grew rapidly, and at Easter 1960 and 1961 about 100,000 people took part in the marches from Aldermaston. Many of them were young and a significant proportion were working class. CND groups provided an initiation into politics for a whole new generation of young people. Most of them had little experience of the Labour Party, though some of them later moved into its youth movement. (The Communist Party was absent in the early years of the campaign, arguing that it was 'divisive', but joined CND by Aldermaston 1960.)

For the Socialist Review Group this new upsurge offered the chance to go beyond the routine of Labour Party and trade union work. Without abandoning its fundamental orientation on the working class, *Socialist Review* (now printed fortnightly) tried to find an audience among those newly radicalised by the CND.

Socialist Review's rejection of capitalism East and West—summed up in the slogan 'Neither Washington nor Moscow but International Socialism'—clearly meant that it condemned equally British, US and Russian H-bombs. This distinguished it from the Communist Party, and from certain 'orthodox' Trotskyist groupings—notably Gerry Healy's SLL—which argued that the Soviet possession of H-bombs (and by implication their possible use against Western workers) was somehow different. The *Socialist Review* position was certainly close to the impulsive reactions of the majority of CND supporters, even if most of them didn't have a very clear analysis to back up their feelings. As a result of its politics and activity, the Socialist Review Group was able, in the early 1960s, to recruit a new set of cadres to supplement the small number who had survived the pressures of the 1950s.

Towards the end of the 1950s and beginning of the 1960s, a new opening beckoned. In February 1960 the Labour Party decided to launch a new national youth movement, the Young Socialists (YS), five years after the disbandment of the Labour League of Youth. By the spring of 1961 there were 726 YS branches, and the first national conference had over 300 delegates.

Although Socialist Review Group members were active both in the CND and in the YS, the latter offered much greater opportunities. First of all branches of the YS met weekly, unlike the CND. Secondly, it allowed discussion of a variety of subjects, not only the bomb. Finally its composition was far more working class. We especially put great emphasis on the importance of the apprentices' strike of 1960, whose main centre was Glasgow.

The dominant theme of discussion in the YS was the nuclear bomb. There were three positions: the right wing, followers of leader of the Labour Party Hugh Gaitskell, who was in support of the Western powers' bomb, and the followers of Gerry Healy, who argued that Russia should keep its bomb, as it was a workers' bomb. The *Socialist Review* members denounced all bombs. We argued that we were not pacifists, and hence we did not oppose all weapons. However the H-bomb was inherently reactionary. A gun in the hands of British troops oppressing a colonial nation, is reactionary. A gun in the hands of colonial rebels is progressive. Alas, the H-bomb cannot differentiate between the two camps. It will annihilate all. I remember I used to recite a song of the Russian Red Air Force from the 1930s. The song went, 'While we bomb your bosses, workers of the world, we distribute leaflets to you.' I used to add, 'The leaflet should be short, as you will have only four minutes to read it.' You cannot have a progressive H-bomb any more than you can have progressive racism, as the bomb does not differentiate between capitalists and workers, rich and poor. *Young Guard*, our youth paper, carried a big headline: 'No Bombs, No Bosses'. Another headline I remember was to an article supporting the Russian bomb. The editor, with a good sense of humour, gave it the heading 'The Workers' Bomb for You and Me'.

The question of nuclear disarmament was the point of departure of the development of many youth. However, their interest was not confined to this. The relation between the bomb and capitalism was of interest to them. The relation between war industry and civilian industry, the fact that, to use Marx's words, 'the slaughter industry is part of industry', fascinated them. The productive forces determine the destructive forces. Under feudalism the serf used a horse and a wooden plough, so the knight had a horse, perhaps a better one than the serf, and a wooden lance. The armies of millions of the First World War could not come into being without millions of workers being mobilised into the munitions industry.

The first time I came into serious contact with a member of the Labour Party youth was in 1958 when I met Roger Cox, who was then 18 years old. He was the son of a railwayman who used to be taken by his father, when he was a child, to union meetings. Now he was an apprentice motor mechanic and member of Shoreditch YS. He used to come every Sunday to our house. We had dinner together and would then spend hours talking. I used to give him lectures for half an hour, or an hour, or even more, at a time. I taught him Marxism, economics, historical materialism, etc. It was a joy to see him developing. He taught me a lot about conditions at his workplace, the workings of the engineering union, the thoughts and feelings of young workers, and so on. In this microcosm I saw the whole world of young workers. More recently I asked Roger what motivated him to come and listen to my lectures on Marxism. He said it was the workers' uprising in Germany in June 1953 and the Hungarian Revolution in 1956.

Besides Roger, another six or seven members of Shoreditch YS used to come every Sunday to sit in the tiny room we had and listen to my lectures on Marxism. I was also invited to speak to the branch meeting of Shoreditch YS held in the rooms of the Labour Party.

Another group of Labour Party youth I met two years afterwards, in 1960, was in Newcastle. Once a fortnight I would come on Saturday for a day school. I gave them a series of lectures that dealt systematically with Marxism: dialectics, historical materialism, Marxist economics from the labour theory of value to the decline of the rate of profit and the nature of the capitalist crisis, monopoly capitalism and imperialism, state and revolution, state capitalism, permanent arms economy. Everyone in the school received a duplicated pamphlet containing a synopsis of every lecture. We took things very seriously indeed. The same pamphlet was used afterwards more widely in the education classes that we held for youngsters everywhere. It is interesting to note that 40 years later everyone I interviewed for writing the present book mentions with real excitement the education in basic ideas such as state capitalism and the permanent arms economy that he or she got at the time.

In Newcastle there were about 15 comrades in the room, all of them youth with the exception of Terry Rodgers, a leading militant in the engineering factory C A Parsons, who was in his early 40s. Five quite quickly joined our group: Terry, John Charlton, Jim Nichol, Jim Hutchinson and a fifth one whose name escapes me. Of these four are still with us.

Meeting Jim Nichol while engaged in preparing the present book, I reminisced with him. He reminded me that he was aged 15 at the time. Two issues in the main motivated him to come to the meetings: state capitalism and the permanent arms economy, the first because of the Hungarian Revolution—the same issue Roger Cox mentioned— as he wanted to understand how and why the Russian Revolution was followed by the victory of Stalin. Jim was interested in the theory of permanent arms economy, because he wanted to understand how and why Western capitalism went through a very long boom with full employment, rising wages, social services, etc.

He reminded me of an incident during my talk on state capitalism. I gave figures on the Stakhanovist movement in Russia where Alexei Stakhanov, the model miner, cut a massive quantity of coal in one shift, serving as a benchmark for other miners to emulate. I explained how Stakhanov achieved those fantastic figures. A specifically selected group of miners prepared a very thick seam with good machinery ready for Stakhanov's work. The line of carriages was in perfect order, and everything else perfect and at the ready. Then Stakhanov came, accompanied by the press and photographers. Jim was staggered by the figures I gave about Stakhanov's output. He was at the time working for the National Coal Board, in an office administering two neighbouring pits. He came from a miners' family; both his father and his uncle were miners. I assuaged Jim's doubts about the figures for output, when I opened a book and showed him in black and white that the figures were authentic. He was convinced, but later said, 'I did not know you were the author of the book you were quoting from. Had I known, my doubts might have persisted.'

I came to Newcastle every fortnight, and this went on for months.

Besides the London group of youngsters and the Newcastle ones, I came in touch with Young Socialists in Glasgow. Some time in the winter of 1961 I was invited to a dayschool organised by the Gorbals YS. The subject was 'The Soviet Union'.

There must have been some 40 to 50 people in the room. The youngsters were overwhelmingly working class, many of them engineering apprentices. A short time before they had been involved in a very large apprentices' strike which covered the whole of Glasgow and also Newcastle. Among those present was Gus MacDonald, an apprentice in the shipyards who played a leading role in the strike. I am bound to admit that he was not only a leading member of the strike, but also a leading member of our youth, and was one of four who represented us on the National Committee of the Young Socialists. At present he is in the House of Lords.*

I started with the following words, 'I can't speak on the Soviet Union because in Russia there are no soviets—they were liquidated by Stalin—and the country is not a union but an empire. The four letters USSR represent four lies: it is not a union; it is not a soviet; it is not socialist; and there are no republics.'

My meeting in Glasgow was followed a few weeks later by the surprise visit of Glasgow apprentices turning up at our home in London. Within a few weeks 42 Glaswegian apprentices had turned up at our tiny house. They all took off their boots to go to sleep on the floor—the atmosphere was heady. Eighteen stayed for breakfast for a period. We had an enormous problem understanding what they said with their working class Glaswegian accent, especially their constant jokes, which had to be repeated over and over for us till they were jokes no longer. Gradually they were absorbed into the workforce and got their own accommodation.

I was very serious in relating to our contacts. I thought every one of them was invaluable. To illustrate this I shall relate a sad story. One day we got a letter from Glasgow, from a man who came across *Socialist Review* and was interested in our group. I decided to visit him, but being poor and unable to afford a rail ticket, I got a comrade to take me on the back of his motor bike. After a long, uncomfortable journey from London we arrived in Glasgow and met the man. He was a very impressive worker in his seventies. We had a very good discussion. But we never heard from him again—a few days after our visit he died.

I was prepared to, and did, travel up and down the country to speak to and recruit contacts. These events were not always guaranteed to run smoothly and efficiently. For instance, I was asked to

* By the way, the most effective leader of the apprentices' strike was Alex Ferguson, today manager of Manchester United Football Club. He not only brought the apprentices at work out on strike, but completely stopped work in the entire factory, Remington Rand, which encouraged the strike in other places. However, Alex Ferguson was not one of the people who came to the meeting I addressed.

speak in Liverpool by Peter Sedgwick, a fine and longstanding comrade. I travelled up, met Peter in the pub and waited. No one turned up. After a long wait I asked to see the leaflet advertising the meeting. An excellent leaflet. There was only one little snag—the leaflet did not give the date of the meeting.

The meeting was rearranged. I travelled up, met Peter in the pub and waited. No one turned up. After a long wait I asked to see the leaflet advertising the meeting. An excellent leaflet with the correct date. There was only one little snag—the leaflet had no place for the meeting.

On one occasion I travelled up to Northampton to speak. The town hall, seating 1,500, was booked. On the platform were the three speakers, of whom I was one, and the chairman. Below was the audience, numbering exactly seven!

Once I spoke in York to an audience of about 30. The chairman was more than friendly. He introduced me and told the audience what I would be talking about—for five minutes, ten minutes, 15, 25, 40 minutes (despite urgent notes to stop). The audience drifted out. By the time I got to speak, there were 10 minutes left, and 10 in the audience.

Contact visiting was sometimes comical. We got a letter from a person who had read *Socialist Review*, explaining that he was interested. We decided to visit him. It was seven or eight in the evening. We knocked on the door. A woman opened the door and we asked if we could see the person. She replied, 'He's in bed, fast asleep.' We asked, 'Is he on an early shift?' to which she replied, 'No, he's ten years old, and he was tired.'

Comrades reading the story about our serious attitude to contacts, the readiness to patiently spend a lot of time and effort with them, could learn something from this. When Lenin wrote, 'There cannot be a revolutionary movement without revolutionary theory,' he meant that one had to take Marxism seriously—education classes are very important indeed. When Trotsky adapted Marx's term 'primitive accumulation of capital' and from it coined the term 'primitive accumulation of cadres', he meant that you have to look after every individual contact seriously.

Another thing. It is extremely important that the person teaching Marxism never forgets that above all he has to raise the confidence of the pupils. This is quite unlike leadership in a reformist organisation.

Even if we ignore the out and out careerists (of which there are many), even the best seek to represent within themselves the rank and file, to gather to themselves the strength and initiative of others. The revolutionary sees progress the other way round—as based on the self activity of the working class, and for this the key thing is self confidence.

There could have been a problem here. For while it was a real joy to meet the YS members, the age gap between them in their teens and me in the mid-40s was very big, psychologically greater than at present when, at 82, I talk to comrades in their 40s or 50s. The danger of talking down, of patronising, was there. I knew that this would be the worst crime that could undermine the confidence of the youngsters.

A few experiences outside the YS helped me. I remember having an argument with my daughter Elana when she was four or five. I don't remember the issue, but I do remember that she said to me, after a few minutes' discussion, 'You must be right, because you are older and cleverer than me.' My answer was, 'If I'm more clever than you and you'll be more clever than your child, people will become more and more stupid.' I know, however, that I did not always win the argument with my kids. I remember one day when Elana was five years old, she asked me, 'Do you believe God exists?' I said, 'I don't think God exists.' 'Why do you think that?' I replied, 'If he exists, how can he see us when we can't see him?' She gave me the coup de grâce: 'We see the people on television, but they can't see us.' No answer.

A meeting I had a few years later, speaking to a group of Punjabi workers in Birmingham, taught me a lot. At the beginning of the meeting, one of them, said, 'I must apologise to you for our poor English'. I answered him swiftly, 'You don't have to apologise to me. I have to apologise to you. You know some English. I don't know a word of Punjabi.' Only then could we look one another in the eye as equals.

Another incident: I spoke to a well attended meeting in Manchester. At the end of my speech the first person to speak from the floor was a middle-aged working class woman. She started, saying, 'I was very disappointed with Tony Cliff.' This depressed me. But then she went on to say, 'I thought he was young, tall and handsome.' This did not disturb me, as I have no illusions about my looks. She then ended her speech with these words, which made me really happy, 'When he spoke I felt nine feet tall.' I would have been very disturbed if she had said after my speech, 'I felt Tony Cliff was nine feet tall.' That would have meant that I had made her feel small.

The members of the YS learnt from me, but I also learnt hugely from them. With some individual members I had very warm relations. The revolutionary party has to lead the working class based on all the experience of the past. So the party teaches the workers, but then the simple question arises: 'Who teaches the teacher?' It is extremely important to understand that we can be taught by the working class. All the great ideas come from the workers themselves.

One example is Marx. If you read his *Communist Manifesto* he speaks about the need for a workers' government, the dictatorship of the proletariat. Then in 1871 he writes that workers cannot take hold of the old state machine, they have to smash it—the old standing army, bureaucracy and police—to establish a new kind of state. This is a state without a standing army or bureaucracy, where every official is elected, where every official gets the same rate of pay as the average worker. Did he find this out because he worked so hard in the British Museum? Not at all. What happened was that the workers of Paris had taken power—the Paris Commune—and that is exactly what they did. Marx learnt from them.

The Stalinists always claim that Lenin invented the idea of the soviet. Indeed, according to Stalinist literature Lenin invented everything. They had a concept of religious hierarchy. Lenin's correspondence shows that when workers established the first soviet in Petrograd in 1905 he asked, four days later, 'What the hell is that for?' In the struggle the workers needed a new form of organisation. They learnt the hard way that if they had a strike committee in one factory it was not effective in a time of revolution. You need a strike committee which covers all the factories. And that is what the soviet was: delegates from all the factories meeting together to run the show. They did it. Lenin followed them. The party has always to learn from the class, always.

The reader must have noticed that up to now, when I refer to our activities around the Labour Party youth, I all the time use the pronoun 'I', not 'we'. This is not an accident, and it is not the result of my being big headed. I describe the situation as it was. For perhaps six months I was the only member of the Socialist Review Group involved with Labour Party youth. To give a lead, one has to create facts. Action and argument must come together. It is no good saying, 'Comrades should do this, that or the other,' unless one points to experience to support the suggestion. If there are ten people in a group, one or two will be ready to experiment, to try new things; one or two are so conservative that even a successful experience will not convince them, while the majority will vacillate between the two extremes, and will learn through experience. The key is to be part of the one or two ready to experiment, to find new ways to take things forward, and if successful, to win the majority for the new direction.

When I came to the conclusion that the groups of youth connected with us, however small they were, needed a paper of their own, as *Socialist Review* did not fit them and could not serve as their organiser, the idea of *Rebel* was born. The members of the Socialist Review Group were going to be very reluctant to undertake this venture: after all we had only 60 members, and that after ten years of existence! So I convinced Chanie to buy a tiny Adana hand-printing machine. We set the text for the first *Rebel* letter by letter. This took hours and there was an urgency, as the new *Rebel* was needed for a coming demonstration. We had to put one sheet at a time in the machine. I remember the blue paper, and also how agonising the job was. Each sheet had to be laid out on the floor or on furniture separate from the next, so that the ink would dry, as we somehow could not get the thickness of the ink right. For the other side of the four page paper we had to repeat the process.

I tell this story because throughout my political activity I had to use the same method again and again: dare to act. Action and argument should come together. One example: Jim Nichol reminded me how during the miners' strike of 1972 he and I and the other two members of the Administrative Committee decided to appoint 15 full timers for the Yorkshire mining area (Sheila McGregor and Bill Message among others). At present Chris Bambery acts within the SWP in basically the same way as I used to—creating facts as the priority.

One has to avoid being stuck in a niche; every comrade has to do any task needed. There is no place for a hierarchical attitude in a revolutionary organisation. I took it for granted that I undertook many manual jobs, such as printing on the Adana machine. Or again, our monthly paper had six pages, printed commercially. To save money— I think £1 a month—together with other comrades I used to fold the outside pages and insert the middle page. I never understood why one should not speak to youth, to miners, to engineers, to building workers, on any subject under the sun, from historical materialism to payment by results in industry, from the Russian Revolution to the history of the British Labour Party.

Our experience of the YS was of great significance in our development. Prior to our intervention in the YS our membership grew very slowly indeed: from 33 in 1950 to 60 in 1960. Now, by 1964 our membership was 200, a modest but good success. The experience of the Socialist Review Group in the YS produced a qualitative advance. Even more important, the new recruits played a leading role in what was a mass movement. They learned how to intervene in a mass movement.

When Labour came to office in 1964 and Wilson supported the US intervention in Vietnam, the YS withered. We did not make a fetish of owning a Labour Party membership card, and now we did not make a fetish of tearing it up. We had originally entered the Labour Party because the tiny size of the Socialist Review Group did not allow us to pursue many independent initiatives outside the Labour Party. Now, having grown, there was no need to remain.

In December 1962 the Socialist Review Group became the International Socialism Group.

Chapter 4

The turn to industry, students, and the founding of *Socialist Worker*

Although the youth movement was at the centre of the arena during this period, the International Socialists (IS) never dropped their concern with the industrial struggle. More workers were being recruited to IS, though they were being recruited as individuals on the basis of general politics rather than on the basis of an industrial strategy. In any case, most of them were too young to have any decisive influence at their place of work. But they provided the basis of a new industrial cadre for the future.

The industrial orientation was also encouraged by the launching in 1961 of a new paper, *Industrial Worker*, soon to be renamed *Labour Worker*. It was intended to be more agitational, more geared to ongoing industrial struggles, than *Socialist Review* had been.

It was clear to us that with the coming to office of Labour under the leadership of Harold Wilson in 1964 an offensive against the workers and trade unions would occur. Britain lagged more and more behind its rivals. While British industrial production rose by 40 percent between 1951 and 1962, France's doubled, that of West Germany and Italy went up two and a half times, and that of Japan quadrupled. Britain's exports rose 29 percent, France's 86 percent, Germany's 247 percent, Italy's 259 percent and Japan's 378 percent. British national income fell below that of Germany and France.[1]

In 1963 Harold Wilson offered a vision of resurgent modern capitalism under dynamic management. He promised economic planning not based, as traditionally accepted in the Labour movement, on the nationalisation of industry, but on a national incomes policy, ie the imposition of wages control. Straight after his victory Wilson introduced a six month standstill on wages, to be followed by a further six months of 'severe restraint'.

Harold Lever, the Parliamentary Labour Party's leading economics expert, pleaded for business confidence: 'Clause Four or no Clause Four, Labour's leadership…knows as well as any businessman that an engine which runs on profit cannot be made to run faster without extra fuel… [Profits, then] must and will, over a longer period, increase significantly… For their part, businessmen should show less sensitivity and more sense. It is time they realised that a ringing political slogan is often used as a sop to party diehards or as an anaesthetic while doctrinal surgery is being carried out'.[2]

Labour's incomes policy was dressed up as fairer to the poor, but this was totally false. The proof was that the conservative weekly paper the *Economist* supported 'a profit conscious and profit seeking' Labour in the 1964 election.[3] The Tory economist Sam Brittan also recommended a Labour vote because 'paradoxically, one of the strongest arguments for a Labour government is that, beneath layers of velvet, it might be more prepared to face a showdown in dealing with the unions'.[4]

For incomes policy to be effective, Wilson had to weaken the unions. As early as 1963 a Fabian Tract explained, 'Acceptance of an incomes policy will also have implications for the right to strike. Clearly, to be operable, such a policy cannot have hanging over it the threat of a strike by a dissatisfied union'.[5] Two years later the *Economist* said the same: 'The price of securing an incomes policy in Britain will be a willingness to stand up to strikes',[6] adding later, 'quite bluntly, blacklegging must become respectable again'.[7]

Above all, Wilson wanted to weaken the power of the shop stewards. They were the main motors of wage rises and they reflected the strength and confidence of a working class which had been working in conditions of boom and near full employment for two decades. A few examples from our own comrades illustrate this point.

One day the guillotine at our printshop broke. We needed a new piece for it. Roger Cox agreed to make it up. At that time he worked in CAV, a car accessory factory. He was not a fast worker and it took him days to produce the piece needed, but one day it arrived. I asked him how it was possible. Wasn't the foreman looking on and noticing what was going on? Roger's reply was that the foreman might know he was doing a 'homer', but he wouldn't dare comment on it.

Geoff Carlsson, as has been mentioned, was the chair of the shop stewards of ENV, the north London engineering works. A new manager was installed. He called a meeting of the shop stewards in his room and told them that now, 'We are one happy family.' After a time he went to the toilet. When he returned he found Geoff sitting in his chair with his feet up on the table. He was furious. Geoff replied, 'But you said we were one happy family. At home I always put my feet up.' And he added, as a warning, 'I have got rid of more managers than I've had hot dinners.' That was the sort of power that the ordinary workers felt in the boom conditions of the 1950s and early 1960s.

For years national agreements between the trade unions and the employers merely established a minimum wage level. This was supplemented by wage drift—the topping up of incomes by plant bargaining around piece rates, bonuses, etc. Settlements by strong shop stewards committees would set a benchmark for other workers inside and outside the industry.[8] Incomes policy, it was clear, would have to weaken the unions in national bargaining and the shop stewards in plant bargaining. And that is exactly what Barbara Castle, the employment secretary in the Wilson government, tried to do with her white paper, "In Place of Strife", issued on 17 January 1969.

Such a general offensive by government and employers, we argued, would meet with a generalised defence by workers. Up to now the pattern of strikes was that of atomised struggles covering one plant or even one shop in the plant, led by a few shop stewards, or even just one. From now on things would change. It would take some time and would be slower under Wilson than under Heath (1970-74). Nevertheless, the trend was already visible. As Colin Barker and I wrote:

> The first essential task for any worker is that of ensuring that his own immediate organisation is in fighting shape; that every factory and place of work has a joint stewards committee (including all stewards regardless of their union membership, and covering white collar workers like draughtsmen too); that every company with different factories is covered by combined stewards committees to coordinate activities and prevent 'splitting' activities by the employers. More broadly, the rank and file must find forms of organisation—area rank and file committees, etc—that can do the job the trades councils used to do. Only the new organisations must be based on the factories rather than on geographical place of residence.
>
> Most of these tendencies are in their infancy, but the threat to the shop stewards is now so acute that the implementation of these basic tasks must be accelerated and largely achieved in a relatively short

time, creating the conditions for the formation of a national shop stewards movement—an idea which, since the First World War, has existed almost solely in the minds of some of those whom Harold Wilson calls 'wreckers' and whom we see as the potential builders of the mightiest socialist movement yet in the history of Britain.[9]

From words we moved to deeds. One path open to me to approach trade unionists was that of the NCLC—National Council of Labour Colleges. This was an educational organisation that served the trade unions. I was a voluntary tutor, and was invited to different branches of the union to speak on a variety of subjects in which the members were interested. Among the most useful were lectures on incomes policy, trade union legislation, the role of the trade union bureaucracy, etc.

However, far more important was our link with ENV. I was invited to speak to the shop stewards in this very well organised workplace, which not only enjoyed wages above the district level but had a reputation for giving traditional solidarity to other workers in struggle. The shop stewards took time off from their work, some two hours, to listen to me. As already mentioned, we had one member in the factory, Geoff Carlsson.

The shop stewards committee was dominated by members of the Communist Party. As the political differences between Geoff and the rest were well established, there was hardly any political argument between the two sides: 'We know the arguments, so why reiterate them?' And so Geoff was politically isolated among the shop stewards. Now an opportunity arose. The shop stewards wanted me to explain to them how to read a company balance sheet. Having worked in Palestine in an economic research institute, I knew quite a lot on the subject. Instead of speaking in generalities I decided to take the balance sheet of ENV and analyse it. The result was that I argued that the profit of the company was far greater than the company claimed. The shop stewards committee issued a leaflet to this effect. The management reacted by issuing a reply, which they stuck on the factory noticeboard. I then wrote a long article on the same subject, which was printed as a broadsheet. It ended with a challenge by the shop stewards to the management to come to the canteen and have a debate on the subject in the presence of all the workers and managers. Each side had the right to bring its own expert. Of course, the management declined.

After this incident I started coming to the factory every week to meet a number of the shop stewards to discuss different subjects. Eventually we built up a group of twelve in ENV. It was on the basis of this that the IS branch in ENV was able to take an important initiative. The convenor, Geoff Mitchell, was involved in a legal dispute, and following action to support him the ENV shop stewards committee decided to launch the London Industrial Shop Stewards Defence Committee. The meeting was held on 16 January 1966 and attracted some 200 people, about three quarters of them industrial workers, from 23 different unions.

The platform speakers included two IS members from ENV, Geoff Mitchell and Geoff Carlsson, and another IS member, Jim Higgins of the POEU. There were also two Communist Party members. One was Reg Birch, an AEU divisional organiser, former long-standing Communist Party militant and, at that time, a Maoist. The other was Jim Hiles, chairman of the building workers' Joint Sites Committee.

The resolution unanimously adopted by the meeting was remarkable in bringing together what were to be the main issues facing British workers over the coming decade:

■ This conference of rank and file trade unionists is deeply perturbed at the proposed, and actual, intervention by the government into established wage negotiations.
■ We equally deprecate the threats of legislation against the trade unionists and rank and file militants who have been mainly responsible over the past years in improving the wages and conditions in industry.
■ We are opposed to the government incomes policy, which has nothing in common with socialist planning; as likewise we are opposed to those trade union officials who support the government on these issues.
■ It is our belief that the so called incomes policy, the threats of legislation and the interference in wage negotiations can only strengthen the employers in their efforts to smash the shop stewards and the rank and file movements.[10]

The secretary of the London Industrial Shop Stewards Defence Committee was Geoff Carlsson. A couple of months after the conference launching this committee, it published the book *Incomes Policy, Legislation and Shop Stewards*, written by myself and Colin Barker, with an introduction by Reg Birch.

The book set out in a clear and non-sectarian manner the main lines of the analysis IS had been developing over the previous couple of years. It began with a general consideration of the economic situation that had led the ruling class to start imposing incomes policy. It then looked at the existing situation on the wages front, and in particular showed the importance of the phenomenon of wage drift in the preceding period. It contrasted the role of shop stewards with the full time union officials, who were shown to be becoming increasingly conservative and impotent. Finally, it looked at the pattern of strikes over the preceding period, in which working class strength had been reflected by the predominance of short, unofficial and generally successful strikes, and predicted that with the introduction of legislation against trade union rights the situation would have to change. The book closed with a call to action, stressing the need for 'a political as well as industrial response'.

The book sold like hot cakes. Some 15,000 copies were sold, the great majority to factory workers. The dozen IS members in ENV spent a week going around factories in north London pushing the book. (The shop stewards organisation in the factory was tough enough to prevent management disciplining them, or even deducting pay for the time they spent going round factories.) Many other members of IS did the same. Chanie spent three months when unemployed doing the same. By and large we did not sell single copies, only in bulk. Approaching the shop stewards from outside, both at the factory gate and the trade union branch meeting or the trades council, was very successful.

The IS membership increased significantly. Ian Birchall writes:

> By the end of 1967 the membership had increased slowly but significantly—over 400 as against 200-odd when Labour came to power. More important, it was a membership geared not simply to arguing the line, but to making interventions, albeit usually very low level ones, and to servicing the ongoing struggle. Without the base and, even more importantly, the orientation established in this period, the breakthrough of 1968 could not have taken place.[11]

To launch the book, a meeting was held in Hanson Hall, Willesden, with two speakers, Reg Birch and me. There were nearly 300 people in the audience, the large majority engineers from the huge industrial Park Royal area.

The struggle at the universities

This period also saw the development of mass college sit-ins, strikes and demonstrations throughout the world, in Berkeley in 1964, Berlin in 1966-67 and Paris in 1968. Tokyo students were involved in large-scale militancy. British students were first involved in March 1967 when London School of Economics (LSE) students had a sit-in.

1968 was a year of momentous events. In January the National Liberation Front in Vietnam launched the Tet Offensive, winning great victories against the far superior military forces of the US. In May the largest general strike in history took place in France, with the occupation of factories, triggered by a rebellious mass movement of students. In August the Russian invasion of Czechoslovakia led to a deep internal upheaval in the Stalinist parties across the world. A number of them dissociated themselves from Moscow for the first time in their history.

The role of students in society has changed radically over the last two generations. Hitherto the most enduring image of students among working class militants in Britain remained that of Oxbridge under-graduates scabbing on the General Strike in 1926. Trotsky had long ago dismissed the revolutionary potential of students. In 1910 he wrote:

> The intensification of the struggle between labour and capital hinders the intelligentsia from crossing over into the party of labour. The bridges between the classes are broken down and to cross over one would have to leap across an abyss which gets deeper every passing day…this finally means that it is harder to win the intelligentsia today than it was yesterday, and that it will be harder tomorrow than it is today.[12]

In 1968 students played a completely different role to that envisaged by Trotsky.

The explanation for the change in the mood of students since Trotsky wrote his article and since the 1926 General Strike is above all rooted in the change in the social composition of students. As a result of changes in capitalism and in the employment of intellectuals, the majority of students are not being trained any more as future members of the ruling class, or even as agents of the bosses with supervisory functions, but as white collar employees of state and industry, and thus are destined to be part and parcel of the proletariat.

A central aspect of the 'third industrial revolution' is the integration of manual with mental labour, of intellectual with productive work: the intellectual element becomes crucial to the development of the economy and society. But this productive force comes into increasing conflict with the irrational nature of capitalism. The conflict expresses itself in university life as a contradiction between the demand for the streaming of education dictated by the immediate needs of industry and the need to allow a certain amount of intellectual freedom. This applies especially to the social scientists, who have to 'solve' capitalism's social problems—according to the theory of the ruling class—and at the same time have to understand, at least to a certain extent, what generates the revolt against capitalism.

Under capitalism a commodity has both a use value and an exchange value, as Marx said. The first is natural and intrinsic to the commodity; the second is specific to the capitalist order of society. In the university this is reflected as a contradiction between the ideal of unlimited intellectual development, free from social, political and ideological restraint on the one hand, and the tight intellectual reins imposed by capitalism on the other. The real purpose of education clashes with its capitalist content.

Because students—or, even more, graduates who have left the university—are more and more pivotal to the development and salvation of all advanced industrial countries, it is more and more essential for these countries to ensure that students and technologists fulfil their assigned role. And this means that any attempt by these groups to put forward demands on their own behalf which conflict with the needs of capitalism will inevitably be resisted by the ruling class. Increasing international competition and the narrowing of profit margins combines with the need to produce more graduates. As a result the pressure is fierce to cut expenses per student, which involves greater streamlining of courses, regimentation of standards, and increasing resistance to students' claims.

Another factor fanning the revolt among students is the feeling of insecurity as to what the morrow of graduation will bring in their personal lives. The student of a previous generation knew in advance the slot into which they would fit—in the higher brackets of society. Not so the student of today. At the university they do not find the kind of education that was awaited, and after graduating it is more and more difficult to get the kind of job they were led to expect. The feeling of instability, of uncertainty, creates unease, which easily combines with other factors to create a revolutionary combustion.

The feeling of insecurity among students was clear in 1967-68 when I spent weeks talking to LSE students. Again and again a raw nerve was touched when I said, 'I see before me a number of BA unemployed, or BA failed.' I knew very well about the last category as I myself was a BA failed. (I never got a degree as I was arrested in 1939 on the eve of my finals in the Hebrew University in Jerusalem. Who knows, if I had got a degree perhaps Alex Callinicos would not have been the only professor on the Central Committee of the SWP.)

Another important element encouraging student rebellion is that students are more and more concentrated in the same areas. This was particularly the case in Nanterre, where 12,000 students were gathered in the same buildings, many living on the university campus all the year round.

'The special medium in which the student is trained—theorising and generalising—facilitates the synthesis of the different elements of unease and rebellion'.[13]

Another significant characteristic of students is their youth. Nowhere else in capitalist society are young people separated off and pooled together in the same way. There are no factories containing only young workers. But late capitalism concentrates growing numbers of students into special institutions. This has many disadvantages for the long term development of a student movement—isolated from the mass of the population, it can easily be taken on by the authorities without receiving outside help, and it is incapable by itself of really damaging the ruling class through attacking their profits. It also lacks the tradition of sustaining struggle that some sections of workers have. But this lack of tradition also means lack of inhibition by outdated modes of struggle or past defeats. Youth alone can confront late capitalism with the resources of unlimited imagination. It is not weighed down by the past. When young workers occasionally do struggle for their own ends (as in apprentices' strikes), they too display some of this initiative and ability to learn quickly. Yet it is only in the colleges that these qualities are really concentrated. That is why students have been the first to respond without inhibition to the much wider disenchantment with past political forms.[14]

In 1966 the Socialist Society of LSE, which included among its members Chris Harman, John Rose and Laurie Flynn, published an intermittent magazine, *Agitator*, and held meetings on Rhodesia, incomes policy and the seamen's strike.[15] In October 1966 *Agitator* organised a campaign against the appointment of Walter Adams, previously director of University College in Rhodesia, as director of the LSE. This caused outrage, as the LSE was a multiracial college. In March 1967 a sit-in took place in protest against Walter Adams.

The IS members of the Socialist Society in LSE were active in founding the GLC Tenants' Action Committee, formed to fight the rent rises which led to a rent strike; they were also involved in actively supporting building workers in the Barbican dispute.[16]

Activities were intermixed with very serious discussion of ideas. I spent something like five hours every day in the canteen over a period of weeks. The number of cups of tea I drank probably kept a Ceylon tea plantation going.

The IS members in the LSE and other colleges had been 'known...for the line of taking students off to the picket line and factory gate'.[17] IS, and later the SWP, were more than once accused of 'workerism', or a contempt for ideas, because of our insistence on the centrality of the working class. But the accusation was misplaced, and the orientation misunderstood. It would be the most stupid thing for a student to pretend that she or he was a worker. It was a question of social circumstances that led to the direction we followed. Because of their life experience, workers tend to go from the specific—wages and conditions—to the more generalised issues. Intellectuals begin from ideas. The most important thing for the development of the students (as well as our implantation in the working class) was for the students to learn from direct contact with the workers' movement.

In 1896 Russian social circumstances were comparable, to a certain extent. Lenin had to move from operating in Marxist circles to economic propaganda. Krupskaya describes how one worker said that Lenin was worse than two employers, because he always asked so many questions. He produced four handwritten copies of a factory leaflet. Two reached the hands of workers, the other two were seized by the employers. But Lenin did not want the party to limit itself to immediate economic concerns, and two years later he had to attack the narrowness of 'economism', which had taken the organisation too far in one direction. That would be a danger for us too—that orientation on the working class would lead to a worship of the limitations imposed by the prevailing ideology on many workers. To give one example, there was a time when the Socialist Review Group was tiny, with between 25 to 30 members only. A worker wanted to join.

He liked our programme, but he thought that our opposition to immigration controls would prevent other workers from joining. I said, 'You join the group over my dead body.'

Student occupations took place in more and more colleges, from Manchester to Bristol, from Hornsey Art College to Hull and Essex.[18] However, by far the most important focus for student activity was opposition to the Vietnam War. IS branches in the localities helped to prepare the demonstration in October 1967. The result was some 30,000 people in Grosvenor Square (outside the US embassy), a confrontation with the police, and the Vietnam Solidarity Campaign's name firmly on the political map (two more massive demonstrations followed, in March and October 1968).[19] On the day before the mass demonstration on 27 October, an occupation took place in the LSE to provide sleeping accommodation and first aid facilities for thousands.

The demonstration was a very important test. Three Trotskyist groups were present, but each took a different position. The Socialist Labour League (SLL), followers of Gerry Healy, came to the demonstration for one purpose only—to distribute a leaflet entitled 'Why The Socialist Labour League Is Not Marching'. The argument was that it was not led by Marxists and not composed of workers: 'The Socialist Labour League refuses…to participate in the demonstration. Our task is to direct all young workers and students towards serious consideration for the theory and role of Trotskyism and the Fourth International towards the building of the revolutionary party'.[20]

Then there was the International Marxist Group (IMG), whose characteristic was to overlook the revolutionary potential of the working class and look for the agents of socialism elsewhere: the national movement in the colonies, the peasantry, and now the 'student vanguard'. The talk was about turning the universities into 'red bases'.

The orthodox but ossified 'Marxism' of the SLL assumed that the question of how students would behave in 1968 was made clear by their behaviour during the 1926 General Strike, or by Trotsky's article of 1910. If that is so one does not need theory, only memory.

For the impressionistic 'Marxism' of the IMG, on the other hand, everything changes completely. There is only change, no continuity. Hence one cannot have a theory, as one cannot generalise. The ideas of Marx shaped in the 1840s about the centrality of the working class in liberating itself, and liberating society, have no relevance for 1968.

IS members were deeply rooted in Marxist theory, but we did not live in an ivory tower. So we were quite conscious of the changes that took place. For us it was clear that students could not be a substitute for the working class but could only aid the working class in its liberation. We always looked to the student movement as a detonator.

On the 27 October 1968 demonstration IS distributed a leaflet that aimed to link the anti-war struggle with the class struggle at home:

> ...the battle against the wage freeze; against social service cuts; against bad housing and rent increases; against bad hospitals and schools; against unemployment; against the government's racialist policies is the same as the battle against the Vietnam War... In the factories workers are fighting against the wage freeze and unemployment. On the housing estates tenants are resisting rent increases. If we are to help the Vietnamese we must go on from Grosvenor Square to fight these struggles. 'A blow against the boss is a blow against the Vietnam War.'
>
> Today on Sunday we are demonstrating against the war in Vietnam. What will we do on Monday? We will have to go to the factories, the docks, the bus depots, to connect with the workers' fight.

Out of the three Trotskyist groups—the SLL, the IMG and the IS—only IS built significantly out of the demonstration.

The SLL declaration of disdain for the demonstration would not have encouraged anyone among the demonstrators to join it. The IMG did not say anything the demonstrators disagreed with, but it did not raise any argument to convince the demonstrators to go beyond the point they were at at the beginning of the day. To say, 'Victory to the National Liberation Front' was obvious to anyone who came to the demonstration.

This has parallels with intervention in a strike situation. For example, you can stand on a picket line and next to you is a worker who makes racist comments. You can do one of three things. You can say, 'I'm not standing on this picket line. I'm going home because no one makes racist remarks there.' That is sectarianism, because if 'the emancipation of the working class is the act of the working class', you have to stand with workers on a picket line against the boss.

The other possibility is simply avoiding the question. Someone makes a racist comment and you pretend you haven't heard it, and you say, 'The weather is quite nice today.' That is opportunism.

The third position is that you argue with this person against racism, against the prevailing ideas of the ruling class. You argue and argue. If you convince them, excellent. But if you don't, still when the scab lorry comes you link arms to stop the scabs, because 'the emancipation of the working class is the act of the working class'. You cannot choose between activity and argument. Activity alone is blind. Argument alone is futile. Both must be combined in a dialectical unity, one with the other. To give a lead one has to go with the stream three quarters of the way, and against it a quarter of the way.

Our leaflets did not convince the 100,000 demonstrators, but they must have impressed a few thousand, made them think. IS was with the demonstrators but at the same time arguing with them.

Tariq Ali was better known and more popular than any IS member on the demonstration. But he did not bring forward any convincing argument why anyone should join the IMG. Leadership is a dialogue, and dialogue contains both agreement and disagreement. We recruited hundreds to IS at the demonstration and straight afterwards. The students we recruited in the Vietnam campaign were recruited on the basis of orientation on the working class.

At the end of 1974 there were about 90 IS student societies. The founding conference of the National Organisation of IS Societies (NOISS, subsequently changing its name to Socialist Worker Student Society—SWSS) at Leeds in November 1974 was attended by delegates from 28 universities, 11 polytechnics, six colleges of education, and six colleges of further education and technical colleges. Its journal, *Agitator*, had a circulation of about 3,000.[21]

Ian Birchall writes:

IS had grown dramatically in the course of 1968. It had begun the year with 447 members, and ended with something in excess of a 1,000 (the pace of recruitment and turnover were so hectic that precise figures are hard to get). The monthly *Labour Worker* had given way to the weekly *Socialist Worker*, with a vastly increased circulation. A number of full time workers had been employed both for the paper and as regional organisers. The pace of growth had taken the members by surprise.[22]

It was largely students recruited during 1968 and the following couple of years who built a sale of *Socialist Worker* in the factories, who recruited workers into the organisation, and who played a crucial role in establishing IS factory branches and rank and file groups.

An encounter with growing racism

When, in April 1968, Enoch Powell made his infamous racist speech about 'rivers of blood', thousands of London dockers came out on a one day strike and demonstration in his support. The Communist Party, which had considerable influence in the docks, declined to use it to fight Powell. Danny Lyons, one of the leading Communist Party militants, had so little confidence that he brought along two clergymen, one Catholic and one Protestant, to try and dissuade the dockers.

IS had only one docker in the organisation, Terry Barrett. He took a very strong anti-racist position. However, I remember having a very long discussion through the night about the tactics he wanted to adopt. He was convinced he should cross the dockers' Powellite picket line and go to work. I was convinced that although his feelings were admirable, the tactic he suggested was wrong. If he violated the democratic decision, however wrong, of his mates, and was paid for the day, what would we say when in other strikes—and they were far more numerous—another docker decided to scab. Finally we came to an agreement. So Terry issued an IS leaflet that he and a number of IS members, including students, distributed among dockers who supported Powell. They got insults as a result, but I am still very proud of this leaflet, which argued a clear class line against Powell:

> Who is Enoch Powell? He is a right wing Tory opportunist who will stop at nothing to help his party and his class. He is a director of the vast National Discount Company (assets £224m) which pays him a salary higher than the £3,500 a year he gets as an MP.
>
> He lives in fashionable Belgravia and writes Greek verse.
>
> What does he believe in?
>
> ■ Higher unemployment. He has consistently advocated a national average of 3 percent unemployed.
>
> ■ Cuts in social services. He wants higher health charges, less council houses, charges for state education and lower unemployment pay.
>
> ■ Mass sackings in the docks. Again and again he has argued that the docks are 'grossly overmanned'.[23]

Sadly, Powell had quite an impact in the country. Racist microbes spread widely. Coming back to Terry Barrett, he got a lot of support from LSE students at the time he needed it to fight Powellism. Terry reciprocated the help he got from them. Again and again he came to LSE to argue revolutionary politics with them.

The civil rights movement in Ireland

I had connections with a number of people who played a key role in the civil rights movement in Northern Ireland in 1968-69. One was Gerry Lawless and his old Irish Workers' Group which, despite some of its flaws, included as members both Michael Farrell, who was the key person in leading People's Democracy (PD) in Belfast, and Eamonn McCann in Derry, who played a central role there from October 1968 to August 1969. Through McCann we got quite close connections with Bernadette Devlin. She became famous when, as an MP newly elected to the Commons on a civil rights ticket (17 April 1969), she crossed the benches and punched Reginald Maudling, the Tory minister. The British state happily deals out repression. It does not expect to be confronted in its own home. Bernadette Devlin did several meeting tours with us, and her meetings were always very well attended.

Michael Farrell's relationship with us was close in the period 1969-70. He spoke at one of our conferences. We took collections for PD. I remember a discussion I had with him and some other people at my house in early 1969. It was just after the Burntollet march, where the civil rights marchers were ambushed and beaten up by several hundred Loyalist bigots, including a number of part time police of the B-Specials. At that time Farrell and Devlin, as well as McCann, were strongly committed to the idea of building a non-sectarian revolutionary movement in Northern Ireland, but they were enormously confused as to what to do. This is shown by an interview they did for *New Left Review*. They did not, for instance, seem to want to say anything about the border. I failed to convince Farrell that they had to say something about it, to find ways of putting across an argument against partition which linked national and working class issues in a way that could build support among workers in the South and so find a bridge to Protestant workers in the North.

For a successful revolutionary strategy these issues could not be ducked. On the surface it is true that the problems the workers in the South face—bad working conditions, poor housing, poor social services—have no direct relation to the presence of British troops in the North. Equally it appears, superficially, that the fight for civil rights for Catholics in the North also does not relate to the day to day struggle of workers in the South. Yet the issues of the border and of class politics are inextricably linked because the hold of reaction in the South is reinforced through Green nationalism. In the North the sectarian division of Protestant and Catholic workers because of partition damages the interests of both groups.

Thus Green nationalism has no attraction for Protestant workers in the North, who do not see why they should aspire to a united Ireland. With the Green Tories ruling Dublin, why should the Protestant workers of Belfast wish to join them? Home rule looks like Rome rule. This leads Protestant workers to identify their interests with the British state and its symbols, such as the monarchy. In the South workers are also held back. When I lived in Dublin (1947-52) I remember visiting a number of trade union offices, and I was really shocked to see at their entrance a statue of the Madonna and the infant Jesus. How could a Protestant worker, or an atheist or agnostic worker, find himself at home in such a place?

The civil rights movement could not avoid these questions and succeed. To demand civil rights for Catholics, in other words equality between Catholics and Protestants in job opportunities, housing, etc, also would not convince Protestant workers to aspire to join the Catholics if it looked as though it would be merely the sharing of misery. Catholic workers' advance under such conditions looks as if it is at the cost of Protestant workers.

To break down the walls of the Catholic ghetto in the North one has to mobilise the workers in the South on class issues that challenge the power of the Green Tories and the Catholic church. The route connecting the Shankill Road and the Falls Road goes through Dublin (the Shankill Road is the centre of the Belfast Protestant working class, while the Falls Road is the centre of Belfast's Catholic workers).

Michael Farrell paid lip service to Marxism, to the working class, to the need to unite Protestant and Catholic workers. Alas, in reality, he did not go beyond the civil rights movement in the North. This movement in itself was only a reformist movement that, in the end, could not break through the walls of the ghetto to unite Catholic and Protestant workers, to unite the workers of the South and the North.

A revolutionary party, of course, is not a sect, and therefore has to participate in progressive movements. But it has to be a distinct, separate entity. Two examples have already been mentioned: while Socialist Review Group members participated in the CND march to Aldermaston in 1958, making up a contingent of some 50 in a crowd of 50,000, we carried a banner that the majority of CND supporters would not have agreed with. It said, 'Industrial action against the bomb. Black the bomb. Black the bases.' Ten years later, in October 1968, in the Vietnam Solidarity Campaign (VSC) demonstration, we issued a leaflet stating, 'A blow against the boss is a blow against the Vietnam War.' We had a clear class position in the latter campaign.

The independence of the revolutionary party is also a question of survival. It cannot afford to dissolve itself into such movements. A movement rises and falls: CND rose, and then declined, as did the VSC. If the boundary between the revolutionary party and the movement is fudged, the decline of the movement must lead to a deep crisis and even disintegration of the revolutionary organisation. It was a great error for Farrell's PD to merge completely with the civil rights movement.

My failure to convince Farrell was possibly connected with the relative size of our organisations. IS had about 1,000, while the civil rights movement in Northern Ireland consisted of tens of thousands and was very much in the news. Farrell did not understand that under such conditions PD was bound to rise like a rocket but fall like a stick two years later. Nevertheless, the strategy I argued for was not without a basis. Eamonn McCann, in his brilliant book *War and an Irish Town*, lists many occasions in the history of the North when Catholic and Protestant workers joined forces. This was at times 'when they have had something to fight together for'.[24]

In 1973 McCann wrote the following about the civil rights movement of 1969:

> There never was the slightest possibility of a movement demanding 'fair play' [for Catholics] in Northern Ireland engaging the support, or even securing the neutrality, of Protestant workers. In terms of strict economics the only programme with any potential to undercut sectarianism would have been one which linked the demand for fair distribution of the relevant commodities to demands designed to increase absolutely the number of jobs and houses available for distribution… In a phrase, it would have involved the elaboration of a comprehensive anti-capitalist, not just anti-Unionist, programme.
>
> If any group had fought consistently…for such a programme, the all-class Catholic alliance, which is what the civil rights movement

became, could not have held together. And such a programme...would not have attracted immediate mass support; but it might have enabled those of us in Derry at least to go on talking to Protestants...in 1969.[25]

Alas, PD did not build a real organisation. It was a very loose grouping. Farrell, Devlin and McCann led a mass movement, but they had no organisation to speak of. McCann, writing about the Housing Action Committee in Derry, said:

> We called a meeting of 'the local organisers' for Tuesday night in the City Hotel. The index of our political and organisational chaos was that, having called the meeting, we were not at all certain who would have the right to attend. At the time that did not seem very important. We would as always muddle through... In the nature of things there was no mechanism whereby our loose group could convene itself and arrive at a joint attitude.[26]

PD had very incoherent views. McCann writes:

> It was a loose organisation, without formal membership and with an incoherent ideology comprising middle-class liberalism, Aldermaston pacifism and a Sorbonne-inspired belief in spontaneity. [27]

> ...while maintaining a separate existence the PD...was for a long time effectively submerged in the mainstream of civil rights agitation, establishing itself not as an organisation with a programme qualitatively different from that of the 'moderates', but as a lively and aggressive ginger group within the same broad movement. To the mass of the people it was clear that the PD in Belfast and White, Finbar Doherty, myself, and others in Derry were more militant than the NICRA [Northern Ireland Civil Rights Association] or the Derry Citizens Action Committee. But it was not clear what we were being militant about.[28]

After the demise of the civil rights movement, McCann drew the right conclusion:

> We have learned that mass 'influence' or prominent involvement in mass agitation is, despite sometime appearances to the contrary, meaningless and fruitless unless one is in the process of forging the political instrument necessary to lead such agitation to victory over the opposing force. We have learned that it is impossible to do that if one

is not forearmed with a coherent class analysis of the situation and a clear programme based on it.[29]

In a phrase, we need to build a mass, revolutionary Marxist party.[30]

McCann ends his book with the following words:

The future in Ireland lies with the small, but at last steadily growing, forces of Marxism. To make the revolution we need a revolutionary party.[31]

Sadly, 20 years later, in 1993, in a preface to a new edition of his book, McCann admitted that he had done very little to achieve this target:

I ended the book in 1973 by suggesting that the future lay with the small but steadily growing forces of Marxism. This was something of a cheek, since at the time I was doing little to encourage this growth. It wasn't until 1983 that I joined a Marxist organisation.[32]

McCann joined the Socialist Workers Movement, the sister organisation of the British SWP.

The civil rights movement disintegrated and was absorbed into two separate organisations: the Republicans on the one hand and the SDLP on the other.

The Republicans cannot unite Catholic and Protestant workers, as for them the struggle for a united Ireland has nothing to do with bread and butter issues. The Irish equivalent of the Labour Party and trade union leadership also see the issues compartmentally. They have nothing to do with the national question, being mediators with the bosses and the state. They take a Green colour in the South and an Orange hue in the North. So the struggle for a united Ireland remains confined largely to the Catholic ghetto in the North. This fits the Republicans perfectly.

People's Democracy, composed as it was of students who were influenced by movementism, did not go further than paying lip service to the working class. A revolutionary organisation must be orientated on the working class. Although a tribune of the oppressed, it must relate also to other sections of society. Alas, the discussions with the leadership of PD did not bring lasting results.

When all hell broke loose in Northern Ireland, with the armed attacks on Catholics, including the Belfast pogroms of August 1969, we did our best to help PD by printing literature for them and so on. There were, however, serious problems, as McCann later explained in *War and an Irish Town*. The PD leaders were able, at a particular point, to head a massive movement. They spoke to huge meetings. Bernadette Devlin was elected to the House of Commons. But that is not the same as leadership. They never succeeded in building anything like a stable organisation capable of evaluating what it was doing and putting forward a coherent socialist policy as an alternative to the pull of mere nationalism. So there was not even an organisational link between the socialists in Derry and those in Belfast, let alone with any socialist organisation in the South.

After August 1969 they were fairly rapidly marginalised by the SDLP on the one hand and, more importantly, by Republican forces that had seemed moribund in 1968. They had started an avalanche but then did not know what to do, or how even to organise themselves. So it was that over time they all drifted off to Republicanism or inactivity, apart from Eamonn McCann, who still puts across a revolutionary socialist line.

When the British troops were brought into Northern Ireland in 1969, we in IS were faced with a dilemma. We insisted British imperialism was the root of Northern Ireland's problems. But the Paisleyites were the loudest voices shouting 'Troops Out', meaning 'leave the RUC, the B-Specials and the Orangemen to kill Catholics'. And there was even some shooting between troops and Orangemen in the Shankill Road. Meanwhile, the Nationalist population were initially friendly to the troops. We had to find a way of putting forward anti-imperialist demands without sounding the same as the Orangemen. We did this in *Socialist Worker* with the headline, 'Keep The Barricades', and by arguing very strongly that people should not rely on the troops to defend them. An editorial in *Socialist Worker* of 21 August 1969 had the following headings:

The Barricades Must Stay
Until B-Specials Disbanded
RUC Disarmed
Special Powers Act Abolished
Political Prisoners Released

The editorial in *Socialist Worker* of 11 September 1969 said:

Defend The Barricades
No Peace Until Stormont Goes
The breathing space provided by the presence of British troops is short
but vital. Those who call for the immediate withdrawal of the troops
before the men behind the barricades can defend themselves are invit-
ing a pogrom.

The moment the honeymoon between the troops and the Catholic
population came to an end, early in 1970, we then raised the slogan
'Troops Out' as a central demand.

Activity around the Irish issue was quite central to us in the
years 1968-72—the Irish Civil Rights Solidarity Campaign, the
Anti-Internment League and so on, and the big and bitter demonstrations over Bloody Sunday. But after 1972 it became difficult to
get more people than our own members on demonstrations and
protests. This was because Republican bombs in Britain had the
effect of making the Irish population in Britain keep their heads
down, especially after the Prevention of Terrorism Act (late 1974).
The bombs removed an important way of getting the argument
about the oppression of the Catholics in the North and the problems caused by partition across to other workers.

Problems of growth

One has always to fight against conservative inertia which plagues
even the most revolutionary organisations.

As I have said, between April and October 1968 the membership
of our organisation grew from 400 to 1,000. This quick growth brought
about a serious crisis in the organisation. We were forced to have
three national conferences in 1968. The first, in the spring (before the
May events), was held in the Africa Centre, and had an attendance
of about 200 people. The second was held in the Beaver Hall in October with some 300 comrades present.

There were deep splits all over the place. We had recruited hundreds of students in the previous months and they had all sorts of
ideas. What is more, the effect of the May events was to create enormous spontaneism and illusions in the immediate revolutionary possibilities. (I remember Akiva Orr, who had only just joined us and left
soon after, saying, in true C L R-James-type fashion, 'Socialism already
exists in the factories.' He was not the only one to be attracted to such

ideas—Ian MacDonald and three people who had been working with us around tenant and anti-racist work were very much influenced by similar ideas.)

Had the comrades waited a few weeks they would have found out that the revolution did not win in France, that capitalism survived the spontaneous action of the masses.

It is true that on 20 May the largest general strike in history began. One million people demonstrated in Paris. But the French Stalinists controlling the union bureaucracy did not disappear. Frightened of the thought that the revolutionary students would mingle with the workers, they insisted on separating the two groups by creating a cordon of 20,000 stewards holding arms to separate them. Ten million workers did go on strike, but the strike committees were not elected. They were appointed by the trade union bureaucracy. It is true that millions of workers occupied the factories, but right from the beginning of the occupations, the union bureaucracy insisted that only a small minority of the workers should stay in the factories while the majority were sent home. If the workers had remained in the occupation the strike would have been active. Now it was passive.

Tragically, there was not in existence a large revolutionary organisation that could overcome the bureaucracy. In Russia in March 1917 the Bolshevik Party had 23,600 members, and this number increased by August to 250,000. The French industrial working class was significantly large than the Russian working class in 1917. Had there existed a revolutionary organisation of some tens of thousands, it could have argued that the workers' contingents on the demonstration should not be separated from the students. It could have called for democratic elections of strike committees and convinced the millions occupying the factories to remain inside the factories, creating a collective force many times stronger than when these same workers were simply an aggregation of individuals. Alas, the total number of revolutionaries in France could be counted in hundreds.

Therefore it was not long before the government got the unions to agree to a compromise with the employers on a wage rise. The occupation of the factories ended, the strike was called off, and the ground was prepared for the return of the president, General de Gaulle. When the factories were occupied de Gaulle was so demoralised that he flew out of the country to find refuge with the French troops in West Germany. But now he came back to rule once more. On 30 May a right wing demonstration of half a million took place in Paris. The police seized back the TV and radio stations, threw out occupying workers, attacked any continuing demonstrations, and even killed two workers and a school student. Again and again during 1968 the revolutionary potential, which could have gone far, stopped well short of victory. And this has been the pattern in other revolutions.

The debates at IS conferences in 1968 were heated. Symptomatic of the extremes of the libertarians was a resolution put forward by one branch of the organisation that headlines of *Socialist Worker* should be determined by delegates from all the London branches. At present Chris Harman and the rest of the *Socialist Worker* editorial board decides these. Each branch has a different composition and works in different situations. If the headline was put to a debate of 30 or 40 branches every week the paper would never appear.

Symmetrical to the libertarian tendency was 'toy Bolshevism'. A number of old timers—and I use this word loosely, to describe people who had been in the organisation four or five years—started complaining loudly about the 'dilution' of the membership. At the Beaver Hall conference a motion was proposed to introduce probationary membership. The chairperson called one speaker in support of the motion, one against, and so on. The last speaker was myself. When the chairperson asked for a comrade to support the motion over probationary membership I put my hand up. Comrades were stunned. I said, 'I am for introducing probationary membership for everyone in the organisation who has been a member for four or five years. It is dangerous if they exhibit conservative inertia. They should be put on probation and then excluded if they fail.' I was the last floor speaker and we won the vote overwhelmingly against the introduction of probationary membership. A revolutionary does not live on his past or his promises for the future. What is decisive is what he or she is doing this week, next week, and what was done last week. Toy Bolshevism is a danger threatening small revolutionary organisations which become impatient and too hard.

The October 1968 conference lasted a number of days. I did not speak at all on the factional issues because the moment I spoke it would only serve to unite all the factions in their anger and disappointment at the leadership not delivering the goods as quickly as the comrades, in their inexperience, had expected. The need was to consolidate the group. Therefore the question of democratic centralism (rather than everyone for themselves doing their own thing) was very important. Democracy that does not lead to common action results in bureaucratic anarchy, where the person with the loudest voice predominates or there is action which pulls in many directions and cancels itself out.

The most impressive intervention at the conference was by Duncan Hallas. The comrades there did not know who he was, as he had left the organisation in 1954 and had now reappeared. The comrades who argued against Leninist democratic centralism on the grounds that Leninism leads to Stalinism were all very young and inexperienced. Therefore when Duncan, who was in his forties, spoke with real authority, it was extremely impressive. What he said was short and sharp and included the question, 'If Leninism led to Stalinism, why did Stalin kill all the Leninists?' His speech was absolutely riveting. Still he was heckled by some delegates.

The atmosphere of the conference led me to propose an adjournment of the conference for a couple of months. So it was that the issue of leadership and democratic centralism was not finally settled until what was in effect the third conference of the year (again in Beaver Hall), where we carried the argument without any splits. To help the process I wrote a short document on democratic centralism.

It was not perhaps very well argued, but I myself was panicked by the situation. What is so important about democratic centralism? First of all, it is important to understand why we need democracy. If you want to go from London to Birmingham you need a bus and a driver. You don't need democratic discussion, because the route has been followed before and all that is needed is one good driver and one good bus. The problem is that the transition from capitalism to socialism is something we have never experienced before. We do not know the issues that will arise on the way and what the party will have to do to carry the struggle forward.

If you do not know, there is only one way to learn—by being rooted in the working class and learning from the class. It is not that democracy from below solves every problem. Marxism, in so far as it is a science, does not need to revisit every discovery of Marx and debate every concept in his books. If you want to know if there is a decline in the rate of profit, if Marx is right, you do not need to go to the vote. The same applies to other questions of principle such as anti-racism. However, there is another category of things that must be put to the vote. Everything that is connected to our struggle must be put to the test, because we simply do not know the right answers. If the emancipation of the working class is the act of the working class, the working class through its own experiences will teach us, and this must be expressed within party debates and shape the strategy that is followed.

There is a beautiful description of how Lenin had to learn from the class in 1917. He describes what happened when he was in hiding after the July Days in 1917. The Bolshevik Party was illegal and its press smashed. The Bolsheviks were accused of being German agents. Lenin did not know how far the power of reaction had been consolidated. He describes eating with a worker he was in hiding with. The worker gave him bread and said, 'The bread is good. They, the capitalist class, are frightened of us and don't dare give bad bread.' Lenin wrote, 'The moment I heard him I understood about the class relation of forces. I understood what workers really think—the capitalists are still frightened of us. The victory of the counter-revolution is not complete'.

If you want to know if the workers are confident you cannot decide from the top down. How do you know? You cannot have a ballot in the press—they do not provide the opportunity. You cannot survey every individual. For a working class revolution you need a deep democracy. And what the revolution is about is raising the working class to become the ruling class, about creating the most democratic system in history. Unlike under capitalism, where every five years you elect someone to misrepresent you (because they are completely in the power of capital), here it is a completely different story. Under capitalism you elect the MPs but not the employers. Under capitalism we do not vote on whether to close a factory. We do not elect the army officers or the judges. In a workers' state everything is under workers' control. Everything is in workers' power. It is the most extreme form of democracy. Therefore, within the revolutionary party there must be democratic debate which reflects the experience of the comrades, who themselves are part of or linked to the working class.

If this is all true, why do we need centralism? First, the experience is uneven. Workers have different experiences. You have to collect that experience together. Even in the revolutionary party the members are influenced by different pressures. They are influenced by the general picture and by the section of the workers to which they belong. As I wrote in 1968, 'Marx argued that as the prevailing ideology under capitalism is the ideology of the ruling class, revolutionary politics does not reflect the current ideas of the class'.[33] There must be a clear picture of the current state of class consciousness, but the role of the party is to overcome the sectionalism, the narrow experience. You need to centralise all the experience.

Again you need centralism because the ruling class is highly centralised. If you are not symmetrical to your enemy in power of organisation then you cannot win. I was never a pacifist. If someone uses a stick on me I have to have a bigger stick. I don't believe a quotation from Marx's *Capital* will stop a mad dog who attacks. The power of our organisation has to be symmetrical to our enemies'. That is why I cannot understand the anarchists when they come and say that after a revolution we will immediately abolish the state. The capitalists elsewhere will still have a state. How do you maintain workers' power in the face of organised capitalist opposition without a state for the workers? Anarchists always deny the issue of the state. Yet during the Spanish Civil War, when confronted by Franco's state, they immediately joined the bourgeois state opposing him. They should have tried to oppose Franco with a workers' state.

Democratic centralism therefore involves the freest debate and discussion about how to take the struggle forward based on an estimate of the possibilities of the moment, combined with a centralised carrying out of the decisions reached. Between conferences the Central Committee is responsible for leadership. In bourgeois parties the leadership is rarely accountable for its actions. MPs cannot be removed between elections. Governments hide behind blaming 'the world economy' or 'economic forces beyond our control' for their failures. They depend on the passivity of their party memberships, who are there only to canvass at election times or give standing ovations. The Central Committee of the SWP is accountable for its political line every week through the pages of *Socialist Worker*. Because we are an organisation of activists, if the Central Committee took a wrong position on an issue the comrades would soon let us know about it. Every week the comrades know where we stand on the key issues of the moment.

I wrote elsewhere:

There is a dialectical relationship between democracy within the party and the party's roots in the class. Without a correct class policy and a party composed of proletarians, there is no possibility of healthy party democracy. Without a firm working class base all talk of democracy and discipline in the party is meaningless verbiage. At the same time, without party democracy, without constant self criticism, development of a correct class policy is impossible. Lenin said, 'We have more than once already enunciated our theoretical views on the importance of discipline and on how this concept is to be understood in the party of the working class. We defined it as: unity in action, freedom of discussion and criticism. Only such discipline is worthy of the democratic party of the advanced class' (Lenin, *Collected Works*, vol 9, p230). Again: 'The proletariat does not recognize unity of action without freedom to discuss and criticise'. (ibid, p321)

If democracy is essential in order to assimilate the experience of the struggle, centralism and discipline are necessary to lead the struggle. Firm organisational cohesion makes it possible for the party to act, to take initiatives, to direct the action of the masses. A party that is not confident in itself cannot win the confidence of the masses. Without a strong party leadership, having the power to act promptly and direct the activities of the members, a revolutionary party cannot exist. The party is a centralist organisation which leads a determined struggle for power. As such it needs iron discipline in action.[34]

The arguments in 1968 were not just about democratic centralism as an issue standing on its own; they were about reorienting the student recruits towards industry with factory sales, bulletins, etc. The book I wrote on productivity deals at the time (*The Employers' Offensive: Productivity Deals and How to Fight Them*) was part of the same process. The turn to the working class in the late 1960s and early 1970s led to serious distortions in our activities. It encouraged the wholesale abandonment of student work, justified by 'workerism', which was especially rampant among ex-students. Chris Harman, Alex Callinicos and Simon Turner had to fight to get student work taken seriously again in the mid-1970s. This tendency for ex-students to turn their backs on student work is still with us in a number of groups outside Britain belonging to the IS Tendency.

Chapter 5

Building in the upturn

Rank and file groups in the unions

When the Tories won the elections in 1970, a new impetus was given to workers' generalised resistance to the bosses and the government. Union militancy had mushroomed in the face of economic difficulties and the failures of the Wilson government. It was given further impetus by the policies of the new Tory government led by Edward Heath. Legislation on industrial relations and a determination to control public sector wages produced a series of strike explosions. An Industrial Relations Bill was introduced in December 1970 which had affinities with Labour's 'In Place of Strife'.

The union leadership reacted far more sharply against the Tories than under Labour. The TUC held a series of national, regional and local meetings, a rally in the Albert Hall, and many open-air demonstrations, including a 140,000-strong march on 21 February 1971. The TUC called on the unions not to register under the act, and practically all sizeable unions responded. All unions employed the draft clause suggested by the TUC for collective agreements, stating, 'This is not a legally enforceable agreement.'

However, when Labour is out of office union bureaucrats do not change their spots entirely. The TUC still rejected industrial action. In spite of this, one day protest strikes did take place. They were organised by the rank and file and involved 600,000 workers on 8 December 1970, 180,000 on 12 January 1971, and about 1,250,000 on both 1 March and 18 March 1971.

One high point in workers' struggle was over sackings at Upper Clyde Shipbuilders (UCS). On the afternoon of 24 June 1971 more than 100,000 workers in Glasgow stopped work over the looming crisis in the yard. Half of them demonstrated through the city. This was the largest Clydeside protest since the General Strike. A month later John Davies, the industry secretary, announced that the number of jobs at UCS would be cut from 8,500 to 2,500. Next day the workers of UCS took control of the four yards.

On 10 August a meeting of more than 1,200 shop stewards from all over Scotland and the north of England unanimously endorsed the plan for a work-in, and appealed for financial support for the workers of UCS. On 18 August, some 200,000 Scottish workers downed tools, and about 80,000 of them went on a demonstration. The shock to the government was immense. David McNee, head of Strathclyde Police, phoned Downing Street and made it clear he would not take responsibility for civil order unless the government kept UCS open. Heath obliged by making a U-turn.

In July 1972 five London dockers were imprisoned in Pentonville for breaking the industrial relations law. All 44,000 dockers around the country struck unofficially. Fleet Street followed suit and a number of engineering workers also came out. It seemed the union bureaucracy might lose control unless it acted. On 26 July the general council of the TUC called a one day strike for 31 July. The government took fright, and on the very day the general council issued the call the House of Lords took the dramatic step of altering the law to get Heath off the hook. The men were freed immediately, and the TUC dropped the call for a general strike.

There were more than 200 occupations of shipyards, factories, offices and workshops between 1972 and 1974. Workers also won important battles on the wages front. The most significant battles were the magnificent miners' strikes of 1972 and 1974.

The first of these involved a great deal of rank and file activity and industrial solidarity which culminated in the 'Battle of Saltley Gates'. Thousands of miners, assisted by some 20,000 striking engineers, shut a strategic Midlands coke depot and thereby ensured the success of the strike. The second miners' strike, during the winter of 1973-74, though more passive than its predecessor, finally precipitated the downfall of the Tories and forced the general election which returned Labour to office.

A generalised attack by the government had led to a broadened defence by workers in which economics and politics fused. Workers themselves moved to generalise, to think in class terms rather than sectional terms.

This gave a massive impetus to the rise of rank and file union groups organised by IS members. Looking at this development in retrospect, the nature of our intervention becomes clear. In one sense the idea of a rank and file movement is part of the continuity of the

British labour movement. At its high points it has thrown up this sort of organisation, such as during the First World War (though this example was not foremost in our minds). The concept arises not so much from memory but from conditions which repeat and so generate the same response.

The British working class is one of the most organised in the world in terms of trade unionism. Consequently it suffers from the inevitable effect of bureaucratisation.

The role of the union bureaucracy means that for the class struggle to advance beyond strict limits it is necessary for action to be organised independently of the officials. During the 1950s and early 1960s, such was the confidence of ordinary workers that this action was common. But it did not lead to an organised movement because the employers were prepared to make concessions in conditions of boom. Isolated action (or what we called at the time 'do it yourself reformism') was enough. With the return of the economic crisis, and the political and ideological offensive under Wilson and later Heath, things had to go beyond isolated action to succeed.

The IS became involved in rank and file organisation not only because our worker members were brought to this conclusion by outside events, but also because of our general emphasis on the concept that 'the emancipation of the working class is the act of the working class'—the red thread running back to the lessons of the theory of state capitalism and beyond to Marx.

A rank and file orientation meant organising around shop stewards (or their equivalents in non-industrial unions). In the late 1960s shop stewards combined three things: they were part of the ordinary workforce (this being before their incorporation during the mid-1970s); they were the elected rank and file leaders of that workforce; and they were the lowest rung of union organisation.

One approach to them came from the Communist Party which was fast throwing away its past achievements on the industrial front. As Alex Callinicos writes:

> The CP's relationship to shop stewards organisation was an ambivalent one. On the one hand, many leading stewards were party members, and the CP and its Broad Left caucuses in many unions and localities acted as a network linking together the best militants. On the other hand,

the party never pursued a serious rank and file strategy after 1928... Communist strategy was one of winning official positions in the unions in cooperation with left wing members of the Labour Party. In the early 1970s the CP found itself virtually paralysed by the increasingly glaring contradictions between the trade union bureaucracy and the rank and file which ran through its own ranks. Thus while its indus- trial front, the Liaison Committee for the Defence of Trade Unions (LCDTU), led two large unofficial stoppages against the Wilson gov- ernment's anti-union proposals in 1969, followed by two others in 1970-71, it made no effort to link together rank and file militants during the much greater struggle which followed.[1]

If the CP emphasised the shop steward's role in the union ma- chine and sought to use them as a channel for bureaucracy from above, there could be the opposite danger, of seeing the steward in syn- dicalist terms. Though not an organised presence since 1910-14 (except for the tiny Solidarity group), syndicalism as an idea is con- tinuously regenerated in industrial struggles. This stresses the self ac- tivity and self reliance of workers but avoids the 'divisive' issue of politics. At any time this is a disaster, because it prevents struggles going beyond the immediate issues of wages and conditions. In the late 1960s it would have been particularly misplaced. The context of the struggle was set by the conscious attempts of the state (under both Labour and Tory governments) to attack the working class. Our first short book on the issue already showed how IS sought to steer clear of the trap of syndicalism, its title being *Incomes Policy, Legisla- tion and Shop Stewards*.

We argued long and hard for the need to build rank and file or- ganisations. In his *History of the Russian Revolution* Trotsky explained how revolution had been achieved: 'The party set the soviets in motion, the soviets set in motion the workers, soldiers and to some extent the peasants. What was gained in mass was lost in speed... [You can] represent this conducting apparatus as a system of cogwheels'.[2] Even in non-revolutionary situation the analogy applies. The work- ing class needs three cogwheels. The revolutionary party and trade unions are two of them. But to connect them we need a third one— the rank and file organisation. In an article after the freeing of the Pen- tonville Five, entitled 'The Battle Is Won But The War Goes On', I wrote:

Three cogwheels: the trade union movement with 11 million members and 250,000 shop stewards is a powerful cog, with by far the strongest shop organisation of the working class anywhere in the world.

Let us assume that we have in this country a revolutionary socialist party, a combat organisation, steeled in struggle and schooled in the art of strategy and tactics for the overthrow of capitalism. Let us assume that we, the International Socialists, while building such an organisation, had 50,000 members.

There is no question that this would indeed be a powerful cogwheel. However, one cogwheel of this size could not have moved a cogwheel of 11 million. If it tried it would only break its cogs. A connecting cogwheel is necessary between the two.

This is the organisation of militants in different unions and industries who work together round specific issues, issues wider than those affecting a small group of workers in one place of work, and not going as far as to aim at the complete emancipation of the working class by the overthrow of the capitalist system.

IS members participate in building such a cogwheel in the form of rank and file organisations round papers like *Carworker*, the *Collier*, and *Rank and File Teacher*. The aim of these is to influence the policies of the trade unions.

The rising conflict will disclose to workers the magnitude of the struggle, will widen their horizons, and will help to clarify their ideas. It is very important for members of IS to do their best to recruit militants into our political organisation as well as to strengthen all existing rank and file industrial and trade union organisations.[3]

The capitalist class uses two arms to defend its interests: the economic arm and the political arm. The economic power of the capitalists is their ability to hire and fire workers, to open factories and close them, etc. The political arm is the power of the state—army, police and courts—and propaganda via press, television and radio. The workers also have to use both arms, their economic and political strength. *Socialist Worker* reported my speech to the IS Industrial Conference on 11 November 1973 in the Belle Vue Hall, Manchester, attended by 2,800 people:

Build New Leadership—With Socialist Politics
We need a new type of leadership, rooted in the rank and file...

But Cliff rammed home the message that the struggle ahead was about more than just rank and file organisation: 'To mobilise millions we need strong rank and file movements—plus a central cog to bind them together.'

That cog was socialist politics. 'We need a socialist outlook,' he declared, 'so that militants think, I'm a socialist first, a miner second, a socialist first, a docker second,' and so on.

The rank and file papers created in recent years could not survive without IS policies—even though our members are in a minority on their editorial boards.'

He ended with a ringing call that won sustained applause: 'We are fighting a political battle. We need a workers' party'.[4]

The first rank and file paper initiated by IS members was *Rank and File Teacher*. Until the early 1970s it was the only regular rank and file paper. There were a couple of issues of *Dock Worker* in 1968-69, and a couple of one-off publications: *Grading* and *Contracting Sparks* (electricians), and the pamphlet on the Barbican strike (1967) written by Paul Foot and entitled *Anti-Cameron Report*. By March 1973 there were 16 rank and file papers published regularly:

Rank and file papers, March 1973[5]	
Publication	**Print Order**
Carworker	6,000
Collier	5,000
Hospital Worker	6,000
Platform (bus workers)	3,000
Textile Worker	1,500
Case Con (social workers)	5,000
Journalists Charter	2,000
NALGO Action News	6,000
Rank and File Teacher	10,000
Redder Tape	3,000
Scots Rank and File	2,000
Tech Teacher	2,000
Dock Worker	5,000
GEC Rank and File	8,000
Building Worker	2,000
Electricians Special	2,000

There were other rank and file papers not mentioned in the above list, like *Steelworker*, *Post Office Worker*, *Printworker*, and a couple of others.

The IS conference of March 1973 passed the following resolution: 'We should work to convene a rank and file conference in the autumn/winter, ideally jointly sponsored by all the rank and file papers on which we have some influence'.[6] And, accordingly, a rank and file conference was held in Birmingham on 30 March 1974.

The Industrial Report to the 1974 IS conference stated:

> The Rank and File Conference held in Birmingham on 30 March was quite clearly the most important venture we have ever undertaken... 318 trade union bodies applied for credentials: a real credit to the three months of hard slog in the branches and the Industrial Department. For these 318 trade union bodies that were won for the conference there was probably the same again, if not more, where our comrades or contacts were defeated, usually by a combination of the right wing and the Communist Party. Clearly a very high proportion of our industrial (manual and white collar) members took the conference very seriously indeed.
>
> Some 500 delegates from 270 bodies actually turned up and participated in the conference. Of these, nearly two thirds were manual workers, and of all the delegates only half were IS members. These figures speak for the development of IS over the past year—in March 1973 such a response would not have been on the cards. In particular it is a tribute to the establishment of factory branches, the strengthening of the fractions, and the work of the rank and file papers. It also demonstrates the basic correctness of our orientation. Our stress on a democratic national rank and file movement fighting for independent working class politics actually corresponds to the consciousness of militants.[7]

The report was quite satisfied with the state of the National Rank and File Movement: 'The NRFM is a genuine transmission belt operating at a very modest level within the working class.'

The self destruction of the Communist Party had left the field increasingly open to us. There was no time in which militant workers were so open to us as in 1970-74 under the Heath government—not before and not since. All this progress was assisted because of the process of generalisation taking place in the working class. Workers were changing in struggle.

Why did this happen? Take the example of the picket line. Workers do not initiate violence here. It is when police and scabs try to break through that they will fight back. Workers look for the path of least resistance. So long as the path of reform is open the path of revolution is closed. It is only when tinkering will not work any more that people will go to the extreme. Ultimately this is a revolution, which is not a tea party. It is a fantastic risk and sacrifice, and the masses will only do it when there is no other way. So long as fragmented struggles gained results workers did not generalise. But when faced with crisis the employers would no longer give concessions, and workers had to raise the level of struggle, Thus they changed to broader class struggle from sectional struggle and this changed the workers themselves. It meant that an important number of workers learned how the state organised to defend capitalism, about how the media reports strikes, how the reformist MPs stand on the sidelines, and so on.

A few weeks after the great miners' victory in 1972, I went to Barnsley to meet the three IS members in the National Union of Miners (NUM). I expected they would bring three or four contacts. I was really astonished when over 100 miners turned up, including a member of the NUM national executive, Peter Tait, and Arthur Scargill, at the time on the Yorkshire NUM executive. The meeting convinced us of the need and possibility of a rank and file paper in the mining union. John Charlton reports that the March 1972 rank and file miners' conference called by IS had been attended by 56 miners from various parts of the country, 'and as a result we could look forward to a rapid growth of a strong rank and file movement around the new paper, *Collier*, which had been very well received. A number of leading miners have now joined IS'.[8]

We held a meeting in Grimethorpe, a mining village. We had no members there. The meeting was held under the auspices of IS, and the title of the meeting was 'The miners' strike and the struggle for socialism'; 500 people turned up.

When the five dockers were imprisoned in Pentonville for breaking the Industrial Relations Law in 1972, the London Port Shop Stewards' Committee wanted to print a poster protesting against the imprisonment. They contacted the Communist Party printshop, but it refused to do the job as it was the weekend, when the printshop was closed. The reluctance of the CP printshop to print posters was a symptom of a general malaise. The CP and its industrial front, the

Tony Cliff aged 24

Tony Cliff and his wife, Chanie Rosenberg, outside Buckingham Palace, October 1946

Aldermaston march for nuclear disarmament led by Canon Collins with Michael Foot behind, Easter 1960, and (above) one of the very earliest editions of *Socialist Review*, May 1951

Anti Vietnam War demonstration in London, October 1968 (left), and the battle at Grosvenor Square (above)— anti Vietnam War demonstrators battle with police outside the US embassy, October 1968

Dockers marching to parliament in support of Enoch Powell after his 'rivers of blood' speech in 1968, and (left) one of the early editions of *Socialist Worker*, September 1966

Workers from the occupied Upper Clyde Shipbuilders arriving in London, June 1971. Jimmy Reid is standing next to Tony Benn

The turning point in the 1972 miners' strike, the Battle of Saltley Gates

Print workers on strike against the *Sun*, Fleet Street, 1972

East London teachers, including Chanie Rosenberg, outside Pentonville prison in support of the five dockers jailed under the Industrial Relations Act, 1972

The first
national
Rank and
File
conference,
March 1974

Marching against unemployment under the hated Heath government

The Anti Nazi
League
demonstrating in
Trafalgar Square
in the late 1970s

Marching in support of the Great Miners' Strike, April 1984, and
(inset) the final miners' march at the end of the strike, February 1985

Nurses at Charing Cross Hospital protesting against the poll tax, May 1990, and (below) the poll tax riot in Trafalgar Square

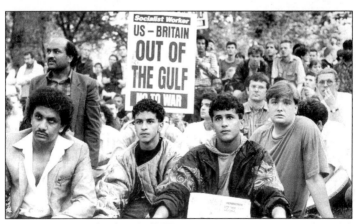

Protesting against the first Gulf War in 1991

Marching to the Anti Nazi League carnival, May 1994 (left). 150,000 people came to the carnival following the election of the Nazi Derek Beackon in the Isle of Dogs. Protesting (above) against the Criminal Justice Bill, October 1994

Singing the Internationale at the SWP's May Day Rally in Alexandra Palace, 1992

The lobby of the Labour Party conference in 1999, and (below) Tony Cliff on a pensioners' demo, December 1997

Militant demonstration of Linksruck supporters in Germany

LCDTU, were more or less inactive, because they tailed behind their left friends in the bureaucracy.

Our printshop, a tiny outfit at the time, was contacted. Our printing comrade phoned me and asked, 'Is it alright if we work throughout the weekend?' My answer was, 'Certainly. If need be we should work throughout the night.' The poster, 'One docker in the dock, all dockers out of the docks', was printed and widely flyposted.

The dockers were very friendly to us even before the arrest of the five in Pentonville. It was Laurie Flynn who, in *Socialist Worker*, broke the story that the Midland Cold Storage Company, which was being illegally picketed by the five jailed dockers, was not the innocent little firm portrayed in the papers. It was owned by the giant Vestey family with their fabulous wealth.

A few days after the Pentonville Five were freed from prison, IS held a dockers' victory meeting in Stratford, east London, to welcome them back. Three of the five Pentonville dockers—Tony Merrick, Connie Clancy and Derek Watkins—were on our platform. Two other dockers were also on the platform—Mickey Fenn and Tony Delaney. I was also one of the speakers.[9] At that time the total IS docker membership was one! Shortly afterwards Mickey Fenn and Eddie Prevost—a very serious docker—joined us. Sadly, Mickey Fenn is dead. Eddie is still an active member of our organisation, although he is not working in the docks any longer.

Another case: the TUC called a lobby of parliament for 2 November 1972 to demand higher pensions. All work at the huge Anchor Steelworks construction site in Scunthorpe stopped in the afternoon, and 2,000 workers marched from the site to the town football ground for a mass meeting to demand higher pensions. They were supported by workers from the Drax power station site and delegations of trade unionists from all over Yorkshire. Some 5,000 workers assembled. I was one of the people invited to address the meeting.

I remember I started my speech with something like this: 'I had an alternative. I could have gone to lobby parliament or come here. I had to show respect to the dead, so I did not go to parliament, but came here to the living and fighting.'

I said I was proud to be present at 'a day in the history of the working class movement. The tears of Jack Jones break my heart. But they will not give higher pensions. The only way to help the pensioners is to fight through strike action.' I went on to say, amid loud cheers, 'We are the army of the working class. I believe that the rank and file is strong enough by industrial power to raise pensions now. I believe that the rank and file, by industrial power, can smash this Tory government'.[10]

Significantly, straight after the mass rally, I was invited by the shop stewards committee of Anchor Steelworks to come some time later to a half day shop stewards school to discuss with them the issue of productivity deals (more on this subject below).

Between 1968 and 1974 my meetings around the country inhibited our home life. My daughter Anna asked: 'Why didn't I have a daddy between my fourth and tenth birthdays?' Because politics had always dominated our conversation at home, and because we had television and radio news practically 24 hours a day, the children were full of politics. But quite often they caught the wrong end of the stick. For example, on one occasion Chanie, Donny and I were in the car passing near Camden market. Chanie said, 'Let's go into the market.' Donny asked, 'Is that the Common Market?' We laughed. More embarrassing was when Chanie and I went to the South Bank construction workers' picket line in 1958 with Donny. When the police roughed up the building workers, Donny, aged four, announced in a piping loud voice, 'Daddy, I want to be a policeman!' Another incident: during the 1972 miners' strike, the television news reported that the miners were holding the country to ransom. Our daughter Anna burst into tears, terrified of what was going to happen to her. That was not the 'politically correct' attitude!

Sometimes these family jokes could turn out to be useful. One example concerned Donny, who must have been a stupid boy. We gave him a bulb to plant in the garden. One day Chanie saw him pulling the bulb out of the earth. She asked him why. 'I do this every day. I want to see how well it is growing,' he said. I've reminded comrades of this when they show impatience and seem to be getting no visible results from what seems a heavy expenditure of political time and effort. You cannot harvest where you did not sow.

Favourable conditions for growth

The electoral defeat of the Tories in 1974 was the culmination of a mighty advance of the working class. When it came to our expectations regarding IS, again they were very high indeed. The previous few years had been very good for the organisation.

At the Easter 1970 conference, IS had a membership of 880. By Easter 1972 this had risen to 2,351, and by 1974 to 3,310. The social composition of the membership also changed radically for the better. In 1970 IS was composed mainly of students and white collar workers, with a smattering of manual workers. The students, then and later, played a very important role in selling *Socialist Worker* round factories and trying to recruit workers.

The Industrial Report to the 1974 IS conference gave the following picture:

Membership and Social Composition[11]			
	March 1972	March 1973	March 1974
Manual and white collar	613	746	1,155
Students	381	617	591
Housewives	58	87	146
Unemployed	109	106	94
School students	51	41	49
National members		100	54
Miscellaneous	314	144	120
Total	2,351	2,667	3,310

Union composition[12]			
Manual fractions	March 1973	Dec 1973	June 1974
AUEW (engineering)	200	235	275
Buses	25	35	37
Docks	3	6	7
EETPU	40	60	90
Motors		150	180
NUM	50	67	70
POEU			15
Steel			20
UPW			30
Manual and white collar			
Health	30	100	130
White collar			
APEX			30
ASTMS		120	160
ATTI		150	150
AUEW (TASS)	30	50	70
Civil servants	40	46	56
NUT		260	230
NUJ		37	48
NALGO		120	160

In March 1974, of the 2,000 membership forms analysed, 200 comrades were manual worker shop stewards and 125 were white collar union workplace representatives, 250 held positions in their trade union branches, and 92 were on district or divisional committees. A significant proportion (10-15 percent) of our members now had a constituency in the wider working class movement, and it was to them increasingly that we needed to turn for leadership at local and national level.[13]

Lenin wrote that in the revolutionary party there was no rank and file—everyone was a leader. Unlike reformist parties, where the leadership regards the members as sheep to be passively led, the revolutionary party seeks to get the class acting in its own interests, and this means intervening in debates on 'what is to be done' at every level. Therefore you cannot be a leader if you are solely tied up with the internal life of the party. It is a matter of how the organisation relates to non-members. This is the test of leadership.

Many times I have argued with comrades and they have disagreed, but then half an hour later I might hear the same comrades repeating my arguments to non-members in an effective way. This shows both the friction and the agreement needed to lead in a practical situation. Leadership is a dialogue, and there is no dialogue with people who agree in advance with 100 percent of what you are saying. Leadership is about how to have an argument with people who agree with you 50 percent and through argument you are able to raise the level to 60 percent or more.

Socialist Worker played a crucial role. In September 1968 the paper was launched as a weekly. It had four pages, cost two old pence and looked somewhat scruffy. It was sold mainly by students outside the gates of factories and on council estates. Slowly the paper was improved. It grew to six pages in 1969, eight in 1970, 12 in 1971 and 16 in 1972. Its sale increased from 8,000 a week in August 1969 to 21,000 in July 1972, and 31,000 in October 1974.

The 1974 Pre-Conference Industrial Report stated, 'In June last year we decided to use *Socialist Worker* to test the water for a genuine bona-fide trade union conference. We called for a *Socialist Worker* Industrial Conference in November. This rally demonstrated beyond any doubt that our periphery was substantial, serious and working class.' Around 2,800 IS members and contacts filled the Belle Vue Hall in Manchester, and the organising experience gained was considerable.

Politically the rally also indicated that *Socialist Worker* did carry the commitment of many workers who were not (yet) IS members. The considerable increase in the number of workers contributing to *Socialist Worker* since April was an indication that at least part of this development had been successful. But it was then still too early to be able to argue with any certainty about the consequences of this shift.

The move to factory branches

Despite its orientation on industry, and despite its impressive growth, the IS organisational structure in 1972 was still a geographical one. Members belonged to branches according to the area they lived in. At the end of 1971 I came to the conclusion that this structure had become an impediment to the correct functioning of the organisation. Organisation on a geographical basis fits electoral politics; for an organisation based on struggle at the workplace it is inadequate. The ENV branch was the only factory branch that existed in 1966. Now even this one did not exist, as the factory had closed. At the Easter 1972 conference I moved a resolution to build factory branches. After a heated discussion the conference initially rejected this. The opposition came from two sources: those who opposed factory branches in principle, and those who thought it was premature to establish them.

An organisation, to survive, needs inertia. The more developed the organisation, the longer it exists, the more widespread is the inertia. This is a source of strength but, dialectically, the other side of the coin is that it is a source of weakness. One of the reasons why human beings survived while the dinosaurs did not was that the dinosaurs developed certain characteristics to an extreme point, but they therefore could not change when circumstances changed. Humans are miserable little creatures—they have no fur to protect themselves against cold weather, so they put coats on. But if the weather changes they can take the coats off. A human being is not carnivorous or vegetarian, but can be both. For a revolutionary organisation the danger of rigidity exists—it was natural that the members, having expended so much effort in building the organisation, were worried about a change, worried about dilution of the membership, worried that factory branches would lead to economism or pure trade unionism. Under such conditions we had to 'bend the stick' hard. This phrase comes from Lenin, who repeated more than once that in bending the stick you could go too far. But he always corrected the problem after winning his position.

The idea of forming factory branches was eventually won, and the way this was achieved is instructive. The art of leadership comprises a number of elements. One is the recognition of contradictory consciousness. If it was the case that workers were convinced that capitalism should be abolished, then leadership would be unnecessary—it would happen straight away. If it was the case that workers believed that absolutely nothing could be done against capitalism, leadership would again be unnecessary, because it would be futile. Because workers have a contradictory consciousness comprising both elements, the need for a revolutionary party arises. However, within the party there is contradictory consciousness and unevenness as well, for there is a mixture of the inertia needed to maintain organisation and the will to advance and break new ground in the struggle to win the working class for socialism. In his approach to leadership Lenin followed the Napoleonic dictum, 'On s'engage et puis on voit' (first get stuck in and then see what happens). Of course, this method must lead to mistakes being made, but at the same time it is essential if there are to be breakthroughs, forward jumps into new ways of doing things. This was the case for factory branches. Comrades had not experienced these, and the only way to find out if they would work was to try.

To summarise the initial experience of the branches, in September 1973 I wrote a pamphlet which stated:

> Workers' power lies mainly in the factory, docks and other places of work. A revolutionary socialist organisation must be built not as a collection of local branches but as a union of factory branches. It can lead the decisive sections of the working class if it has strong party branches in the factories, especially the big ones. The factory branch will be responsible for carrying the party's policy to the workers in the factory on all current questions, as well as on the party's long term programme, thus ensuring the unity in action of its immediate and final aims.
>
> The factory branch should be the driving force in raising the class consciousness of the workers round it, developing their political education, their organisation, their initiative, enthusiasm and fighting ability, so that from the factory they are drawn into the struggle of the

working class as a whole. Factory branches should organise the vanguard of the working class at the point of production. The factory is the best centre of the organisation of the working class in struggle, not only in the factory itself but around it. The factory branch should consist of the party members employed at the same place, in which they represent the party as a whole. The branch is not simply a collection of individuals who hold the same views, who merely meet to discuss points that especially interest them. The members have a collective responsibility to win the workers in their place of work to the party policy as a whole.[14]

It is necessary for comrades from factory branches to take the lion's share in the district committee. This will strengthen the district leadership, and at the same time will strengthen the factory branches through broadening their outlook, seeing the struggle of the working class in wider terms and helping to prevent a narrow industrial outlook.[15]

The factory branches pamphlet summed up the general guide to factory branches thus:

First of all, a factory branch has to unite the socialists, the militants in the factory…

Second, the factory branch will relate the advanced socialists to the majority of the workers… The IS branch, with the help of leaflets, bulletins and the rank and file papers relevant to the industry, will try to influence the mass of workers in the factory.

Third, the factory branch has to hold regular meetings to discuss how IS members should fight for resolutions and policies that are laid down by the national organisations…

Fourth, the branch has to hold regular meetings to discuss how IS members should fight for shop stewardships and other important positions and delegations in and from the factory.

Fifth, the branch has to hold regular political meetings to discuss a basic education programme and current events, features in *Socialist Worker*, *International Socialism* or any other publications of the International Socialists.

In addition, 'a central theme of the work of the factory branch must be the attempt to win the leadership of the workers in the factory'. An important part of this task was that 'every factory branch should produce a programme for the factory'. The basic aim of the IS factory branch was to do in the specific what IS as a whole tried to do generally—that is, 'raising the consciousness, the self activity and organisation of workers at their place of work'.[16]

The most significant decision at the following year's conference in 1973 was to build at least ten factory branches over the next year. The results were much more impressive than the target of ten indicated. At the 1974 conference it was reported that 'we now have 38 workplace branches with at least 300 members',[17] or an average of eight members per branch—a very impressive result.

> In the Leyland combine we now have six factory branches, in the Ford and Chrysler combines we now have three. In Lucas we have two, and in ICI, the steel industry and RTZ we have one each and a number of scattered members and contacts.[18]

What was very exciting about our factory branches was that they did not limit themselves to fighting against their own bosses but went outside the gate of the factory to lead battles on general social and political issues. This was essential. Lenin had always insisted that Bolsheviks were not just fighters for the interests of the working class but acted as 'the tribune of the oppressed'. Just as it was essential for students to escape from abstract theory to intervene, so it was vital for workers to look beyond the limits of syndicalist or workerist ideas. I shall give two examples of how this worked in practice.

In Ossett in Yorkshire we had a good branch in an engineering factory which produced car accessories. They learnt that at the local school the dinner arrangements were extremely unfair: children who paid for their meals were in one queue, while those who got free meals were put into a separate queue. Each queue had a different coloured card to present for their meal. Our factory branch convinced the workforce that they should go on strike in protest. They won a quick victory: the mayor of Bradford rushed to the factory and announced that the local authority was cancelling the dinner arrangements.

Another example: after the Birmingham pub bombings in 1974 a tide of anti-Irish hatred swept the workplaces. Of course we opposed the idea of putting a bomb in a pub visited by working class people, including Irish workers. It was not part of a military camp. At the same time we were for the withdrawal of British troops from Northern Ireland, and for an end to British imperialism's role there. In Birmingham at the time we had five IS factory branches, including a strong one in Longbridge and another in Lucas. The comrades called a meeting to discuss what to do. Over 50 engineers turned up, and a very clear, effective strategy was adopted. They decided to organise a day of mourning for the victims of the pub atrocity. As a mark of respect for the dead no placards or slogans were allowed, and the march was to be in total silence. It was to start some time before the pubs opened, and end some time after the pubs closed to avoid digression into drunkenness. The route of the march avoided Irish areas.

The fight against productivity deals

In 1970, in my book *The Employers' Offensive: Productivity Deals and How to Fight Them*, I explained that the failure of Harold Wilson's incomes policy to stem significant wage rises led the employers and the government to use a more indirect attack—the trap of productivity bargaining. Management and government came to the conclusion that payment by results (or piece-rates) was the main driving force behind the wage drift and rise in wage levels.

In 1968 the Coventry District Employers' Association published an extremely interesting study entitled *Working Party Report on Wage Drift, Work Management and Systems of Payment* (known as the Coventry Blue Book). It explained that payment by results was a strong weapon in the hands of workers to raise wages and cut profit margins. In addition it undermined management's prerogative to manage:

> It slowly and surely wrests from management an area of control that is essentially a management function, until inevitably shop floor management have little or no control whatsoever and workmen are then able to reach that point where they can achieve their rate of incentive payment by negotiation and work at whatever rate suits them best.[19]

The struggle over piece-rates illustrates Marx's argument that the class struggle goes on always, whether in open or hidden form. Time rates had been very common, but bosses decided that this encouraged workers' unity, as each worker earned the same. Time rates, they felt, did not encourage productivity rises, as you earned as much whether or not you worked hard. Payment by results was designed to divide worker from worker and rack up output. It was the bosses' trump card. But in the hands of a well organised working class movement their master strategy was blunted and then turned into a weapon of the workers. The creative initiative of the working class showed itself once more.

The main argument against payment by results was repeated by Allan Flanders, publicist of the pathbreaking productivity agreement in the Fawley refinery. For Flanders, one of the main aims of productivity deals was to put an end to the 'abrogation of management by management'.

> This is the aspect of productivity bargaining that I particularly want to stress. I find it difficult to see how the accumulated disorder, which is the heritage of two decades of post-war growth in the unofficial system of collective bargaining, can be cleared up without the help of productivity agreements. The re-establishment of order and control is central to my case for productivity bargaining, because in the long run this may be far more important than the immediate gains that can be found in terms of increased labour productivity.[20]

He concluded that productivity bargaining was 'a logical first step towards a modern, viable system of managerial control and effort'.[21]

Productivity deals also meant the more effective screwing of workers to work harder. A central feature in practically all productivity deals is increasing flexibility in the use of labour. This labour flexibility boils down to one worker having to do the job of two.[22] Involved in productivity deals was the introduction of time and motion studies and speed-up.[23]

Productivity deals undermined the power of the shop stewards, as they replaced piece-work by national or plant bargaining. Thus they took away the stewards' most basic function—that of negotiating the rate for the job. They inevitably increased the role of full time convenors. As I wrote:

> A most insidious trend appearing in recent years is the increase in the number of full time convenors, shop representatives, deputy convenors, works committee members, etc, who spend an increasingly long period away from their increasingly nominal jobs. In many factories the ordinary worker who is elected shop steward very rapidly finds himself (if he's good at representing his men) taken away from the shopfloor more and more often. Then he gets put on a 'soft' job, to allow management to take him away without disrupting production. It's no wonder that many get completely divorced from their base. With factory convenors this is particularly strongly felt. Often the only contact they have

with the workers is when they appear to try and persuade the men not to walk out over a grievance.[24]

The full impact of productivity deals on the overall militancy of the labour movement was only to become clear to us after 1974. Therefore the optimism of the Industrial Report to the 1974 IS conference was undimmed. It was also quite rightly proud that the organisation was very interventionist in workers' struggles: 'The list of disputes in which IS, supportive rank and file organisations and IS comrades played a significant role or distinguished themselves reads like a working class history of the time: the hospital ancillary workers' dispute, the GEC victimisations, Fine Tubes, the Chrysler strikes, the Perkins dispute, struggles involving black workers at STC and women workers at GEC, Con-Mech, Shrewsbury, the Glasgow firemen, the ambulancemen, the miners, Strachans, the [teachers'] London weighting disputes, solidarity with Chile, the nurses and the wage threshold struggles'.[25]

Chapter 6

Setbacks

From beautiful spring to freezing winter

The years 1970-74 had been the best years of my life. As we have already seen, the working class won massive victories: two victorious miners' strikes—the first, in 1972, got rid of the Tory incomes policy, the second, in 1974, got rid of the Tories; the five Pentonville dockers had been freed as the result of a national docks strike; the strike of Fleet Street workers; and a massive strike in the engineering industry, turning into a near general strike. The 8,000 workers occupying UCS won a glorious victory, followed by some 200 other factory occupations. IS had also done very well indeed. Our growth was impressive. Many of our members were shop stewards. And around our membership a much greater number of workers were collecting, organised in rank and file groups.

And yet after this the working class offensive turned into a retreat which we called a 'downturn in the class struggle'. To understand the collapse of militancy one has to take into account economic and political factors, and grasp the dialectical relation between the two elements.

Back in 1964 Harold Wilson's 'Statement of Intent on Productivity, Prices and Incomes' had failed to stem rising militancy. Ted Heath tried unsuccessfully during his term of office from 1970-74 to impose an incomes policy . Now, in Wilson's term of office after 1974, this was going to be introduced voluntarily through the Social Contract with the blessing of the union leaders.

The Social Contract was supported strongly by the left leaders of the unions, Hugh Scanlon of the engineers' union and Jack Jones of the TGWU. An integral part of Labour's pre-election programme in 1973, this 'far-reaching Social Contract between workers and the government' was planned so that it could be renewed each year as circumstances and new opportunities presented themselves. What Heath with his aggressive policy failed to achieve Wilson and Callaghan, with their softly-softly approach, hoped to do.

So when, in October 1974, Labour won the second general election of the year, Heath's policy of confronting the unions was replaced with the new strategy. It included significant concessions to the unions. To facilitate the co-option of the unions Harold Wilson took into his government people with left wing reputations: Michael Foot, Tony Benn and Eric Heffer. The miners won their wage claim. Altogether wages rose by 16 percent in the first year of the Wilson government, while prices rose by 8 percent.

Michael Foot, the minister of labour, went on to repudiate most of the articles of the Tory Industrial Relations Act in reaction to a strike of all members of the AEU against the court seizing the assets of the union. The 'crime' of the AEU had been that it supported the strike of the relatively small Con Mech engineering factory in Surrey.

As groups of workers continued to fight closures and redundancies, Tony Benn, the minister of industry, promised aid to workers' co-operatives in Triumph Meriden, KME (formerly Fisher-Bendix) in Kirby, and the *Scottish Daily News*.

In July 1975 Healey imposed stage one of Labour's wage control policy and introduced cash limits on public spending. This was the first real move to what would later be called Thatcherism. Then, on 1 August 1976, stage two of the incomes policy was introduced: a 4.5 percent increase in wages at a time when the rate of inflation was 16.5 percent. This meant a serious cut in real wages. Yet not a single union officially challenged it.

Looking ahead, it would become clear that there were limits to how much the rank and file would endure. By stage three, crucial union conferences—those of the engineers, the TGWU, NUM and many others—decided to oppose any third year of wage restraint. From the summer of 1977 the government was obliged to police this phase on its own. However, the union leaders still tacitly collaborated. Only one union resisted stage three with strike action—the Fire Brigades Union, which began an eight week strike for a 30 percent pay claim in November 1977. The Labour government mobilised all its forces against them, including the use of troops. Despite wide public support, the firemen were defeated. When the government tried to impose stage four in August 1978—a 5 percent pay limit—the floodgates broke. The result was the 'Winter of Discontent'. Nevertheless, Wilson and Callaghan could still pat themselves on the back. They had achieved *de facto* union cooperation in incomes policy over a long and

tough period, 1975-78. The strategy had succeeded in turning the
great advance of the working class in the years of the Heath government into a catastrophic retreat.

The chief architects of the disaster on the union side, Scanlon
and Jones, were themselves wholeheartedly supported by Communist
Party activists, who had great influence among the rank and file. One
product of this was trade union collaboration with the employers,
now called 'participation'. The influence of 'participation' on workers' militancy was pernicious.

Here the advantages of Labour's carrot over the Tory stick were
shown graphically. Govan, the new name for three of the four former
UCS yards (the fourth becoming Marathon), had been a pioneer in
the field of 'workers' participation'. Stewards sat on a joint union-
management committee monitoring a harsh productivity deal. They
signed a 31 point agreement which contained elaborate no-strike
pledges and massive concessions on work practices which gave management the right to impose compulsory overtime.

When shipyard workers at Swan Hunter on the Tyne refused a
tough management package tied to a large Polish ship order, Govan
scabbed on them. Jimmy Airlie, Govan's Communist convenor, had
led the UCS occupation in 1971 and asked at that time, 'Are the
other shipyards going to accept our orders and let my men starve?' But
in 1978 he sang a new song: 'If Newcastle are losing six ships through
disputes, we will build them. If not us, then the Japs will.'

Participation also became the rage in the car industry. It led to
blacklegging becoming respectable at Longbridge, British Leyland's
biggest factory, and for decades by far the most militant plant in the
car industry. In 1975 senior stewards accepted a three tier system of
participation accompanied by an announcement that 12,000 jobs
had to go. Now, instead of seven full time senior stewards, Longbridge had more than 50. A gap was created between them and the
members. The *Financial Times* published fulsome praise of the Longbridge senior stewards.

Derek Robinson, the Longbridge convenor, chairman of the British
Leyland Combine Committee and a leading member of the Communist Party, was more profuse in his praise of 'participation' than anyone
else. More and more he spoke as the partner of management: 'We still
haven't won the conception amongst the broad masses of people on
the shop floor that they've got a vested interest in efficiency no less than

we have. It is one of our problems…if we are able to…make Leyland successful as a publicly-owned company, then it is self evident that that will be a major political victory.'

Under Robinson, the Longbridge works committee, instead of serving as a transmission belt for channelling workers' demands upwards, came to serve the interests of the employers, transferring their orders downwards. 'Participation' weakened shopfloor organisation, increased sectionalism and, finally, made scabbing an official tactic. In February 1977 2,365 toolmakers throughout British Leyland went on a one month strike for separate bargaining rights and restoration of differentials. When the government threatened to sack them, engineering union president Hugh Scanlon declared that the sacking 'has the full backing of all the unions'. Robinson agreed and encouraged all workers to cross the toolroom workers' picket. In August 1978 the toolroom in the company's SU carburettor plant came out on strike. Again, both union officials and the leadership of the combine lined up with management.

Two other examples of official scabbing by unions during the 1974-79 Labour government deserve mention. In March 1977 535 electricians at BSC Port Talbot struck for higher pay. Other members of the electricians' union at the plant, along with 6,500 other trade unionists in the plant—members of the engineering union, TGWU and other unions—were instructed by their leaderships to cross the picket line. The strike went on for more than two months. The second example was the strike of 5,000 maintenance engineers at London's Heathrow airport (1 April to 27 April 1977), when 54,000 other trade unionists, members of the TGWU, GMWU, EETPU among others, were instructed to cross the picket line.

The years of participation did terrible damage. The government appointed a tough new manager at British Leyland, Michael Edwardes. He proposed 12,500 redundancies in January 1978. Mass meetings were held in protest, but soon the majority of senior stewards and union officials decided to accept. In November a strike called by the Longbridge shop stewards committee against the government's 5 percent limit on wage rises petered out without a murmur. On 10 September 1979 Edwardes, with the support of the leadership of the Confederation of Shipbuilding and Engineering Unions, exploited the gap between the shop stewards and their members and initiated a ballot over the heads of the stewards. This simply asked workers, 'Are you in favour of the Leyland survival plan?' without even pretending to spell out what that meant. The vote was 'yes' by seven to one.

Now Edwardes no longer needed 'participation'. On 19 October he sacked Robinson. In spite of everything Longbridge was solid, and 57,000 workers came out on strike in British Leyland as a whole. But the picket was small, and little effort was made to spread the strike elsewhere. On 27 October the engineering union leaders called it off, and Robinson himself backed down, leaving behind a terribly demoralised shopfloor. In short, the strength of the Longbridge workers' organisation, which had played a key role in supporting the miners in 1972, had atrophied disastrously.

In the case of the miners, the measure used to undermine their ability to struggle was an incentive scheme, a sort of productivity deal giving widely differing incomes between coalfields, and even between individual pits. In September 1974 the National Coal Board and representatives of the miners' union executive submitted details of a draft agreement. In a ballot, 61.53 percent of NUM members rejected this.

But the government, represented by energy secretary Tony Benn, and the Coal Board kept the pressure up. NUM president Joe Gormley obliged them by breaking the union's constitution and balloting again. He hoped to overrule the previous decision, but once more the majority (55.6 percent) rejected the scheme. Now the NUM executive allowed separate areas to negotiate their own local incentive schemes, which Nottinghamshire and others rapidly proceeded to do. This, more than anything, created the deep divisions that were to take such a heavy toll in 1984-85. The seeds of the scabbing in that strike were sown by the Labour government in 1977.

The Labour government went further than just encouraging scabbing. When the Glasgow dustcart drivers came out on strike in March 1975 the government sent in troops to break the strike, and the army was used again against the firemen in the winter of 1977-78.

Labour's link with the trade unions now meant that it could use the union bureaucracy to police the working class far more effectively than could Heath's industrial relations courts and all the paraphernalia of the state.[1]

There was a massive collapse of militancy throughout the mining industry, as can be seen from the following figures: the number of strike days 'lost'—over 10 million in 1972 and over 5 million in 1974—collapsed to 52,000 in 1975, increasing to 70,000 in 1976,

88,000 in 1977 and 176,000 in 1978.[2]

Another aspect of this process (warned of in my 1970 book, *The Employers' Offensive*) came to the fore at this time. Productivity deals meant shop stewards were excluded from wage negotiations while convenors were transformed into full timers, thus increasing the power of the trade union bureaucracy over the rank and file. The number of full time convenors had recently increased dramatically. A study published in 1978 showed this clearly. It was based on a survey of 453 workplaces employing 330,000 GMWU manual workers across a wide range of manufacturing and service industries. Of the total number of workers in the sample, 73 percent were in manufacturing industry and 23 percent in public service (principally gas, water, electricity, NHS, and national and local government).

The study showed that in manufacturing 62 percent of all plants employing more than 500 workers had full time convenors, while the corresponding figure for engineers was 69 percent, and for the public sector 21 percent. The study reckoned that there were now four times the number of full time convenors than there were in 1966—about 5,000 in manufacturing establishments (in addition, there were another couple of thousand in other places of employment). Thus the number of full time convenors was about two and a half times the number of full time officials.[3]

Of course, the position of full time convenors is not identical with that of full time union officials. But quite often there is a greater similarity between these two categories than between either of them and the rank and file workers.

The years 1974-79 confirmed the analysis of *The Employers' Offensive*, but being correct was little comfort. Sadly we, the members of IS/SWP, had far too little influence compared to the CP.

The massive rise in unemployment also undermined workers' confidence in their ability to fight. The impact of unemployment is double edged. It can cow workers or spur them to fight. The dominant political forces in the labour movement tilted the balance towards retreat. In January 1975 there were 678,000 people out of work; by December 1975, this figure had risen to 1,129,000; by December 1976 to 1,273,3000; and by September 1977 to 1,609,000.[4]

Facing the great rise in unemployment from 678,000 in July 1975 to 1,273,000 in September 1977, we decided to launch the Right to Work Campaign. Alas, the success of the Right to Work Campaign in raising the struggle against unemployment in no way stopped the general retreat of the working class.

The extent of this retreat becomes clear if one follows what happened to wage levels. 'Never since the Second World War had the real wage of workers declined as much as under the Labour government of 1974-79'.[5] There were many industrial disputes under the Labour government of 1974-79. But they were radically different to those of the preceding period. The disputes were far more bitter and lengthy; the employers were far more aggressive and quite often unready to concede anything except after a long battle; lockouts were back with a vengeance; and the proportion of disputes ending with workers' defeats or partial defeats was much greater than in previous years.

Last, but not least, the working class retreat in 1974-79 was caused by the political ideas dominating the class. As I wrote elsewhere:

> ...in the years 1968-74 there was an unstable balance between the political generalisation on the employers' side—incomes policy and industrial relations legislation—and the industrial militancy on the workers' side. Such a situation cannot last for long. The unstable equilibrium can lead to one of two outcomes: to the political generalisation of industrial militancy, or to the decline of sectional militancy. In fact, the unstable equilibrium in the following few years was destroyed by the politics dominating the British working class—Labourism—the nature of which is summed up in the banner of the Kent NUM: a miner outlined against a pithead and looking towards the Houses of Parliament. This is the essence of what Labourism represents in the relations between industrial action and politics. The logic of this dichotomy between economics and politics is that if workers have a claim that brings them up against a Tory government there is the alternative of a Labour government. But if the claim brings them headlong against a Labour government they have no alternative but to retreat.[6]

Some time in the 1950s my friend Jabra Nicola, ex-editor of the legal Stalinist paper in Palestine who joined our Trotskyist group, came on a visit to Britain. We were comparing the fate of the British Empire with that of the French. He put it very well: the French had suffered massive explosions in their colonies in Indochina (Vietnam, Laos, Campuchea) and Algeria. As a result the French capitalists lost practically all their investments. As against this, the British withdrew from places like India and the Middle East practically without losing a penny and keeping all their investments intact. Jabra explained the difference very clearly: when the pressure was rising in the pipeline the French said, 'We are not going to retreat', and they screwed the tap tighter. Eventually the whole structure exploded. The British rulers were more experienced and adaptable, so that if there was pressure in the pipeline they opened the tap. When the pressure decreased they tightened the tap. Wilson and Callaghan were incomparably more effective in delivering capitalist policy with their softly-softly approach than Heath with his confrontation with the unions.

Reading the first draft of this book I had the strong impression that the reader would ask, why is such a lot of space given to the twists and changes in the economic, social and political setup, and in the balance of class forces?

As a disciple of Lenin I learnt well that strategy and tactics have to change according to changes in the objective situation. The driver of a car on a twisting mountainous road must carefully follow the twists and turns in the road if he wants to avoid a mishap. For a revolutionary adjusting to the objective situation is much more difficult than for the driver of a car. Imagine if a fog engulfed a winding road so that it was very difficult to make out the twists and turns in it. Grasping the changes in economic, social and political reality is a very complicated task, and quite often a very difficult one. We have to learn from Lenin that a revolutionary is not a person who commits no mistakes but one who admits his mistakes and corrects them swiftly. If over the last three decades or so we had not grasped the continuous changes in the objective situation in the level of the class struggle we would have been doomed. We would have drifted either into right wing opportunism (thinking that revolution would never come and that tiny reforms were all that could be achieved) or ultra-leftism (believing that socialism could be won immediately).

The danger of opportunism is obvious. Regarding ultra-leftism, one can be a pure revolutionary but completely useless. If one is completely isolated from workers one can easily adopt an extreme position, but it is a meaningless one. If I wanted to buy a car I would have to calculate how much money I could raise for this purpose, and I would probably find that I could afford nothing better than a clapped-out 1970s Ford. If I just wanted to daydream about a car, I certainly would not say to myself, 'I wish I had a clapped-out 1970s Ford.' I would say, 'I wish I had a gold plated Rolls Royce.' The more isolated revolutionaries are from the working class, the less their positions can be corrected by workers in struggle, and the greater the attraction of extreme, hollow sloganising. Only practice reaffirms one's ideas, one's theory.

It might still be said that the preceding account of changes in the class struggle still belabours the point. Is it not obvious what happened?

With hindsight 20:20 vision is easy. But writing history or biography one has to develop the theme chronologically, to put oneself in the shoes of somebody active at the time. Describing how I wrestled with the problems of the shape of the class struggle at the time is of much greater educational value than simply telling the reader what is obvious with hindsight.

Thirty years ago there were many groups claiming to be revolutionary, both Trotskyist and Maoist. IS was not the largest of the groups. Today we are the only significant one, both in terms of size of membership and influence. Our understanding of the twists and turns in class struggle was a decisive element determining this.

I learned from Lenin that with any radical change in the class struggle one has to be clear about the key link in the chain of development and grasp it hold of it. But we could not assimilate Lenin's approach except through our own struggle to analyse contemporary reality. We borrowed a lot from Lenin in this regard, but what we made of the borrowing depended on our own experience and our own thinking. This was not, however, the only element involved. At the same time, in the zig-zags we followed, we might easily have lost sight of the ultimate destination if we did not hold clearly and with passion to the general theory given us by Marx, Engels, Lenin, Trotsky and Luxemburg.

High expectations misplaced

The 1974 IS conference had quite high expectations for the future. Not only would the industrial upturn continue, but so would the growth and influence of IS, the factory branches and the Rank and File Movement. The Industrial Report to the conference stated, 'We should aim to have 5,000 members by annual conference 1975, of whom at least 2,000 should be manual workers'.[7] Remember, at the 1974 conference IS membership was 3,310. The target for factory branches was to double the number over a year so that there would be 80 factory branches by October 1975.[8]

In retrospect it is clear we were radically wrong in our prognosis regarding the shape of the class struggle, and hence our fate. Thinking long and hard about our misjudgment, I cannot think how we could have come to a more correct prognosis at the time. We inevitably refer to the previous few years to shape the perspectives for the next few years. We could not have avoided this. Alas, if history just repeats itself we do not need theory—memory will do. On the other hand, if history never repeats itself one cannot generalise—and hence theory is impossible. The sharper the break in continuity, the more difficult it is to get a reliable prognosis. Hence at all breaking points in the past we find that the best Marxists got things wrong.

For instance, after the end of the 1905 revolution, at the beginning of June 1906, Lenin wrote, 'It is quite evident that we are now passing through one of the most important periods of the revolution. Signs of a revival of the broad mass movement against the old order have been visible for a long time. Now this revival is reaching its climax'.[9] And in July he still saw the revolution rising: 'The possibility of simultaneous action all over Russia is increasing. The probability of all partial uprisings merging into one is increasing. The inevitability of a political strike and of an uprising as a fight for power is felt as never before by large sections of the population'.[10]

In fact, a bloody counter-revolution took place.

Again, one remembers Marx writing after the 1848 revolution that as the crisis of capitalism in 1847 had triggered the 1848 revolution, the next crisis of the economy would lead to a new revolution. In 1857, however, there was a slump, but it did not trigger any revolution. I still believe that we could not have come to any different conclusions at the beginning of the Wilson-Callaghan government. Our real crime was that it took us far too long to rectify the errors.

The impact of the downturn on the IS/SWP

Some IS/SWP activities were more affected by the downturn than others. Factory branches, depending on the confidence of rank and file workers versus the bosses, were affected most, and most quickly. The Rank and File groups were less affected but became resolution-mongering bodies, concentrating on passing motions through committees, and being pulled away from the rank and file. The Right to

Work Campaign was affected even less. To borrow Trotsky's analogy once more: instead of the system of cogs working to transmit energy from the small wheel of the party to move the bigger cogwheel of the class, the retreat of the workers exerted counter-pressure back on the party through the larger intermediate cogs. IS/SWP itself, although active in all the other fields, got conflicting signals, depending on whether these came from factory branches, the National Rank and File Movement, the Right to Work Campaign or the Anti Nazi League (more on this below).

Factory branches declined very swiftly. In the Industrial Report to the 1974 IS conference we were told that we had 38 factory branches with about 300 members, ie on average eight members per branch.[11] A couple of years later we were told that at most three or four of the factory branches survived with an average of two or three members each.

The downturn affected the factory branches in the most direct way. The factory branch is put to the test daily. If workers lack confidence in facing the boss the branch will prove impotent and its members are bound to be demoralised. In an upturn the strength of the rank and file in the factory gives a fillip to the factory branch. In a downturn the workers put pressure on the members of the branch and demoralise them.

The Rank and File organisations were more immune than the factory branches to the pressure of the downturn, as they did not face a daily test of their ability or otherwise to deliver in the face of the bosses. Members and the leadership of IS/SWP were for a long time conscious of the weakening of the Rank and File organisation. But we suffered from schizophrenia: 'Yes, things are very bad in every section. But if we add them together it will be alright.' One is reminded of the baker who is asked, 'How much do you make on a loaf of bread?' 'I lose a penny on every loaf I sell.' 'So how do you make a living?' 'I sell lots of loaves.'

Depoliticisation affected the Rank and File groups severely. Because the class struggle was going down, the Rank and File groups either disappeared, became husks or became completely non-political.

After 1974 the introduction of the Social Contract, supported above all by the left union leaders Jack Jones and Hugh Scanlon, blunted the rank and file militancy which had gripped the working class under Heath. The Communist Party and its organisation, the union

Broad Lefts, tailended Jones and Scanlon. This led to a great move to the right in the movement. One byproduct of this situation was a demoralisation among significant sections of our own members. They lost heart. Some left the organisation without any statement of disagreement (like Mike Kidron and Peter Sedgwick), but some, like the former national secretary Jim Higgins, and former editor of *Socialist Worker* Roger Protz, led a split that included 150 members. This was the largest split in the history of our organisation.

They accused us of ultra-leftism because we argued that we had to steer left. Even if we did not understand the downturn, we recognised, as early as 1975-76, the importance of standing out clearly in political opposition to the Social Contract. A group of engineers in Birmingham who played a very good role during the Saltley battle in 1972 now, precisely because they were rooted in shop stewards organisation, felt the left union bureaucracy's gravitational pull to the right much more strongly than other sections of our organisation. No doubt, with hindsight, it is clear that our shifting left saved us from being sucked into the general move to the right that engulfed not only the Communist Party but also many revolutionaries, like the IMG (which dissolved in the process). It is quite instructive that hardly any of the 150 people who followed Higgins and Protz are active politically.

On 26 November 1977 a conference of the National Rank and File Movement ook place in Manchester. Over 200 delegates representing 200 trade union bodies participated. The conference passed a resolution unanimously calling for a day of action in support of the striking firemen on 7 December 1977.[12] When it came to it, this day was a damp squib. I do not know of any workplace that came out on strike (although I did hear that one school had an hour's strike. I don't know if that is true). And no workplace came out on strike for the firemen till the very end of the strike in January 1978, when they were beaten.

The delegates to the Manchester Rank and File conference were no doubt honest. With hindsight one is astonished that Ian Morris, the engineering union shop steward from Heathrow, could vote for a resolution for a one day strike when he had just come out of a very serious defeat a year previously. The 4,000 members of·the engineering union had come out on strike, while the 16,000 members of the TGWU crossed the picket line on union instructions and all other trade unionists did the same.

I know of only one delegate to the Manchester conference who refused to vote for the resolution. That was Terry Rogers of CA Parsons in Newcastle. He did not speak at the conference, but after its end he told Dave Hayes, who is now a member of the SWP's Central Committee, 'I could not vote for the resolution because I knew I could not convince my mates to come out.'

The failure of the 1977 National Rank and File Movement conference's one day strike in support of the firemen had a very demoralising effect throughout the movement. A Central Committee statement in 1978 pointed out, 'Our lack of industrial muscle was starkly illustrated by the dilemma of the Rank and File conference: what, concretely, can we call for to support the firemen? What can we actually deliver? The answer turned out to be, in terms of industrial action as opposed to lower level solidarity work, effectively zero.'

A new slogan was coined to try and fit the reality that had been denied for such a long time about the state of the class struggle and the Rank and File organisation: 'Small is beautiful... Meticulous attention to detail. Concentration on small problems: this fraction, that workplace branch, even this or that individual. In short, a sustained effort to make small gains, to deal only with immediately soluble problems in industrial and trade union work first of all, but also in black work, women's work, and so on'.[13]

The problem with this was that the whole concept of a rank and file movement is to think big: beyond the shop in the factory, or even beyond the individual factory. Now the target changed completely. What had this new target to do with the concept of a rank and file movement as a weapon to mobilise the rank and file of the trade unions against the bosses and the government, acting independently of the union bureaucracies?

The relationship between the downturn and the Right to Work Campaign is interesting. There were two parents to the Right to Work Campaign: first, the rising unemployment, and second, the failure of the National Rank and File Movement. The role of the first was self evident.

The second was more complex. The failure of the National Rank and File Movement was crucial to the rise of the Right To Work Campaign because, as the SWP Central Committee stated in May 1977:

Almost as soon as the second Rank and File conference wound up its business towards the end of 1974, the Rank and File Organising Committee it elected was isolated and left on the shelf—inevitably so, as the level of industrial struggle dropped from year to year.

In an attempt to keep the Organising Committee's presence felt various initiatives were taken: Chile solidarity work, a series of health and safety schools. Small positive results were obtained, but the central tasks—organising solidarity, developing real rank and file networks—could not be carried out.

It was in these circumstances that we made the turn—at the beginning of 1976—towards the Right to Work Campaign. That campaign was a success and greatly added to our credibility in the movement. But the child swallowed the parent. The NRFOC disappeared into the RTWC. It was not that we had 'dropped the rank and file perspective' as various people inside IS/SWP and outside argued. It was the pressure of circumstances—the NRFOC was impotent and the RTWC was viable.[14]

After the child, the Right to Work Campaign, replaced the parent, the National Rank and File Movement, it itself went into terminal decline.

The Right to Work Campaign started off very well. Its first march was in Manchester at the end of February 1976. After demonstrating all day through the city, arguing with workers at factory gate meetings, the marchers came to a rally in the Lesser Free Trade Hall.

Four hundred people burst into wave after wave of enthusiastic applause as the platform speakers emphasised the importance of the march. Veteran campaigner Harry McShane, after one of the finest speeches in a lifetime of socialist agitation, was greeted with a standing ovation.

John Deason, secretary of the Right to Work Campaign, said the march was not a hunger march. 'It is more of a flying picket,' he said. 'Our job is not only to remind workers of the desperate plight of the unemployed. It is also to encourage employed workers to throw their strength behind policies which can stop unemployment.'

Eighty unemployed marched 340 miles from Manchester to London. This march was sponsored by over 400 trade union bodies, including 70 shop stewards committees.

The campaign had to be based on direct action as well as on propaganda. It had to show that initiatives, albeit on a small scale, were possible even in the immediate short term. The first Right to Work march was significant not just for the support it obtained but for the style it adopted. Throughout its course marchers joined picket lines and even entered factories where sackings were being threatened in order to encourage workers to fight against unemployment. This marked a big step forward from the 'hunger marches' of the 1930s, which had great difficulty in making contact with employed trade unionists and scarcely ever succeeded in actually entering workplaces.

The success of the first march was shown not only by the 5,500 people who turned out to greet it at the Albert Hall but by the fact that the march had sufficiently irritated the upholders of 'law and order' for the police to attack it as it entered London. At Staples Corner in London the police, freely wielding their truncheons, made four unprovoked assaults on the march. Some 35 marchers were arrested, along with nine local trade unionists who were part of a delegation.[15] A number of marchers were sentenced to imprisonment, but the campaign against the repression provided an important focus for the Right to Work Campaign in the coming months. The most serious charges, against campaign secretary John Deason, were dropped after a big campaign outside the court.

Incidentally, the Right to Work supporters who picketed the Old Bailey in support of Deason celebrated the acquittal by travelling to the Grunwick factory in North London and staging what was to be the first mass picket of that factory. One struggle thus fired another.

Alas, the trajectory of the Right to Work Campaign, after an impressive start, was continuously downwards. The first Right to Work march, from Manchester to London (March 1976), had 570 marchers. The next, from Liverpool to Blackpool to the TUC in September 1977, had 700.[16] The third, from Liverpool to London (13 June 1978), had 50.[17] The fourth, to the Tory conference in Blackpool in October 1979, had only 40.[18]

Having swallowed the National Rank and File Movement, the Right to Work Campaign itself then died.

The downturn, the collapse of militancy, had less impact on the SWP than on the National Rank and File Movement. The SWP was also involved in Anti Nazi League (ANL) activity and in making general propaganda, selling papers, etc. It had its eggs in many baskets, and so was bound to be less affected by the decline of one sector of its activity. But still the crisis of militancy affected the SWP very deeply.

A Central Committee document entitled 'Building the Periphery:

A Discussion Document', of November 1979, was very realistic and very gloomy indeed: 'The overall picture suggests that we are relating to fewer, not more, people.'

We moved to stand parliamentary candidates in by-elections. The initial decision to stand in Walsall North reflected a grossly over-optimistic perspective based on the assumption that the gains we were beginning to make out of anti-racist activity in 1976 marked the beginning of a move by left wing workers away from the Labour Party which would provide a political basis for standing candidates.

To stop demoralisation in the ranks we drifted into standing candidates for parliamentary by-elections. It is worth setting out the general issues involved before turning to the concrete situation in 1976. Reformists make participation and success in parliamentary elections their absolute principle. They believe, wrongly, that access to parliament is the be-all and end-all of politics. But parliament is powerless to challenge the immense wealth and influence of the capitalists or their state. The bloody lessons of Chile, and of successive Labour governments, are proof of this. Marxists do not insist either on participation in elections or abstention from them. For us it is a tactical question, and not an especially important one. Lenin wrote, for example:

> The Bolsheviks regard the direct struggle of the masses...as the highest form of the movement, and parliamentary activity without the direct action of the masses as the lowest form of the movement.[19]

With such an approach he could argue both for an active *boycott* of Russia's Duma election in December 1905 and for *participation* in June 1906.

Therefore the question of our standing in elections in 1976 must be judged from a tactical standpoint: was the tactic a success or not? In September 1976 the Central Committee issued a statement:

Parliamentary Candidates—By-Election Campaign
How We Expect To Build

Many active militants are now thoroughly disillusioned with the way this government has attacked the working class. Their anger and resentment is moving them away from the Labour Party.

In almost every part of the country there are Labour activists who put it quite starkly and say, 'I can't be a part of an organisation that causes unemployment, and attacks the poor and the sick.'

They are moving away from Labour but not towards the Communist Party. The CP is part of the whole setup and offers no way of fighting to change things. These militants and activists are looking for a socialist alternative.

It isn't only the activists that are disillusioned with Labour. We are going to put candidates in Walsall North and Stechford.

The hope was:

…that up and down the country militants will take notice of our by-election campaign and will be drawn towards us; that we will make gains nationally to the organisation in the same way as we make gains in the areas concerned, so that we come out of the whole campaign much stronger and with a larger periphery.[20]

This blueprint proved to be completely phoney. We put up a candidate in Walsall North with a promise that we would put up 50-60 candidates in the next general election. The result of the Walsall North by-election was not very encouraging: 574 votes, 1.6 percent of the total, while the National Front got four and a half times our vote. In Newcastle Central we got 184 votes, 1.9 percent of the total. And it went from bad to worse. In the Stechford by-election on 31 March 1977 the SWP got 377 votes, Socialist Unity (IMG) 494, and the National Front over 3,000. The SWP candidate was possibly our most popular comrade, Paul Foot. In the next by-election, in Lady-wood, Birmingham in August 1977, we did even worse. The SWP candidate got 152 votes, the Socialist Unity candidate got 534 votes, and the black nationalist candidate got 336.

The increasing menace from the Tories, now led by the extreme right winger Margaret Thatcher, pushed even critics of the Labour government to close ranks with Labour. With first past the post elections, voting SWP looked like throwing away the vote. Our politics, with its emphasis on workers' self activity, could influence large numbers around specific tactics in struggle, such as anti-Nazi activity. But it did not play so well in the electoral field. Above all the downturn, the collapse of militancy, did not stop at the entrance to the polling booth. But still the Central Committee continued to argue for putting forward candidates.

So why the stubbornness? One reason was the idea that 'if you retreat, if you change your mind, you demonstrate your weakness'. What nonsense! Blind stubbornness is the sign of a weak personality. The truth liberates. We are not Chinese mandarins who dare not lose face.

There were other factors. Notwithstanding the abysmal election results in Stechford, the overwhelming majority of SWP members still supported the continuation of putting up parliamentary candidates. In August 1977 the National Advisory Committee voted to overturn the Central Committee majority, led by me and Jim Nichol, who wanted to pull out of the electoral tactic, and supported the Central Committee minority, who wanted to continue with the tactic. This policy was reaffirmed at the 1978 conference and only abandoned in early 1979. This reflected the more general confusion of the period and the tendency to think big. The row over elections came just after the ANL triumph in Lewisham and the massive publicity the party had received. We had been growing fast before Lewisham, mainly on the basis of anti-racist and anti-fascist activity (I took on the job of membership secretary again). The temptation was to extrapolate from this trend. My argument that we should stop standing candidates seemed to fly in the face of this. We must also remember that this took place before I began to formulate clearly the downturn analysis, so that the proposed abandonment of the electoral tactic seemed like a narrow 'empirical' argument. I was right in fact, but we were all grappling with symptoms rather than causes. As I say below, the situation was contradictory—declining industrial struggle plus Lewisham and the ANL. One should be careful not to make the process of adjustment to the downturn seem more coherent and rational than it was.

It was very difficult to hold on to anyone recruited during the election campaign. The Central Committee statement stated, 'The evidence of all the by-elections is that it is more difficult to hold members won through elections than those recruited in other fields, because there is a tendency during the election campaigns for those involved in the work to become euphoric about the expected results.'

I remember being in Grimsby a few days before the by-election, and the euphoria among our members, both old and new, was astonishing. It was natural. Paul Foot was interviewed on the BBC, and so was Margaret Renn. The SWP public meeting addressed by Paul Foot attracted a larger audience than the Labour Party meeting addressed by Michael Foot. After the pathetic vote we won was announced the demoralisation was extreme. Of the 50 new members we recruited during the campaign, not one turned up to the branch meeting a couple of days after the election. Of the original five members, two left immediately, and a short time afterwards the branch disappeared.

The aim of putting up candidates in parliamentary by-elections was to stop demoralisation in the ranks. The result? It increased it. Today, in different circumstances, SWP candidates are standing again in some parliamentary elections. Not only are the votes higher, but the results are more positive.

To return to developments in 1977: I changed my mind regarding candidates in parliamentary elections straight after the election results from Walsall North and Newcastle Central were announced, and my conviction became much stronger after the Stechford by-election. Watching the results on television I was very angry with myself and with the situation the party found itself in. I paid little attention to the Labour vote, Tory vote or NF vote, and was worried only about whether the IMG did better than we did. I thought completely as a sectarian. Unjustified triumphalism and sectarianism are two sides of the same coin.

No doubt the miserable result of the parliamentary election campaign was an added argument about the downturn. It was a painful lesson to learn, but important nonetheless, because, as Lenin put it, after 'learning how to attack…they had to realise that such a knowledge must be supplemented with the knowledge of how to retreat in good order'.[21]

It took some two years to win the SWP to accept the reality of the downturn in the industrial struggle. It took such a long time not because of the complexity of the argument but because of the emotional resistance to accepting the direct reality.

However, the art of revolutionary politics, as Lenin teaches us, lies in shifting strategy and tactics according to the changing situation. The greatest danger for revolutionaries is to persist in tactics which, though once appropriate, are no more so. Once we understood the objective reality we had to bring radical changes into our activity. We had to retreat from factory branches, the Rank and File organisations, the Right to Work Campaign. The danger was that the retreat would turn into a rout. Hence we had to be very clear about the activities of the branches and the individual members.

In 1979, even after we formally recognised that a radical change had taken place in the balance of class forces, it took us another three years to change the party's way of working. By the 1982 conference we had done it, abandoning all pretensions to building a rank and file movement in the present period:

> Instead we emphasised the following: (1) Politics is central to our ability to build. Without a clear Marxist understanding of society, comrades cannot survive in a hostile world. (2) The geographical branch has to be the main unit of the party. Individuals on their own will move to the right. Hence the need to attend weekly meetings in order to develop a clearer understanding of the world and to get political direction from other comrades on how to intervene in the workplaces. (3) *Socialist Worker* is the key to building a periphery by providing the means to identify the ones and twos who are interested in our ideas.[22]

The emphasis was on theory, on the need for generalised propaganda. When I say propaganda, I use the term in the sense given by Plekhanov, the father of Russian Marxism. Propaganda is putting a number of ideas before a few people, while agitation is putting one or two ideas before a number of workers, leading to action.

But the retreat from the factory branches and rank and file groups, faced us with dangers, above all the danger of sectarianism, of isolation from the working class movement. Without roots in the working class, without routine relations with workers, there is a real danger that ideas and activities will be completely distorted.

To fight sectarianism we had to make our propaganda largely concrete propaganda. What did this term imply? Abstract propaganda, such as 'capitalism bad, socialism good', does not relate to the immediate concerns of workers. Concrete propaganda seeks to relate the general concepts of Marxism to the immediate needs of workers. We insisted that our task was to influence workers, whether in large numbers, or small. The life of the geographical branch was aimed at giving support to individual party members who found themselves quite isolated at their workplace because of the impact of the downturn on the morale of the majority of workers. But the SWP branch is not an asylum for people running away from harsh reality, but a succour or support for comrades fighting to change this reality.

There are two pitfalls we have to avoid: opportunism and sectarianism. After the collapse of Bennism, the danger of adaptation to the Labour left was less serious, but the danger of sectarianism was very great. We could put forward abstract socialist propaganda about the benefits of socialism over capitalism but that was the path to a sectarian dead end, a path trodden many times by the British left, right back to the days of the Social Democratic Federation in the 1900s. We had to relate our propaganda to the experience of workers involved in struggle, even if they made up only a minority, even a small minority.

The propaganda had to be concrete. It had to answer the question, 'What slogan fits the issue the workers are fighting over?' Thus, during the 1984-85 miners' strike, our propaganda was, quite rightly, on the need for dockers, rail workers and others to come to the aid of the miners. But this was not enough. An explanation had to be given as to why this solidarity did not take place: the role of the trade union bureaucracy and of the leadership of the Labour Party. Arthur Scargill called for solidarity of workers with the miners, but he never explained why it never materialised. He never named names—Neil Kinnock, the leadership of the TGWU, the engineers' union, etc. Scargill was on the General Council of the TUC and was bound by the rules of the trade union bureaucracy.

Above all, we had to explain what were the political causes of the betrayal of the miners by the union leaders and Neil Kinnock. We had not only to argue how to win, but also explain to the minority of the class what had gone wrong. The propaganda we had to put forward was qualitatively different to what we did in 1970-74.

On 2 November 1972 I spoke to thousands of workers in Anchor steel plant. The core of what I said was the need for industrial action in support of old age pensioners. During the 1980 steel strike I spoke only once to steel workers, and that was at a meeting called by Rotherham Trades Council with 100 steel workers present. Of course, repeating the speech of 2 November 1972 would not do. It had to be a more thought out explanation of why the state of the strike was so poor and what policies were responsible for it.

We had prepared ourselves for the long slog, above all by understanding the downturn. I wrote elsewhere:

> The Socialist Workers Party tried to come to terms with the changing situation by constantly reassessing the actual balance of class forces and adapting its activity to this. Recognising the downturn after 1974 was not a simple process and the debate was long and difficult. Only experience can prove whether a sneeze is the prelude to pneumonia or only a light cold. The same applies with still more force to the molecular process linking shopfloor developments, general politics and

working class consciousness. With hindsight it is clear that the correct judgment of the situation after 1974 provided the basis for the SWP to continue as an autonomous revolutionary socialist force. Alas, many independent socialist groups evaded the harsh reality of the period and escaped into the Labour Party only to face the onslaught of Kinnockism.[23]

Our propaganda must be an arch connecting two pillars. It must (1) relate to immediate struggles, but it must also (2) carry the battle of ideas, the battle for socialism.

We had to combine argument with action; action alone could lead to adaptation of our comrades to the right. Argument alone could isolate our members and turn us into a sect.

The downturn and the 'movements'

As the labour movement went into retreat, there was a massive pull towards the so called 'movements' which tended towards separate issues of oppression for women, blacks, gays and lesbians and so on. All of them eventually fragmented and disintegrated.

Rising struggle increases unity and generalisation, decline in the struggle leads to fragmentation—between workers in different workplaces, different individual workers, men and women, black and white.

The decline in the class struggle massively strengthened the trend towards separatism. The example of women's separatism was the clearest. In strike action the need for unity and solidarity of all workers, women and men, is always made obvious.

The growth of separatist movements gathered pace after the decline of the Bennite movement and the fall away in industrial struggle. The feminist Bea Campbell now denounced the picket line as 'macho militancy'. The women's movement now accepted the theory of patriarchy. This visualised two struggles—one against capitalism, the other against male domination. Hence its talk about male power and the assumption that all males benefit from women's oppression, and they are therefore defenders of the status quo.

Along with the separatism that was generated by a decline of workers' strength came the tendency of some women to go further in compromising with capitalism. One expression of this was the retreat from fighting capitalism, and leading women to indulge their lifestyles.

The SWP was not exempt from the pressure and a fight had to be conducted to retain the organisation intact. On the one hand we had to keep in mind Lenin's idea of the party as the 'tribune of the oppressed' but not forget that ultimately liberation depends on the success of the working class in overcoming capitalism.

We would have done no favours to women, blacks, gays or lesbians if the party had liquidated itself into these movements. There are two common ways of approaching movements or campaigns independent of the organisation. One is to have nothing to do with them because they do not accept the full revolutionary programme and the centrality of the working class. The other is to act as cheer leaders, saying, 'Hooray!' to everything they do. We had to relate to their struggles without falling into the trap of thinking that spontaneity without consciousness could be more effective than spontaneity with consciousness. Steam without a piston organising its pressure is worse than steam with a piston to direct that energy.

Women's Voice

Women's Voice was a significant enterprise that the SWP was involved with. We published a magazine under this title from 1972. In 1977 it was decided to establish groups round the magazine.

Sadly, although I was in the leadership of the SWP, I was never allowed to be involved in the activity of Women's Voice. I never spoke at a Women's Voice meeting; I never wrote a line for the magazine. I did speak to women, and often, but did so in the context of their being engineers, hospital workers, teachers, students, and so on.

The reason rested on the fundamental disagreement I had with the comrades round Women's Voice. I was steadfast in following the Bolshevik Party tradition of insisting on the common interests of female and male workers. Male workers do not benefit from women's oppression. Imagine a male worker writing to his friend, 'I have good news to tell you. My wife's wages are lousy. To add to my joy there is no nursery for our children. And to fill the cup of happiness to the brim, my wife is pregnant, and we want to have an abortion but she can't get one.'

The Bolsheviks always opposed women's separatism in the same way they opposed the separate existence of the Jewish organisation, the Bund—Jewish workers and Russian workers should belong to the same party.

Krupskaya wrote:

Bourgeois women advocate their special 'women's rights', they always oppose themselves to men and demand their rights from men. For them contemporary society is divided into two main categories, men and women. Men possess everything, hold all rights. The question is one of achieving equal rights.

For the working woman the question becomes quite different. The politically conscious women see that contemporary society is divided into classes. That which unites the working woman with the working man is much stronger than that which divides them... 'All for one, and one for all'. This 'all' means members of the working class—men and women alike.

Anne Bobroff, a historian critical of Bolshevism, complained that Lenin always insisted on the party leadership controlling women's activities. She writes, 'The Bolshevik women who ran *Rabotnitsa* (*Woman Worker*) worked in close association with Lenin. And although the editorial board was both made up completely of women, the editor of *Sotsialdemokrat*—Lenin—had the deciding vote in the event of a tie.' In addition, she says, equal voting rights for the Russian and foreign editorial boards was a device 'to guarantee majority control over editorial policy to Lenin and those women who were in closest contact with him'.

A blatant example occurred at the International Women's Congress in Berne in March 1915:

Lenin sat drinking tea in a nearby restaurant while the women's congress was in session... The Bolshevik women, working under Lenin's direction, introduced a resolution which...called for an immediate organisational break with the majorities in the existing Socialist and Labour parties and for the formation of a new International. Despite the overwhelming opposition of all the other delegates, the Bolshevik representatives refused to withdraw their motion. Because a show of international unity among socialists was desperately desired at that point, Clara Zetkin finally negotiated with the Russian women and Lenin in a separate room. 'Here Lenin finally agreed to a compromise'.[25]

Rabotnitsa was well integrated, politically and organisationally, into the Bolshevik Party. After the October Revolution, the party published a journal entitled *Kommunistka* (*Woman Communist*). Its editorial board included Nikolai Bukharin.[26]

As I was looking from the outside at *Women's Voice* I can say very little about it. But it was an important aspect of our whole work, and as I took a hard position on the subject, avoiding the issue in this autobiography would be a mistake. But I cannot write about things of which I have very little knowledge. So I asked Lindsey German, presently the editor of *Socialist Review*, to write a piece on the subject. This is what she wrote:

> When I first came around the IS (end of 1972, beginning of 1973) there was a women's magazine which we sold along with *Socialist Worker* on industrial sales, etc. There was never total clarity about what *Women's Voice* was for, but at the same time it was clearly linked to the organisation and was very much devoted to working class women's struggles and problems, for example equal pay, but also price rises and rents. We had features on car workers' wives in Coventry, for example (and this, of course, was long before a tradition of wives' support groups grew up with the miners' strike of 1984-85). At the time the assumption was that women were less likely to be political and we tried to counter this in *Women's Voice*.
>
> The paper continued for several years without really finding a niche. The class struggle was rising up to 1974, and there were plenty of women's strikes; however, the rise of the women's movement from the late 1960s onwards was its real impetus, since the argument from many IS women was that we had to show that we cared about women's issues too. While the struggle was high, these confusions did not appear important. After the resurgence of reformism and the crisis of the revolutionary left from the mid-1970s, they became potentially extremely damaging and led to political divisions which lasted for several years.
>
> The *Women's Voice* debate can only be understood in the context of a wider disorientation. The years from 1968 to 1975 essentially saw advances for the left internationally. To most revolutionary socialists, this situation seemed to be going on forever. When it did not, this led to what became known as a crisis of militancy—a sense that the struggles and organisation of those years had proved futile. This crisis of militancy gave a boost to reformist organisations which reasserted themselves under the Labour government. It also gave a boost to feminism. Women who had been caught up in the rush of enthusiasm after 1968 but who were slowly realising that the struggle for socialism

would be long and hard, with setbacks as well as advances, looked to feminism as a new way of organising that could achieve something in the here and now.

This process was most advanced in Italy, where the revolutionary left disintegrated over questions of feminism in the mid-1970s. But in Britain too there were many feminists who abandoned left groups and who developed a 'commonsense' that such politics was inherently male, authoritarian, and could not integrate the demands of women's liberation. Many such people accepted that most women would not trust such organisations to take up their demands and so would be reluctant to join. This was indeed the argument for establishing groups around *Women's Voice* which was decided by the SWP in 1977. An article in *Women's Voice* as early as 1976 stated that 'like men workers, perhaps even more so, women are suspicious of left wing groups'.

The decision to have geographical groups organised round a monthly magazine caused a crisis. There were at least three separate interpretations of the decision. One—the view of Joan Smith, Linda Quinn and it is fair to say the majority of the *Women's Voice* steering committee—was that this was a step towards a completely separate *Women's Voice* organisation appealing to women wanting to organise on the basis of oppression. The second—supported by me—was that *Women's Voice* had to be clearly and closely linked to the SWP and that this was our intervention in the women's movement. The third—backed by most of the leadership—was that the groups had little chance of a viable future. At a series of meetings and conferences throughout 1978 even the second line was only carried through party discipline on those members who did not agree with it.

I was appointed women's organiser in 1979, against much opposition in the leadership. From this point it became increasingly clear that the groups could not work politically and in fact could become a bridge out of the party rather than a means of recruitment.

As I wrote in *Sex, Class and Socialism*, 'The rationale that underlay the creation of the *Women's Voice* organisation was an accommodation to autonomous organisation.' [p222, first edition]. This was reflected in a whole number of campaigns taken up by *Women's Voice*, for example, Reclaim the Night or against toxic tampons. In practice the move was away from class wide demands, or demands which unified women with men.

Although at the 1979 conference those arguing for tighter links with the SWP won their position, there were still bitter political arguments 18 months later. The groups were in a bad state as many SWP women voted with their feet and got on with other political work. At the 1981 party conference a clear majority voted to close down the groups. The magazine folded a year later.

Although the numbers we lost as a result were relatively small, many of those most involved in building *Women's Voice* did leave—many of them extremely embittered to the SWP. However, most women did not, and although the experience of building the groups was basically negative, it taught us a lot. We developed theoretically on women, which was very important. Cliff's book, *Class Struggle and Women's Liberation*, and mine both came out in the 1980s, plus various articles by Chris Harman and others. Part of the appeal of *Women's Voice* was Joan Smith's supposed theoretical justification in her articles on the family which were left unchallenged for a long time—which shows how few women felt confident to write on such matters at the time. My article on theories of patriarchy for the IS was, I thought, relatively uncontroversial, but caused a huge row because it theoretically rebutted the arguments about men benefiting from women's oppression. These theoretical arguments allowed us to eventually win the argument over the groups.

These arguments were also important in reorienting the organisation in the early 1980s. We were helped by the trajectory of most of the left and many feminists into the Labour Party, and their increasing accommodation to the status quo. (We see the result in the women MPs of today.) The slur that we would not take up women's issues and would not develop a women cadre has been demonstrated totally false and we now have a very good reputation on these questions, plus an ability to popularise our theory inside the working class. At a time when feminism is all too often a stalking horse for the right wing, and many feminists accept 'post feminist' ideas, this puts us in a brilliant position for when big issues facing women come to the surface.

In retrospect the mistakes I made in dealing with the issues of *Women's Voice*, and also the black workers' paper, *Flame*, become clear. I always opposed both of them but did not deal with the issues they raised by looking at the large canvas. I wrote a general analysis of the subject in my book, *Class Struggle and Women's Liberation* (London, 1984), long after *Women's Voice* groups were disbanded and the magazine stopped publication. Before that I published only snippets arguing the case, like my articles on Clara Zetkin[27] and Alexandra Kollontai.[28] Above all, I did not argue in writing about the dialectical relation between exploitation and oppression.

Reading the above words in the first draft of this autobiography John Rees commented, 'It struck me as odd that you should say that you weren't involved in the *Women's Voice* debate. I know what you mean in one way, but it would have struck any active party member at the time as wrong. You may not have written as much as you now think you should have, but the *International Socialism* articles were very important. And the debates in the party went on for a long time. I remember the meeting you did to 200 people at Marxism 1981 on Kollontai which was a hard debate.' Terrell Carver, an academic whom we had invited to a debate, stayed at the meeting and said to me in the middle of it, 'This is what the Bolsheviks and Mensheviks must have been like in 1903!'

The oppression of women sharpens the exploitation of working class women. The wealth and power of rich women blunts their oppression. Furthermore, rich women benefit from the oppression of working class women—they pay low wages to the cook, the nanny, the cleaner. Hence no working class woman could call Margaret Thatcher a sister. After the defeat of the Paris Commune, the worst torturers of the women Communards were the rich women walking around and poking with their umbrellas at the eyes of the poor women.

Black separatism

The same arguments about feminism and the working class applied to the issue of the black movement and its trend towards separatism. When it came to the question of our black newspaper, *Flame*, I did even worse at the start than with *Women's Voice*. I wrote nothing. I should have done what Alex Callinicos did so well in his book *Race and Class*. Whether I could have done as good a job as he did is besides the point. The lesson would be that a big crisis in the class and the revolutionary party demands from us to draw the big picture, to develop a general theory.

Black separatism adversely affected our work. The lack of success of *Flame* made us rush to try more and more things without thinking carefully about what we were doing. Inability to face reality led us to undertake a quixotic rush to produce more and more magazines. We entered a paper chase.

The number of SWP publications mushroomed: a Punjabi paper called *Chingari*; an Urdu paper called *Chingari*; a Bengali paper called *Pragati*; a paper for black workers called *Flame;* and a youth paper called *Fight*.

Of course it would have been brilliant if we could have maintained papers in Punjabi, Urdu or Bengali to relate to workers in these communities who could not read English. But for that we needed first of all serious cadres in the communities. Again and again Lenin repeated the argument that the revolutionary party cannot exist without revolutionary theory. We could not have supplied a Punjabi, Urdu or Bengali *Socialist Review* or *International Socialism*. Without that we would be building on sand. Marx wrote that under capitalism there is fetishism of gold. We suffered from fetishism of paper; if you can't act—publish!

Flame was written in English, but still it proved completely ineffective in building IS/SWP membership among black workers. The experience was completely negative.

I was more cautious over women where the situation was extremely delicate and complicated. My guess is that had I argued my position on *Women's Voice* harder in 1977-78, I would have been quite isolated. But on the question of *Flame* I was quite clear from late 1977 that it was ridiculous to have three black full time organisers for a handful of black members. And I did push the argument over the relationship between exploitation and oppression much harder and more confidently on the question of race than on the question of women. Pulling together a group of black members—Mort Mascarenhas and Bruce George in particular—onto my side, the position was at least half won by the 1979 conference.

Chapter 7

Rethinking the situation

The organisation in deep disarray

Part of our problem was that there were still indications of continuing radicalism that ran counter to the idea of a downturn. As already shown, Lenin too was to make a a wrong evaluation of the situation after the 1905 revolution had peaked. Why had he done this? Two contradictory signals came to him: continuous speedy growth of Bolshevik Party membership on the one hand, and catastrophic decline of the workers' strike movement on the other.

At the time of the Fourth Congress of the Russian Social Democratic Labour Party (April 1906) the Bolsheviks had some 13,000 members; by 1907 the number rose to 46,143.[1] What was the pattern of the strike movement at the time?

Year	Number of workers on strike (in thousands)	Percentage of all workers
1895-1904 (av)	431	1.46-5.10
1905	2,863	163.8
1906	1,108	65.8
1907	740	41.9
1908	176	9.7
1909	64	3.5
1910	47	2.4

With hindsight it is quite easy to explain the cross-currents. When a stone falls into water the ripples can grow even after the stone stops moving. The 1905 revolution had such an impact that thousands moved to join the Bolsheviks long after the revolution was defeated and reaction ruled supreme.

Of course, the downturn in Britain from the heights of 1971-74 was a small dip compared to the catastrophic collapse of the working class movement in Russia under the hammer of the counter-revolution after 1905. Nevertheless, the analogy between Lenin's wrong prognosis of 1906 and our complete loss of way in the years of the Wilson-Callaghan government is useful in helping us to face reality and overcome it. One should not, however, fall into the trap of believing that this minimises our mistakes: not every girl without arms is Venus de Milo.

We must remember how the Bolsheviks came to terms with the real situation in the working class. It was not easy or smooth. The leadership of the party disintegrated in the process.

Lenin knew that, to prepare for the great revolutionary battles to come, a revolutionary party must learn how to go through the period of reaction, together with the masses, in their front ranks, without dissolving into them, but also without detaching itself from them. This is also the period in which tough cadres can be trained and tempered. This training cannot, however, be done in a void, in isolation from the struggle, even if its scope and depth are very restricted indeed.

For a long time we did not come to terms with the downturn in the class struggle. Two examples demonstrate our tardiness to face reality. One was my book, *The Crisis: Social Contract or Socialism*, published in 1975. According to *Socialist Worker*, shortly after publication 20,000 copies of the book had been distributed.[3] However, the actual impact of the book was almost zero. Not that its quality was radically different to *Incomes Policy, Legislation and Shop Stewards*, published in 1966, or *The Employers' Offensive*, published in 1970. The timing of publication of *The Crisis* was terribly wrong—after the end of the upturn while still the collapse of militancy was not clear. In revolutionary politics timing is of the essence. It is more significant than tenses in grammar. The timing of the publication of *The Crisis* reminds one of the story of a man coming to his friend, complaining, 'I played beautiful music, and they beat me up.' 'What music did you play?' 'Lovely wedding music.' 'You fool. It was a funeral.' A few days later the chap complains again that he was beaten. 'I played really beautiful music, and was beaten up again.' 'What music did you play?' 'I played funeral music.' 'You fool. It was a wedding.'

Another example was an article I wrote for *Socialist Worker* in September 1977:

Build The Socialist Workers' Party In The Workplace
To start with, we must work hard to establish workplace bulletins. In every factory, pit, docks, hospital, school or office, where workers are

together and there are SWP members, or supporters, a workplace bulletin should be produced...

A revolutionary socialist party must be built not as a collection of local branches, but as a unit of workplace branches...

The widespread production of bulletins should lay the foundation for the widespread building of workplace branches of the SWP. That is where workers' power lies.[4]

I can hardly believe that I wrote those words at that time. But I did. It was especially agonising, because over the previous couple of years, our factory branches either died or withered on the vine. I had direct personal experience that with hindsight certainly should have warned me. In the early 1970s I used to go once a month on a Sunday to Coventry to speak to our engineers and their contacts. There would have been 60 to 80 people in the room. However, from late 1975 or early 1976 I was never invited to a meeting.

The moment of truth

Of course a transition is never clear cut. The upturn did not last until the Tuesday and become a downturn on the Wednesday, or go until the end of January and turn down the next month. Therefore for a time conflicting signals are received. The discussion of the downturn took months, and the organisation was in deep crisis for a couple of years. To lead is to foresee, and if you cannot foresee you cannot lead.

At last I grasped the existence of the downturn. Key to this understanding was the failure of the National Rank and File Conference called in support of the firemen. I asked myself why it happened. The comrades who spoke in support of the resolution and voted for it were sincere socialists. They must have still been in the glow of the events of the year before.

It took a long time for our group to come to terms with the actual situation in the class struggle—the retreat of militancy, the downturn. I first put forward the downturn argument at the National Advisory Committee in February 1978, and then in an interview published in the first issue of the new *Socialist Review*. To begin with, in the Central Committee only Alex Callinicos, Duncan Hallas and Jim Nichol agreed with me. It took some two years to win the organisation.

Initially my position won only minority support among the cadres; in part because it was interpreted cynically as providing a prescription to justify a retreat from standing parliamentary candidates, and in part because it cut across the tendency to extrapolate from our successes in 1977-78 in the ANL.

I understood the difficulty comrades had in accepting the idea of the downturn. It was far less attractive than the alternative. If there are two alternative weather forecasts to choose from, one saying tomorrow will be beautiful, sunny weather, another predicting wind and hail, there is no question what people will prefer to believe in. And so it was with the first suggestions that there was a downturn in the industrial struggle.

I asked myself why I came to the conclusion more clearly and earlier than other comrades. There are a number of reasons that are quite important. An individual member of the organisation of course notices what happens in his or her workplace—school, hospital, factory, and so on. But there is no way they can gauge if it is part of a more general trend. And after all, accidents can play a role in explaining why, say, teachers in a school are less active this year than last. The district organisers, by and large, rely on information gleaned from the individual members. The same applies to the comrades working on the editing of *Socialist Worker*.

In a sense I was in a unique position regarding this situation. During the upturn I spoke to large meetings of workers. I mentioned above my speech to thousands of steel workers in Scunthorpe. I spoke to hundreds of miners in Grimethorpe and many other miners' meetings. I spoke to hundreds of dockers, to a building workers' fraction in Bristol with over 100 workers, to tens of engineers in Coventry on a Saturday every month. And I could continue the list. All those workers' meetings ended some time in the mid-1970s. There was no way I would not notice it.

There was another reason. The past always impinges on the present. And, even when quite young, as in Palestine, I had had to take decisive positions. I had had to do the same later on the question of state capitalism, even though I was only 30 years old. Daring was crucial in all those situations. In 1946-47 I was very worried about the position that Russia and Eastern Europe were workers' states, so I had to stand up and be counted. This time the organisation was not a few individuals, but a few thousand. But still the worry that we misjudged the situation forced me once again to stand up and be counted.

A downturn in working class struggle has a contradictory impact on a revolutionary party, both negative and positive. It can weaken the party, but at the same time it can harden its members and prepare them for future events.

The Russian experience is instructive here. The massive class struggles during 1905 provided opportunities for the revolutionaries grouped in the Bolshevik Party, but it also blurred the difference between Bolshevism and reformist Menshevism. The latter party, at this time, was composed mainly of centrist elements, and intoxicated by the events. Martov's biographer, I Getzer, wrote that, like the Bolsheviks, many Mensheviks:

> ...prepared for a seizure of power and the establishment of a revolutionary provisional government. As Dan wrote to Kautsky: 'Man lebt hier wie im Taumel, die revolutionäre Luft wirkt wie Wein' (One lives here as if in delirium, revolutionary air has an effect like wine).[6]

At this point, as Trotsky wrote:

> The Central Committee of the Bolsheviks, with Lenin participating, passed a unanimous resolution to the effect that the split (between Bolshevism and Menshevism) was merely the result of the conditions of foreign exile, and the events of the revolution had deprived the factional struggle of any reasonable grounds.[7]

However, during the period of reaction that followed, the Mensheviks moved massively to the right. Only now were the Bolsheviks able to demonstrate the political schism between revolution and reform when they held fast to their principles. Now Bolshevism became steeled, successfully passing the most testing times.

During the period of the industrial upturn under the Heath government the Labour Party used the most radical rhetoric. For example, Denis Healey told the 1973 Labour Party conference:

> Our job is to get power, and we join battle armed with the most radical and comprehensive programme we have had since 1945. Its aim is honestly stated to bring about a fundamental and irreversible shift in the balance of power and wealth in favour of working people and their families. (Applause)... We are going to introduce a tax on wealth. We are going to turn the estate duty into a real tax... I warn you, there are going to be howls of anguish from the 80,000 rich people.[8]

Later on, having managed to divert the class struggle into the harmless channels of parliamentarism during the 1974-79 Labour government, Denis Healey was Chancellor of the Exchequer. Now the language was completely different. Healey imposed a wage freeze and for the first time since the war real wages went down.

In the Bennite period the leaders of the left of the Labour Party were spitting fire. A few years later, with few exceptions, they moved massively to the right. (Neil Kinnock, Tony Blair, David Blunkett, Claire Short and Jack Straw were members of CND.) Neil Kinnock collaborated with the SWP, being on the steering committee of the Anti Nazi League. We know where they stand now. The most extreme zigzag was made by Tom Sawyer, the general secretary of the Labour Party, who led demonstrations against James Callaghan's wage restraint policy, and is now a non-executive director of a company which does not recognise trade unions!

We in the SWP saw through the phoney radicalism of Labour's left turn. One consequence was that we were able to emerge from the downturn as a credible independent revolutionary organisation. Many other left groups were deceived by the apparent success of Bennism and driven by the difficult conditions of the downturn into entering into the Labour Party, only then to be witch hunted out of existence.

The SWP was of course damaged by the downturn in the industrial struggle. But it also benefited from the harshest test: the members became more mature, with a better understanding of Marxism, and, above all, with the ability to use Marxism as a guide to action in the economic, political and ideological spheres.

The rise of the Nazi National Front

The downturn, the retreat of the working class in face of the bosses and the government, had a very contradictory impact on the working of IS/SWP. It massively damaged our intervention in industry and the unions, cut recruitment to the organisation, and hit sales of *Socialist Worker*. However, as Marx said, 'man makes history but not in circumstances of his own choosing,' and this applies in bad times as well as good. So, while one consequence of the retreat of the working class under the 1974-79 Labour government was the rise of the National Front, this led, in turn, to the launching of a new organisation with a massive impact—the Anti Nazi League (ANL).

The worsening conditions of the masses led to frustration and helped the Nazis. As I wrote:

> In the five years between 1974 and 1979 Labour turned the greatest advance in workers' struggle for fifty years into a retreat. By demoralising the working class Labour positively assisted an ideological advance of the right...
>
> Mass unemployment, government spending cuts, a decline in real wages and increasing general social deprivation in the years 1975-78 created conditions for the neo-fascist National Front to flourish...
>
> The National Front made substantial electoral gains in 1976. In local elections at Blackburn the National Front and National Party together got an average of 38 percent of the vote; in Leicester the NF got 18.5 percent. In Deptford (Lewisham), in a council by-election in July 1976 the two parties together won 44 percent (possibly over half the white vote)—more than the winning Labour candidate, who got 43 percent.[9]

Chanie, in her excellent article, 'Labour and the Fight Against Fascism', gives the following information: in the Greater London Council elections in May they stood in 85 out of the 92 constituencies, getting 119,063 votes (5 percent—compared with 0.5 percent in 1973) and beating the Liberals into third place in 33 constituencies. An Essex University survey suggested National Front support during this period would have given it 25 MPs under proportional representation.[10]

The NF tried, with some success, to build a base in the trade unions. They made inroads into the postal workers, highly demoralised after a major defeat in 1971. Postal workers in the North London Divisional post office in Upper Street, Islington, which was controlled by the National Front, collected for Tyndall's deposit for the Hackney South and Shoreditch constituency in the 1979 elections. They got so much support that they were able to pay for eight other National Front deposits. In the May 1979 local elections a number of postal workers stood for the National Front. Many wore badges to work. Yet in 1977 it was a Labour Party delegate to the postal workers' union conference who moved a resolution calling for tighter immigration controls. By now, fortunately, the anti-fascist movement had spread its influence among workers. Only 25 out of 5,000 delegates voted for the resolution.

The National Front tried to set up a National Front Railwaymen's Association in spring 1977 and had a presence in the drivers' union,

ASLEF. There were half a dozen National Front shop stewards in Leyland's Longbridge works, which had the biggest National Front branch in the country—70 members. There was even a presence in the NUM (in Barnsley).[11]

With the National Front now a significant and growing movement, it decided to hold a provocative march. It was to be held through the heart of a black area, Lewisham in south London, on 13 August 1977. As noted above, in the previous year's local elections the National Front and National Party had together won 44 percent of the vote here. In true Hitler tradition Tyndall proclaimed, 'I believe our great marches, with drums and flags and banners, have a hypnotic effect on the public and immense effect in solidifying the allegiance of our followers, so that their enthusiasm can be sustained.'

A few months before, the police in Lewisham staged what they called Operation 39 PNH. PNH stood for Police Nigger Hunt. Following early morning raids, young blacks were rounded up on trumped up charges of conspiracy to rob. They formed the Lewisham 21 Defence Committee, which was attacked by the National Front and the police for over two months. To smash it was one of the purposes of the Lewisham march.[12] By this time the anti-fascist forces, led by the SWP, had physically confronted National Front meetings and marches consistently so that it was practically impossible for them to organise without fear of attack. Police protection and assistance were the only way they managed to show themselves at all. The numbers on their national marches had therefore dwindled. At the beginning of 1976 they could mobilise 1,500. Later on, at the first demonstration where they faced united mass opposition—Wood Green in North London—they were down to 1,000; at Lewisham they managed a bare 500.[13]

In Lewisham two counter-demonstrations were called against the National Front march. One was organised by the All London Committee Against Racism and Fascism (Alcaraf) and led by the three main political parties, with Mayor Godsif and the Bishop of Southwark, Mervyn Stockwood, at its head. It ended a mile away from the National Front march. The other was called by the SWP, the Right to Work Campaign and individual members of the Labour Party and Communist Party. It was to meet at the National Front's assembly point before they were due.[14] Our attitude to the issue was that there should be 'No platform for fascists!' To those who argue that this is to deny democratic rights we reply that Nazism exists to destroy the democratic rights of others. It makes use of freedom to march to intimidate and deny freedom generally. Does a cancer cell have equal rights with a normal cell in the body to reproduce and spread?

Two thirds of the Alcaraf march of 4,000 answered the SWP's call to confront the National Front. Very large numbers of local black youth, Labour Party and Communist Party members, even some Cable Street veterans of the Communist Party, made up the numbers. They broke through police lines twice and cut the terrified National Front march in two. It was quickly diverted and dispersed under police protection. The police then violently attacked the anti-fascists in a battle that raged for hours. There were 214 arrests.

The press and the Labour Party treated the National Front and SWP to equal abuse. The *Daily Mirror* said the SWP was 'as bad as the National Front'. The Lewisham East Labour Party delegate at the Labour Party conference that year failed to understand what had happened under his very nose: 'The Law—whether the Public Order Act or the Race Relations Act—must be amended [to strengthen it against the NF], particularly in the London area. Certainly one could say, "The answer is not in violent confrontation with the National Front", and ask, "Who won on 13 August in Lewisham? Only the National Front".'[15]

Sid Bidwell, Labour MP for Southall, which had seen some of the worst clashes with the National Front, could expostulate: 'I have no time for hooligans [in the NF]…and for those crackpot adventurers who have yet to take their part in responsibility in the real Labour movement. We cannot counter them by a strategy of trying to out-thug the thugs of the National Front, because we have the strength to do it otherwise'.[16] Michael Foot, then deputy prime minister, said, 'You don't stop the Nazis by throwing bottles or bashing the police. The most ineffective way of fighting the fascists is to behave like them'.[17] Ron Hayward, general secretary of the Labour Party, appealed to all its members to keep away from the extreme left and extreme right organisations. He saw little difference between the violent demonstrators (ie SWP) and 'NF fascists'.[18] The Labour candidate who won the seat in the Ladywood by-election five days after Lewisham claimed, 'Lunatic elements of right and left are no friends of Labour' and were 'urban guerrillas calling themselves politicians'. The Labour Party West Midlands organiser went on in the same vein about the SWP after an anti-fascist demonstration in Birmingham on 15 August 1977: 'They are just red fascists. They besmirch the good name of democratic socialism'.[19] Tom Jackson, postal workers' leader, added, 'There is little to choose between the SWP and the National Front. Both are political bootboys'.[20]

The truth would be quite different. One sign of the effectiveness of the SWP's intervention in the Battle of Lewisham was demonstrated by the reaction of the National Front. A few days later our headquarters were set on fire. I, being a leading member of the SWP and a Jew, had special reasons to beware of NF revenge. Straight away we turned our home into practically a fortress. First, the front door was replaced with a heavy door without a letter box. The windows in the front and back of the house were fortified with iron grilles. I was exposed to some harassment. Thus numerous phone calls asked us about a Jaguar advertised in the *Evening Standard* for £5, and a few days later a request for payment for the advertisement arrived. We explained the circumstances, so the paper did not persist. For a few nights, again and again late into the night and morning, a cab would turn up at our house saying they had an order for it to pick someone up. I had to put on a certain amount of disguise to avoid entrapment—a slouch cap, and so on.

We also suffered verbal abuse over the telephone. I had one person and Chanie another hurling the foulest possible language at us over the phone through the night, and threatening us with everything, including death. At times the threat was closer than at the other end of the telephone line. When Chanie was working around the Grimsby election campaign she asked our kids to be careful not to leave SWP stickers on the car as there were fascists in the area. But, being kids, they did not listen and, unaware that the side of the car was plastered with them, she drove down a cul de sac at the end of which was a pub. It soon became obvious that this was an NF meeting place. At first they threw paper, and then stones. There was a policeman on a motorcycle just looking on. Chanie wound her window down and begged him to help her escape. He took one look at the car and drove off. In the end she only got away by reversing through the crowd that was still yelling abuse.

The worst case was one day when I came to Leicester for a public meeting. The comrade who drove me from London left me next to the building where the meeting was due to take place, while he went off to buy a sandwich. As soon as he left, I saw two heavily built young men shouting, 'We want Gluckstein!' I guessed they were not friendly. I did not know whether they would recognise me, as it was already getting dark, so I took a quick decision: I rushed towards the building between the two of them, using my elbows to push them aside, and managed to get into the building. They were probably taken by surprise. A short time later a policeman came to the meeting place and told me that there was a complaint against me for using violence. I laughed and said to him, 'I am 61 years old, and a small man at that. The two men complaining are young, tall and heavily built. It was they who started the violence.' The policeman decided to drop the case.

My experience of working in difficult conditions in Palestine probably came in useful at this time. It had done so previously. There was a time in the 1940s, for example, when the British Trotskyists wanted to send literature to comrades in Czechoslovakia who were being brought under the iron heel of Stalinist rule. They were going to send this by ordinary mail. I told them, 'You must be mad. Sending it that way is like signing their prison warrants.' It had not occurred to the British comrades, having lived in Western bourgeois democratic conditions, that the police would open letters and parcels. During the time of the ANL the rest of the comrades also quickly learnt the need for taking elementary security precautions (such as not carrying lists of names and addresses) and acted in a disciplined and coordinated fashion during anti-fascist demonstrations and generally.

On the strength of the Lewisham experience the ANL was born. It was an example of the united front tactic first proposed by the Comintern in the 1920s. We could have seen the rise of the NF and said that, since reformists had the wrong position on capitalism, we would oppose the NF as an isolated revolutionary organisation and not unite with wider forces. This would have been a sectarian mistake and, given our small size, allowed the NF virtually a free run.

Conversely, we could have said that we would unite with the reformists in a vague and general anti-racist campaign with no specific activities and which consisted of passing worthy resolutions through local wards, union conferences and so on. This would have led to a talking shop that provided the Labour Party with a left cover and reduced us to a centrist ginger group. This would have been equally fatal, leading to a political dead end and once again a free run to the Nazis on the streets.

So the ANL was set up as a united front combining the SWP, plus Peter Hain and Labour MP Ernie Roberts and, among other MPs, Neil Kinnock, Audrey Wise and Martin Flannery, who were on the left of the party. Paul Holborow of the SWP was the organiser, and Nigel Harris, also from the SWP, was on the steering committee. The SWP was without doubt the driving force pushing action, organisation and ideas throughout.

The ANL was specifically a one issue campaign. We did not attempt to impose a general programme of revolutionary demands upon its supporters in sectarian fashion, nor did we make do with worthy sounding phrases of opposition to fascism. It was sharply focused, as its title suggested. In November 1977, when the Central Committee of the SWP discussed the launch of an organisation to oppose the National Front we spent time discussing its name: 'Anti-Racist'—too soft! 'Anti-Fascist'—not tough enough! 'Anti-Nazi'!—yes! After all, Hitler went much further in his bestiality than Mussolini.

Thus the target was the hard racism of the NF which, if allowed to thrive, could convert the many more numerous soft racists in British society into the cadres of a mass fascist movement. The ANL united revolutionaries and reformists (who disagreed on many general issues) but who agreed on the need to stop the NF through practical action around the slogan of 'No platform for Nazis'.

The ANL became an immensely popular movement. To give a focus for youth against the NF—the age group they drew most of their support from—the ANL organised its first Carnival in London at the end of April 1978, before the local elections. Its success was beyond everyone's expectations, bringing 80,000 on a march from Trafalgar Square to a music festival in Victoria Park six miles away. Together with Rock Against Racism huge Carnivals were organised in Manchester (35,000), Cardiff (5,000), Edinburgh (8,000), Harwich (2,000), Southampton (5,000), Bradford (2,000) and London again (100,000). The NF vote in the subsequent local elections collapsed. In Leeds it declined by 54 percent, in Bradford by 77 percent. Even in its heartland of London's East End it dropped by 40 percent. There is no doubt that the ANL was largely responsible. ANL groups sprang up all over the country. For instance in one week of May 1978 Oxford set up an ANL at a meeting of 450 people, Bath 100, Aberdeen 100, Swansea 70. From 22 April to 9 December the following ANL groups organised themselves: Schoolkids Against the Nazis (SKAN),

Students, Ford workers, Longbridge workers, civil servants, rail workers, firemen, bus workers, teachers (which held a rally of 1,000), miners (who held a conference of 200 delegates), engineers, NUPE, two Halifax night spots, Footballers Against the Nazis, which held an AGM after some period of existence, and many others.

The ANL was widely sponsored. As early as mid-April 1978, before the Carnival, there were 30 AUEW branches and districts, 25 trades councils, 11 NUM areas and lodges, six to ten branches from the TGWU, CPSA, TASS, NUJ, NUT and NUPE, 13 shop stewards committees in major factories, and 50 local Labour Parties. Numbers grew after the Carnival.[21] The ANL Carnival rallied as many people as CND or the Vietnam Solidarity Campaign had done at their peaks.

An important incident in the history of the ANL was the killing of Blair Peach on a demonstration in Southall. The NF announced that it was going to hold a General Election meeting in Ealing Town Hall. The local Tory council gave the Nazis permission to hold the meeting. A plea to the Labour government home secretary, Merlyn Rees, to ban the Nazi meeting fell on deaf ears. This meeting was a provocation, as the area of Southall was predominantly Asian. The ANL held a counter-demonstration to the Nazis. Blair Peach, a teacher from east London, a member of the SWP and ANL, came to Southall to participate in the demonstration. A massive force of the Special Patrol Group viciously attacked the ANL demonstration and a baton held by one of the policemen smashed Blair's skull and killed him. Blair Peach's funeral was massive—some 10,000 people. Union delegations from across Britain paid their respects. 'There were 13 national trade union banners and TUC president Ken Gill spoke at the graveside alongside Tony Cliff of the SWP'.[22]

By the late 1970s the British Nazi NF was almost totally eclipsed. But years later it began to regroup, this time under the banner of the British National Party (BNP). This took place at the same time as Nazi votes were rising significantly in Europe. Both in Eastern Europe and in Germany, Belgium, Norway and Austria, but above all in France, the Nazis were gaining votes and respectability.

On 4 April 1989 the BNP set up headquarters in Welling. Racist attacks in the area increased by 210 percent, including the murders of Rolan Adams, Rohit Duggal and Ruhallah Aramesh. Faced with this situation the ANL was relaunched in January 1992. It was sorely needed, for on 22 April 1993 Stephen Lawrence was murdered in

Eltham, to be followed only a few months later (16 September), by the election of Derek Beackon of the BNP as a councillor for the Millwall ward in Tower Hamlets. His election was followed by a 300 percent increased in reported racist attacks in east London. Indeed, one week before his election Quddus Ali, 17, was left in a coma after being attacked by eight racists on a main road near the Isle of Dogs.

The ANL was not dormant in this situation. The Sunday after the BNP election success their paper sale was driven off Brick Lane by a huge ANL protest. It had been the only regular BNP sale. Since the ANL protest here there are no other regular Nazi sales anywhere in Britain. On 16 October 1993 there was a demonstration of 60,000 to close down the BNP's Welling headquarters. This was met by a co-ordinated police attack after which 14 anti-Nazis were imprisoned for as much as three years. But our campaigning continued. On 19 March 1994 a TUC anti-racist demonstration took place throughout East London involving 50,000 people. A 'Don't Vote Nazi' campaign was launched in early 1994 and Beackon was kicked out of the council in the 5 May election the same year. On 28 May 1994 150,000 attended the demonstration and ANL Carnival in Brockwell Park.

The fate of the British NF has been completely different to that of the French Front National (FN). At the beginning the FN was much smaller than the British NF. In the elections of 1974 the FN got a mere 0.74 percent of the vote, and two years later, in 1976, even less, 0.33. It was in this year that the French Nazi Le Pen came to Britain to learn from the National Front. Since then the position has been inverted.

With the election of the Socialist François Mitterrand to the presidency in 1981 things changed radically. The disappointment was massive: unemployment more than doubled. The FN mushroomed. In 1984 it polled 11 percent of the votes or about 2 million. In March 1986 parliamentary elections, it won 35 MPs—as many as the Communist Party. Since then the electoral system has changed and the FN has no MPs, but they have over 1,000 councillors, and they control four smallish towns in southern France. In the general election of June 1977 the FN got five million votes, or 15 percent of the total vote.

In Britain, in the local elections of 1997, the total number of votes for the BNP, NF and the Third Way—the three fascist organisations—was only 3,000.

Why is the curve of NF support in Britain radically downwards, while that in France moved sharply upwards? One cannot explain it by referring to differences in the objective situations of France and Britain. The proportion of blacks in Britain is similar to that in France—5 to 6 percent. Unemployment levels are not different. The level of industrial struggle has been much higher in France than Britain. Britain has suffered the longest and deepest downturn in industrial struggle.

For an explanation one has to look to the subjective element—above all the presence of a revolutionary socialist organisation in the SWP which understands the importance of the united front tactic, the nature of fascism and how it grows, and the means of combating it by preventing its marches. Because the SWP was of a size to be able to seriously work with the reformist Labour Party it was able to launch the ANL.

In France an organisation like the SWP is lacking. The main organisation against the Nazis has been SOS Racisme. This organisation hangs on to the coat tails of the Socialist Party. Its leader, Harlem Désir, argues against 'confrontation' with the FN, claiming this will 'play into Le Pen's hands'. He looks to public opinion to uproot racism and expects equal contributions from left and right wing organisations. Though SOS Racisme calls demonstrations, these are not designed to physically confront the FN. The role of Mitterrand in castrating SOS Racisme was central.

One must remember that Mitterrand was an official in Marshal Pétain's government during the war, a government that collaborated with the Nazis, delivering 70,000 Jews to the gas chambers. Later Mitterand became a member of the Resistance. The truth about Mitterand's wartime role is complex and difficult to disentangle, and he may well have been hedging his bets by keeping links with both sides. Mitterand was a classic reformist—a pragmatist, and an opportunist concerned primarily with his own power. So as president he assisted the NF to gain credibility by introducing proportional representation as a strategy to split the parliamentary right and hence weaken the opposition to his government. At the same time he encouraged SOS Racisme in order to draw the anti-racists into the electoral orbit of the Socialist Party and to prevent the far left from taking the lead in anti-racist activity. The consequence, of course, was the growth of the FN, and more attacks on Arabs etc. It was not that Mitterrand was a fanatical racist himself, but because he simply did not care—he was only interested in parliamentary manoeuvres to keep himself in power.

The ANL experience was of tremendous importance. We managed to mobilise hundreds of thousands against the National Front and the BNP. This experience was very positive for the SWP. However, for all its positive aspects, it had negative aspects too.

Adapting to the ANL leads to sharp conflicts over the shape of *Socialist Worker*

So long as we were unclear about the real situation of the working class, we were unable to grasp the nature of the audience of *Socialist Worker*. Because we were not clear at all about the coming to office of Labour in 1974 and the radical change in the objective situation, we started squabbling about the direction *Socialist Worker* should take. Imagine a group of people who have travelled for years in the London Underground suddenly transferred by magic into the Paris Metro, without them knowing what happened. Of course they will quarrel all the time, because the map they have does not help them to arrive at the Gare du Nord.

I felt that something was very wrong. Every field of our activity— with the important exception of the Anti Nazi League—was in decline. I looked for a short cut to get out of the difficulties by simply adapting *Socialist Worker* to the ANL audience. I argued strongly for this through the autumn and winter of 1977, as it became clear that the prospects for the SWP and the working class were much worse than we had believed.

I, and a few other leading comrades, including Paul Foot, the editor of *Socialist Worker*, and Jim Nichol, the national secretary, suggested that if we wanted to succeed, we should simplify *Socialist Worker*. Some comrades quite rightly called it the 'SWP turned into *Sun* edition'. The three of us had quite a standing in the party. I was a founding member, and Paul and Jim had been members for over 15 years, and their prestige was high. Still, at a meeting of the National Committee with some 100 members only five supported our resolution. And thank heaven for that! The comrades had good instincts when they rejected our resolution, because the paper we suggested would in no way have served the intellectual needs of our members.

We must just compare the experience of Trotsky's *Pravda*, published in Vienna in the years 1908-12, with Lenin's *Pravda* published in Petrograd from 1912 onwards. Trotsky intended to address himself to 'plain workers' rather than to politically minded party men, and to 'serve, not to lead,' his readers. Isaac Deutscher comments on this statement, that Trotsky's *Pravda's* plain language and the fact that it preached the unity of the party secured to it a certain popularity but no lasting political influence.[23] The same could not be said of Lenin's *Pravda* which played a key role in schooling the Bolshevik Party and securing it a decisive influence in 1917.

There were many complaints that *Socialist Worker* was boring, the industrial reports especially so. When people are depressed, simple short strike stories will not do. To address the problem I looked for a journalistic solution, instead of asking, why did the industrial reports become boring? A report about a massive, victorious workers' fight is exciting. A report about a tiny group of workers, who lose the battle, cannot but depress. Of course everyone was excited to read about the 1972 or 1974 miners' strikes. But the story of a tiny strike leading to defeat only spreads the gloom. Again, workers writing about their own struggles can be invigorating, but it can also spread demoralisation, depending on the experience.[24]

The argument I brought forward at the National Advisory Committee meeting of the SWP in December 1977 was for simplifying the paper, for orienting it on a youth audience who had very little trade union experience or interest, but were very angry, anti-racist and rebellious. The debate on *Socialist Worker* became entangled with the debate on standing parliamentary candidates, *Women's Voice*, *Flame*, and the downturn. While I am convinced I was right on the last three issues, I was wrong on the first. Thank heaven there was strong resistance in the SWP to my effort to turn *Socialist Worker* into what was called a punk paper. After massive upheavals, including numerous changes of editor of the paper, at last the musical chairs stopped. The final person to take over the editor's chair was Chris Harman, who consistently opposed my efforts to dumb down the paper. We were very lucky in this. For the last 17 years Chris has demonstrated what a brilliant editor he is.

The same mistake that was made in the case of *Women's Voice*— not developing the big picture—was committed by me when we were discussing *Socialist Worker*.

One should not underestimate the damage caused by the row over the paper. It affected people's willingness to listen to me over other issues—above all, the downturn and *Women's Voice*. I well remember that someone as loyal to me as Roger Cox was absolutely inflamed by the 'punk paper'. Similarly Dave Hayes made it clear that he found it embarrassing to try to sell the paper on the shop floor at Caterpillar's.

The sheer confusion was immense. I was right on the downturn, but this analysis was contradicted by the 'punk paper' perspective. What was the point of a more popular paper when the class was in retreat? This highlights a more general problem. No one was clear about what were the practical conclusions from a downturn analysis. Our slogan of the time—'Small is beautiful'—was a good one, but we did not necessarily apply it concretely. It took till 1981 to abandon the perspective that rank and file groups could be built. We only came upon the propaganda perspective—emphasis on theory, big geographical branches, recruitment in ones and twos—empirically, by generalising from the experience of what Andy Strouthous did as Manchester organiser in 1981-83.

Bitter but necessary lessons

The conditions of the downturn led to complete disorientation for some two years in the party. We were not clear about the objective situation. And when I use the words objective situation, I mean not only the economic conditions of the workers, not only the material world, but also the grey matter in the heads of workers—for us these are also objective factors.

Without clarity about basics, secondary issues could loom out of all proportion to their significance. It was all too easy to argue about the arrangement of furniture on the *Titanic*, if you were not aware of the iceberg. Because things were not working out but we did not understand why, arguments became heated. Personal bickering and vilification are bound to aggravate the conflict. However, this does not mean that organisational argument or conflict must be avoided, if it is necessary for progress. As Lenin writes, 'No struggle over principles waged by groups within the social democratic movement anywhere in the world has managed to avoid a number of personal and organisational conflicts. Nasty types make it their business deliberately to pick on "conflict" expressions. But only weak nerved dilettanti from among "sympathisers" can be embarrassed by these conflicts, can shrug them off in despair or in scorn, as if to say, "It is all a squabble!"'[25]

Once, through argument and debate, we did become clear about the objective situation, the cohesion of the party and its leadership would be re-established, and on stronger foundations than ever.

The crisis in the organisation went on for about three years, 1976-79. It is important to see what lessons we can draw from the way we dealt with it. Of course, history does not repeat itself, but similar situations will arise in the future. I would like to draw up a balance sheet of my effort to deal with the crisis: I mean a balance sheet, not a balancing act.

On the positive side, my position proved right on the issue of the downturn in the class struggle, on *Women's Voice* and *Flame*. To understand why the crisis was still so deep and long, one has to look at the other side of the balance sheet, ie, where I was wrong.

First of all, I was far too slow in seeing the existence of the downturn. It is true that my book, *The Employers' Offensive: Productivity Deals and How to Fight Them*, published in 1970, pointed to crucial elements of the downturn that were to be seen clearly in the mid-1970s. This was the withering away of the power of the shop stewards to negotiate terms of employment and the widespread rise of full time convenors, etc. However, I was far too slow in drawing the conclusion. And I was in a better position to gauge the situation than other comrades, practically all of whom had no experience of any period that was not on the way up. The concept of a downturn was not in their vocabulary. Having been a revolutionary since the 1930s, I had less excuse not to see what was happening before our eyes.

Looking back at the years 1968-79, the picture was very mixed: it was not all gloom and doom, but neither was it every day in every way getting better and better. Taking the 11 years together, our organisation improved radically. In April 1968 we had 400 members. At the end of 1979 we had 4,000. In 1968 our membership was overwhelmingly student with a few white collar workers. In 1979 we had a largely working class membership. Our standing in the movement was completely different in 1979 to what it was in 1968.

In 1968 we were not better known than the IMG; as a matter of fact Tariq Ali was the best known person on the far left. In 1968 we were in the same league as the IMG and the SLL. In 1979 the IMG did not exist, and the SLL, with its name changed to WRP, had no more significance than the SPGB that has existed since 1904.

Our organisation in 1979 had hardened cadres who in future could go against the stream, survive the hard years of the 1980s, and be ready to take advantage of the upturn that is bound to come.

Chapter 8

Time to write

The Lenin and Trotsky biographies

I wrote far more books in the period after 1975 than ever before: four volumes of a biography of Lenin (published 1975-79), four volumes of a biography of Trotsky (published 1989-93), *Class Struggle and Women's Liberation* and, in collaboration with Donny Gluckstein, *Marxism and Trade Union Struggle*, *The General Strike of 1926*, and *The Labour Party: A Marxist History*.

In the decade before, I wrote three short books dealing with current affairs: *Incomes Policy, Legislation and Shop Stewards*, *The Employers' Offensive: Productivity Deals and How to Fight Them*, and *The Crisis: Social Contract or Socialism*.

The change in the objective situation—the downturn in the class struggle—left me with a lot of time on my hands. I look back with nostalgia to the period before.

When one writes a biography, it tells you not only about the subject, but also about the author. I will not deal with my biographies of Lenin and Trotsky at length, except to indicate the light they threw on my own political past.

The first volume of Lenin's biography has a subtitle, *Building the Party*. Although I had read Lenin's writings since the early 1930s, only from the 1970s did I really grasp, I believe, many elements in Lenin's writings on the party.

For a very long time I was not a member of a revolutionary party, but of a Marxist circle or at best a little propaganda group. This applied to my 13 years of political activity in Palestine, to the years I lived in Dublin, and to the period between 1950 and the beginning of the 1970s. Marxism, being not only a science, but also an art, cannot be well grasped unless one practises it. A serious tiro painter looks at a picture painted by Rembrandt and tries to copy it, not because he aims at a forgery or has the illusion that he can achieve anything Rembrandt has achieved. He does it because the practice of trying to follow in Rembrandt's steps will influence his painting ability and raise it to the highest level open to him.

Reading Lenin's writings is not enough to assimilate his ideas. What matters is not only what is borrowed, but who does the borrowing. And this depends on the experience and history of the individual borrower and on the activities he has been involved in hitherto.

Only the first volume of my long biography really got to grips with Lenin's theory in its practical application for day to day activity. This is because in the 1970s, 80s and 90s we were engaged in building a revolutionary party. The other volumes, Volume 2, *All Power to the Soviets*, Volume 3, *Revolution Besieged* and Volume 4, *The Bolsheviks and World Revolution*, dealt with political territory I had never visited personally.

When it comes to my four volumes on Trotsky, what was said about the last three volumes of *Lenin* applies also to the first three volumes of *Trotsky*—they cover completely virgin territory for me.

The Lenin biography

A key argument of Lenin was that, because the road between capitalism and socialism is not a smooth straight line, revolutionaries have to learn to change their tactics, to be flexible. But only when one has hard principles can one indulge in changing tactics without becoming an opportunist. I summed up Lenin's position thus:

> Without understanding the laws of historical development, one cannot maintain persistent struggle. During the years of toil and disappointment, isolation and suffering, revolutionaries cannot survive without the conviction that their actions fit the requirements of historical advance. In order not to get lost on the twists and turns of the long road, one must stand firm ideologically. Theoretical scepticism and revolutionary relentlessness are not compatible. Lenin's strength was that he always related theory to the processes of human development. He judged the importance of every theoretical notion in relation to practical needs. Likewise he tested every practical step for its fit with Marxist theory. He combined theory and practice to perfection.[1]

To avoid being lost in a very complicated situation, Lenin always insisted that the critical step was to start by pointing out the most crucial elements, grasping them correctly, while paying less attention, to start with, to secondary factors. Hence one of the main characteristics of Lenin—and he was not apologetic about it—was bending the stick.

This lesson was relevant to the building of a revolutionary party in Britain. Parallels were evident, not only in the external situation, but also in the key strategies need to orientate to that situation.

In 1898 Lenin argued that the one sidedness of *kruzhkovshchina* (the Marxist study circles which emphasised theory above all) had to be corrected. But in the industrial agitation that followed this led to an opposite one sidedness—'economism'. Lenin made this new correction in 1902, in his pamphlet *What is to be Done?* As I wrote:

> Despite the one-sidedness of the factory agitation at the time, Lenin always valued this period as a very important and necessary stage in the development of Russian social democracy. He was ready to admit both its progressive role and the dangers inherent in it...
>
> At every stage of the struggle Lenin would look for what he regarded as the key link in the chain of development. He would then repeatedly emphasise the importance of this link, to which all others must be subordinated. After the event, he would say: 'We overdid it. We bent the stick too far', by which he did not mean that he had been wrong to do so. To win the main battle of the day, the concentration of all energies on the task was necessary.
>
> The uneven development of different aspects of the struggle made it necessary always to look for the key link in every concrete situation. When there was the need for study, for laying the foundations of the first Marxist circles, Lenin stressed the central role of study. In the next stage, when the need was to overcome circle mentality, he would repeat again and again the importance of industrial agitation. At the next turn of the struggle, when 'economism' needed to be smashed, Lenin did this with a vengeance. He always made the task of the day quite clear, repeating what was necessary ad infinitum in the plainest, heaviest, most single-minded hammer-blow pronouncements. Afterwards he would regain his balance, straighten the stick, then bend it again in another direction. If this method has advantages in overcoming current obstacles, it also contains hazards for anyone wanting to use Lenin's writing on tactical and organisational questions as a source for quotation. Authority by quotation is nowhere less justified than in the case of Lenin. If he is cited on any tactical or organisational question, the concrete issues which the movement was facing at the time must be made absolutely clear.

Another of Lenin's characteristics already apparent at [an] early stage of his development is an attitude to organisational forms as always historically determined. He never adopted abstract, dogmatic schemes of organisation, and was ready to change the organisational structure of the party at every new development of the class struggle.[2]

In 1902 Lenin argued that the revolutionary party must be made up of professional revolutionaries. With the outbreak of the 1905 revolution, he bent the stick with the slogan, 'Open the gates of the party.' However, he found the going very difficult indeed among the people he himself had organised and trained. The organisational loyalty of the committee men, which Lenin had cultivated and valued highly, turned into organisational fetishism, and became a serious impediment to Bolshevism.[3] 'Herbert Spencer, the well known naturalist, wisely observed that every organism is conservative in direct proportion to its perfection. Lenin, who knew how to recruit, train and keep the loyalty of the committee men, had to oppose their conservatism during the revolution of 1905'.[4]

The fundamental prerequisite of consistent revolutionary policy, notwithstanding the turns and twists on the road, is for Marxist theory to dominate every action of the party. As I wrote:

A clear scientific understanding of the general contours of historical development of the class struggle is essential for a revolutionary leader. He will not be able to keep his bearings and his confidence through the twists and turns of the struggle unless he has a general knowledge of economics and politics. Therefore Lenin repeated many times that strategy and tactics must be based 'on an exact appraisal of the objective situation,' while at the same time being 'shaped after analysing class relations in their entirety.' In other words they must be based on a clear, confident, theoretical analysis—on science.

Lenin believed in improvisation. But in order for this not to degenerate into simply the shifting impressions of the day, it had to be blended into a general perspective based on well thought-out theory. Practice without theory must lead to uncertainty and errors. On the other hand, to study Marxism apart from the struggle is to divorce it from its mainspring—action—and to create useless bookworms. Practice is clarified by revolutionary theory, and theory is verified by practice. The Marxist traditions are assimilated in the minds and blood of men only by struggle.[5]

One of the saddest things for Lenin must have been the repeated splitting of leaders of the party from Bolshevism at every sharp turning point. Again and again there was a quick turnover in the leadership. Why?

> The very process of selecting people to lead the party has dangers inclined to shape their methods of work, their thinking and their behaviour to fit the specific, immediate needs of the time. The Russian revolutionary movement underwent many changes in course, as a result of changes in the class struggle. A leader who adapted himself to the immediate needs at one stage found himself out of step at the next turn. For instance, Bogdanov, Lunacharsky and Krasin fitted the period of the rising revolutionary storm of 1905. But they could not adapt themselves to the period of reaction and the slow advance afterwards. Zinoviev and Kamenev learned the hard way that it was a mistake to exaggerate the immediate revolutionary possibilities, that one had to undertake the slow, systematic work of organisation and agitation during the period of reaction, and the following period of small deeds—Duma activity, the insurance campaign, and so on. When it came to the stormy events of 1917, Zinoviev and Kamenev were found wanting.[6]

The twists and turns in the class struggle were extremely sharp in Russia: a revolution in 1905 followed by a bloody counter-revolution that annihilated the working class movement, followed by a revival of the movement in 1912, a pause in the revival occasioned by the outbreak of the world war, then two revolutions in 1917, followed by civil war and international invasion. To move from one stage to another was a severe test for the leadership of the Bolsheviks.

The only leader of the Bolsheviks to keep his position from 1903 to 1917 was Lenin. Why did Lenin survive all the turns and twists? The answer was rooted in his flexibility combined with Marxist orthodoxy. He assimilated completely the dialectic that denies, that rejects dogmatic Marxism, because it was clear to him that one should not substitute the abstract for the concrete. So many times he repeated that truth is always concrete. Marx put it differently: theory is grey, life is green.

It is interesting to note that among the lower cadres of the party— the committee men—the turnover was far smaller. The explanation is simple: 'The committee men did not have to take key policy decisions, whereas the top party leadership did. Hence the higher his place in the party, the more the leader was likely to adapt to immediate circumstances, and the more conservative he became'.[7]

A 1922 Bolshevik Party census covering 22 *gubernias* and *oblasts* showed that 1,085 members had joined the party before 1905. A rough estimate puts the number at about double for areas excluded from the census. Allowing for the fact that a large number of party members must have lost their lives during the revolution and the civil war, we see a considerable continuity of membership between 1905 and 1922. These were the cadres who gave the party its stability. For a party working under illegal conditions, in a country where the industrial proletariat numbered only some two and a half million, a cadre organisation of several thousands surviving for many years is a remarkable achievement.[8]

The relative stability of Bolshevism under the most severe conditions, dependent above all on the deep roots it had in the working class, was remarkable. It is true that the revolutionary party has to teach the workers. But who teaches the teachers, Lenin asked again and again. The answer was the working class. One prime example of this was the way that the Russian workers solved the problem of the state and revolution by establishing soviets. This was not a proposal of the Bolsheviks, but was developed by the masses themselves.

Being a disciple of Lenin, I believe I was quite consistent in following him in building a modest revolutionary party in Britain. Standing on the shoulders of a giant, one can see far.

The Trotsky biography

I was as far from the experience of Trotsky in the years 1879 to 1927 as I was from the experience of the Chartists or the Paris Commune. But the fourth volume, *The Darker the Night the Brighter the Star* (1927-40), largely covered a period in which I had become active as a revolutionary.

The centre of gravity of my volumes on Lenin was volume one. With the issues related there I was involved both theoretically and practically. In the case of the Trotsky biography, the centre of gravity is volume four. It touched nerves in me and shaped me in a different way than Lenin's experience in building the Bolshevik Party. The moral courage of Trotsky inspired me more than anything else. It was by far the most painful experience to write this volume, as I always held in my mind the victims of Nazism and Stalinism.

The last 13 years of Trotsky's life were a living hell. When Trotsky stated in 1927 that 'the vengeance of history is more powerful than the vengeance of the most powerful general secretary', he could not have had an inkling of the horrors this general secretary would inflict on himself and his family.[9]

His four children, as well as his first wife, Alexandra Sokolovskaia, were murdered on Stalin's orders. Rosa Luxemburg and Karl Liebknecht were murdered, and the working class movement has many, many other martyrs. But Trotsky's position is unique. He was murdered not once, but again and again. His suffering and courage were unequalled. Prometheus was chained to a rock and the eagle pecked out his liver, but he never yielded or had any doubt about his stand. On 4 April 1935 Trotsky wrote in his diary, '[Stalin] is clever enough to realise that even today I would not change places with him'.[10] Nothing relieved the agony, but still there was no self pity, no pettiness, only a combination of clarity of thinking, passion and indomitable will.

The most decisive event during those 13 years was the victory of Hitler in Germany.

This was the time of the worst economic slump in the history of capitalism, when Nazism was on the march. Trotsky wrote the most brilliant articles, essays and books on the developments in Germany. What is particularly impressive is that the author was far distant from the scene of the events. Still he managed to follow the day-to-day twists and turns. Reading Trotsky's writings of the years 1930-33, their concreteness gives the impression that the author must have been living in Germany rather than very far away on the island of Prinkipo in Turkey. These writings are unsurpassed in their use of the historical materialist method, in their descriptions of the complicated relationships between economic, social, political and ideological changes, the relations between the mass psychology of different sections of German society, from the proletariat, the petty bourgeoisie and lumpen proletariat, to the role of the psychology of the individual, such as Hitler. These writings rank with the best historical writings of Karl Marx—*The Eighteenth Brumaire* and *The Class Struggle in France*. Trotsky not only analysed the situation, but also put forward a clear line of action for the proletariat. In terms of strategy and tactics they are extremely valuable revolutionary manuals, comparable to the best produced by Lenin and Trotsky during the first four years of the Comintern.

Unfortunately, ideas become a material force only when they are taken up by millions. Trotsky's writings failed to do that. His call was like a cry in the desert. Very few in Germany listened to him, or even heard him.[11]

On the eve of Hitler's victory the total number of organised Trotskyists in Berlin was 50, while the Stalinist party had 34,000 members.[12] In France, during the heady days of June 1936—with the general strike and occupation of the factories—the total number of Trotskyists was a couple of hundred, as against the Communist Party's 278,000 members![13] In Spain in 1938, at the height of the civil war, there were, according to the report to the Founding Conference of the Fourth International, ten to 30 members in the organisation, while the Stalinists had 1 million members.[14]

Trotsky demonstrated courage without equal. His agony was extreme. While never affected by self pity, he felt excruciating agony over the murder of his son, Sedov, in 1938, in the midst of the most terrible period of his life. This may be gathered from the obituary he wrote four days after his death, entitled 'Leon Sedov—Son, Friend, Fighter'.

As I write these lines, with Leon Sedov's mother by my side... we are unable to believe it as yet. And this, not only because he was our son, truthful, devoted, loving, but above all because he had, as no one else on earth, become part of our life, entwined in all its roots, our co-thinker, our co-worker, our guard, our counsellor, our friend.

Of that older generation whose ranks we joined at the end of the last century on the road to revolution, all, without exception, have been swept from the scene. That which tsarist hard-labour prisons and harsh exiles, the hardships of emigration, the civil war, and disease had failed to accomplish has in recent years been achieved by Stalin... Following the destruction of the older generation, the best section of the next, that is, the generation which awakened in 1917 and received its training in the 24 armies of the revolutionary front, were likewise destroyed. Also crushed underfoot and completely obliterated was the best part of the youth, Leon's contemporaries... During the years of our last emigration we made many new friends, some of them...becoming, as it were, members of our family. But we met all of them for the first time…when we had already neared old age. Leon was the only one who knew us when we were young; he became part of our lives from the very first moment of his self-awakening. While young in years, he still seemed our contemporary.

The obituary ends with words of remorse for not being able to save his son:

His mother—who was closer to him than any other person in the world—and I are living through these terrible hours recalling his image, feature by feature, unable to believe that he is no more and weeping because it is impossible not to believe… He was part of both of us, our young part… Together with our boy has died everything that still remained young within us.

Goodbye, Leon, goodbye, dear and incomparable friend. Your mother and I never thought, never expected that destiny would impose on us this terrible task of writing your obituary… But we were not able to protect you.

However hard the going, Trotsky's courage and clear sightedness remained undimmed. He never lost the will to struggle whatever the odds. He never understood the meaning of the word pessimism. Thus in a letter to Angelica Balabanoff of 3 February 1937 he wrote:

Indignation, anger, revulsion? Yes, even temporary weariness. All this is human, only too human. But I will not believe that you have succumbed to pessimism…this would be like passively and plaintively taking umbrage at history. How can one do that? History has to be taken as she is, and when she allows herself such extraordinary and filthy outrages, one must fight her back with one's fists.

Trotsky's confidence in the future remained undiminished, and his mind, will and energy were directed towards it. As a young man of 22 he wrote:

Dum spiro, spero! As long as I breathe I hope—as long as I breathe I shall fight for the future, that radiant future in which man, strong and beautiful, will become master of the spontaneous stream of his history and will direct it towards the boundless horizon of beauty, joy and happiness… *Dum spiro, spero!*

Before his assassination, in his testament, Trotsky repeated his optimism for the future:

My faith in the communist future of mankind is not less ardent, indeed it is firmer today than it was in the days of my youth... I can see the bright green strip of grass beneath the wall and the clear blue sky above the wall, and sunlight everywhere. Life is beautiful. Let the future generations cleanse it of all evil, oppression, and violence, and enjoy it to the full.

A short time after, he was murdered. In the biography I wrote that:

No person embodied the triumph and the tragedy of the revolutionary workers' movement more than Leon Trotsky. The torch-bearer of its triumphs had fallen victim to its tragedy.[15]

I have no doubt that in my political life it was Trotsky's moral courage that inspired me most. Many times I made mistakes, many times I was hesitant regarding specific issues, but never for one fleeting moment did I think of giving up the struggle. Of course I was never put to the really hard test, as Trotsky was. If the life of one of my children was on the line unless I gave up my political activity, would I have succumbed? I do not know. But up to now I have never had doubts about the future.

My steadfastness has gained a big fillip from Chanie's revolutionary steadfastness. She is as hard as shoe-leather. One incident connected with my writing of Lenin's biography comes into my mind. I worked a month on writing a skeleton of the book: the sections, the chapters, the subsections of chapters, etc. In addition I made a list of different literary sources I needed for every section. It was really a very hard job. I just finished it on Christmas Eve. A day or so after Christmas I wanted to start working on the book, but I could not find the outline. We looked for it everywhere, and came to the conclusion that one of our kids had thrown the manuscript away. I was so depressed that I stayed in bed for three days. Thank heaven for Chanie! She told me off: 'Snap out of it! Stop your self pity!' I knew she was right, so I followed her order and rewrote the outline.

Literary collaboration with Donny

In 1986 the book *Marxism and Trade Union Struggle: The General Strike of 1926* was published. *The Labour Party: A Marxist History* followed in 1988. Both *Marxism and Trade Union Struggle* and the Labour Party book were co-authored by myself and Donny. It was a real partnership, not that one of us was the main author and the other his assistant. We had equal shares in the enterprise.

The collaboration was very easy. Our styles are practically the same—except for the fact that I still make grammatical and syntactical errors. The way we argue things is practically the same. If the style is the man, we are identical twins, although I was born in 1917 and Donny in 1954.

The conditions of the downturn gave us the time and space to research and write the two books.

The themes of the two are closely related. In passing I must mention another member of our family who played a significant role in the research for *Marxism and Trade Union Struggle*—Chanie. She worked very hard in the TUC Library and the Public Records Office. I know it is embarrassing to mention this, and it looks as if I carry on the Jewish tradition of keeping business in the family. A byproduct of this work was her short booklet *1919: Britain on the Brink of Revolution* which is a serious contribution to Britain's working class history.

This is not the place to sketch the arguments of the two books, but I will mention a few points from them. The trade unions are defence organisations of workers in the framework of capitalism. The trade unions unite workers but also divide them. The fact that they are called trade unions means that they organise only a specific trade but not the whole working class. A teacher cannot join the National Union of Miners, and a miner cannot join the National Union of Teachers.

The unions, even the most militant, are not socialist organisations. Their aim is to improve wages and conditions, not to abolish the wage system. Remember Marx's words: 'Our aim is not a fair day's pay for a fair day's work', but the abolition of the wages system.

A socialist party encompasses only socialists. A trade union, to be effective, has to include any worker who is ready to join, not excluding members of the Liberal or Tory parties.

However democratic the union, it has a bureaucracy, whose first function is to negotiate with the employers. The trade union bureaucrats are neither workers nor capitalists. Unlike the workers, the bureaucrats are not exploited by capitalists, nor are they under threat of the sack. At the same time they are not capitalists either, as they do not employ workers. Rodney Bickerstaffe, general secretary of UNISON, the largest union in the country, does not employ the members of his union. Union bureaucrats, as mediators between the workers and the bosses, vacillate between the two classes.

Of course there is a difference between right wing and left wing union leaders, but the difference between the workers and the bureaucrats is more fundamental. If this is not clear, there is always a danger that the militant workers will adapt themselves to the union bureaucracy, or at least the left section of it. Thus, for instance, during the 1926 General Strike, the Communist Party issued the slogan 'All power to the general council' of the TUC. In so doing it gave up an independent revolutionary role and passed the initiative to the TUC lefts like A J Cook. Cook was the fiery and most left wing leader of the miners' union, and tail-ended other TUC lefts like Alfred Purcell, George Hicks and Alonzo Swales. These three union leaders tail-ended Jimmy Thomas, the right wing leader of the National Union of Railwaymen, who collaborated with the Tory prime minister, Stanley Baldwin, and later, in 1931, would join the Tories in the National Government. The result: the general strike was successfully sold out even though it had massive and growing support.

The revolutionary attitude to all union officials should follow the line expressed by the Clyde Workers' Committee in November 1915: 'We will support the officials just so long as they rightly represent the workers, but we will act independently immediately they misrepresent them'.[16]

Trotsky also put it well when he wrote, ' "With the masses—always; with the vacillating leaders—sometimes, but only so long as they stand at the head of the masses." It is necessary to make use of vacillating leaders while the masses are pushing them ahead, without for a moment abandoning criticism of these leaders'.[17]

The second book, on the Labour Party, was closely related to the one on the unions.

The first question we have to ask about the Labour Party is whether it is a workers' party. Lenin answered the question by defining the Labour Party as a 'capitalist workers' party'. It is a capitalist party because its policies do not overthrow capitalism, but preserve it. So why is it a workers' party? It is not simply because workers vote for it. When Lenin dealt with the subject, at the Second Congress of the Communist International, more workers voted Tory than Labour. And Lenin never dreamt of calling the Tory party a 'capitalist workers' party'. It is a workers' party because it reflects workers' collective urge to face up to capitalism.

Even if the policies of the Labour Party are often indistinguishable from those of the Tories, the rank and file and supporters of the Labour Party express completely different aspirations to the Tory rank and file and supporters. One need but watch the television reports of the two conferences to see the massive differences. At the Tory party conference the floor of the meeting is often to the right of the platform. They give the strongest applause when trade unions are attacked, or black people, or 'scroungers', ie people who live on social security benefit. At the Labour Party conference, the real applause comes when statements are made against poverty, against unemployment, against racism, against fat cats, for union rights, etc. The contradictory consciousness of millions of workers, of both accepting the prevailing ideas in society, ie the ideas of the ruling class, but rejecting many of the consequences of the same, characterises Labour supporters: 'Yes, I believe in profit. The economy couldn't work without profit, but I detest my boss because he's a greedy bastard.' 'Of course high wages are bad, because they cause inflation, but…my wages are far too low.'

The contradictory consciousness of Labour supporters explains the close relationship between the Labour Party and the trade union bureaucracy. At the Second Congress of the Comintern already referred to, a British delegate, William MacLaine, described the Labour Party as the political expression of the trade unions. Lenin intervened in the discussion, saying MacLaine was wrong: 'The Labour Party is the political expression of the trade union bureaucracy.' We drew from this the conclusion that:

> The trade union bureaucracy is a mediating element between the workers and employers. The Labour Party is also a mediating element, except that it is at one remove from the direct struggle at the point of production. In addition the Labour Party leaders are sometimes called upon to run the ship of state: the trade union officials are never given the running of enterprises.[18]

Tony Blair needs Rodney Bickerstaffe to stop strikes. Bickerstaffe needs Tony Blair to justify his stopping of strikes. There is thus a symbiotic relationship between the trade union and Labour Party leaderships which constitutes a powerful bond between them and militates against workers in struggle.

In a short sketch I cannot do justice to the two books. They try to analyse the question of the relation of the trade unions and the Labour Party to the industrial struggle as it changes dynamically. There is an interplay between the conditions of capitalism (its booms and slumps), the ideological pressures of the system and the counter-pressures of class struggle, as well as Labour's position in relation to the state (whether it is in office or not). All this leads to constant changes.

The same also applies to the Labour left. Though incapable of leading this reformist party in a fundamental challenge to capitalism, it still plays an important role. It can be a means of diverting real class struggle into the dead end of parliamentarism, or a focus for workers' aspirations against the right wing of the party. In either case its role must be clearly understood in the concrete circumstances.

No doubt my ability to spend months in doing the research and writing for the two books was dependent on the downturn in the class struggle, so I had time to spare. I still much prefer to participate in efforts to change history than to write history.

Chapter 9

Contrary indications

Political upturn

The catastrophic downturn in the industrial struggle from the mid-1970s had a peculiar side effect. It went hand in hand with a political upturn, expressed in the rise of a new and powerful Labour left wing current centred on the figure of Tony Benn. He had been a minister in the Labour governments of the 1960s and 1970s and was almost unique in his political evolution. Against the established trend of reformist politicians, he did not evolve to the right but to the left. Bennism reflected the fact that, since workers did not have the confidence to take on their employers in the workplace, many of the activists looked for a political solution outside the workplace. They turned to a saviour from on high—the Labour Party.

After Labour's 1979 election defeat the the party experienced its biggest swing to the left for a generation. The January 1981 Wembley Labour Party Special Conference, in which Bennism dominated, made the Labour left ecstatic. To quote some of their papers:

Tribune: 'A watershed for Labour Party democracy'.[1]

Militant: 'Wembley was a great victory for Labour's ranks... The block vote of the union delegations at Labour Party conference will become a vital transmission belt for the demands of an aroused and mobilised working class'.[2]

Socialist Challenge: 'What a day at Wembley...a famous victory for the workers' movement'.[3]

Morning Star: 'It is a momentous decision in the struggle, not only for the return of a Labour government at the next election, but also to ensure a Labour government which carries out the policies of the Labour movement'.[4]

Practically everyone to the left of the Labour Party from the IMG and Socialist Organiser to the women's groups was pulled into the Benn camp and the Labour Party. In regard to the latter I wrote:

The influx of middle class feminists into the Labour Party came when the women's movement was in rapid decline and industrial defeats were shifting the labour movement to the right. If the general argument for New Realism was that strikes do not pay, it took a special form among feminists. To people like the Eurocommunist Bea Campbell, strikes and pickets were macho and typified the 'anti-woman', 'male dominated' working class movement. The focus was no longer collective, but on the individual woman as a victim of men: on rape and other violence against women. The theory of patriarchy—that the enemy of woman is man, that men benefit from women's subordination—came to dominate. Now the women's movement concentrated on personal solutions, on alternative relationships and lifestyles. This naturally appealed to middle class women: working class women could not afford the luxury.

The search for individual solutions led to fragmentation and collapse of the women's movement, so that its remnants shifted away from the politics of movements towards institutional politics, largely towards the Labour Party. Protesting against women's oppression, the product of capitalism, without challenging capitalism *in toto*, they fitted very well into Labourism, which both expresses workers' opposition to the status quo, and at the same time blunts this opposition.[5]

The 1983 general election result pricked the Benn balloon. Labour beat the SDP-Liberal Alliance to third position only by a tiny margin (27.6 percent of the votes to 25.4 percent). Still Benn managed to continue to fool himself. He saw the general election as a triumph:

For the first time since 1945 a political party with an openly socialist policy had received the support of over eight million people…socialism has reappeared once more upon the national agenda… The 1983 Labour manifesto commanded the loyalty of millions of voters and a democratic socialist bridgehead had been established from which further advance in public understanding and support can be made.[6]

Benn's words did not cut any ice even with his own supporters. Labour had received its lowest proportion of votes since 1918. Because there had been fewer Labour candidates in 1918, the number of votes per candidate in 1983 was the lowest ever. And these results followed four years of increasing mass unemployment and attacks on the welfare state.

The moment of truth for the Bennite left could not be postponed for long. The industrial downturn had engineered a political upturn, but it would not be long before the political level of the movement was adversely affected by the low level of class struggle. The Bennites were obsessed with resolutions, with constitutional procedures. This obsession played into the hands of the right. The political activists found it a waste of time and effort to relate to the mass of the workers who did not attend the meetings where the resolutions were passed. They fell into the substitutionist trap of believing they spoke for the millions of block votes cast in their name at Wembley. While Bennites could be counted in the tens of thousands they had not brought millions into active agreement with themselves. The false claim left them vulnerable to the hammering of the media and the right wing.

The 1982 Labour Party conference witnessed a massive decline of Bennism. As *Socialist Worker* wrote after the conference:

> The Labour left are in retreat—a retreat that may well turn to rout. The contrast between this year's Labour Party conference and last year's could not be greater. Last summer all the talk was of Tony Benn. His campaign for the Labour deputy leadership began to look like a triumphal procession, from union conference to union conference, from city to city.

In 1981 his bandwagon had been rolling. Literally thousands flocked to his meetings. The Labour right, battered on one side by the 'Gang of Four' and the other by the Labour left, looked worn and weak. Many started to believe—what so many have wished to believe—that the Labour Party could really be changed. In late 1982 *Socialist Worker* reported:

> One year later the picture is reversed. The talk is now of witch-hunts. The discussion is on just how much of the left will be spared. The Labour right wing are smiles and confidence…
>
> The audiences that last year packed [Benn's] meetings now stay at home. The bubble has burst.[7]

Things went even further to the right during the next Labour Party conference of 1983. *Socialist Worker* said:

> Hattersley, the openly right wing candidate for deputy leader, not only got a massive 67 percent vote, he even got more than half the votes in the constituency parties. Yet only two years ago these were voting four to one for Tony Benn.[8]

The 1983 Labour Party conference demonstrated the complete collapse of the Bennite camp. The left candidate for the position of deputy leader this time was Eric Heffer. He won only 6.6 percent of the constituency delegates, 1.6 percent of the trade union vote and 17 percent of the Parliamentary Labour Party.

But still the left lived in cloud cuckoo land. They did not notice that the attack on *Militant* was the Trojan horse that opened the way for the defeat of Bennism. They ignored the witch hunt in favour of fantasy. After the 1985 Labour Party conference *Tribune* declared, 'The left has never been stronger and the prospect of a radical, left wing Labour government has never been greater.' *Militant* wrote, 'The conference, made up of delegates representing nearly 10 million workers, remained firmly behind radical socialist policies'.[9]

Mad axe-woman on the rampage

In 1974 many capitalists welcomed Labour's election victory. Now in 1979 they rejoiced at its defeat. The Labour government had successfully protected the employers from workers' militancy. Now the employers wanted a new government less beholden to the trade unions. They no longer needed a defensive shield to shelter behind, but a sword to carry their offensive forward against the workers.

But Thatcher was very careful about how she used her sword. In 1978 Nicholas Ridley, her confidant and adviser, wrote an important strategy document. 'The Ridley Plan' argued that Ted Heath had made a great mistake in attacking all the unions in one fell swoop. What was needed was salami tactics—a series of carefully timed, set-piece confrontations, designed to beat the power of key unions, starting in industries where the unions were weak, followed by attacking more powerful groups of workers, and finally, taking on the miners and dockers. And this was the policy Thatcher carried out after coming to office in 1979.

The law was also to be used carefully, weakening the unions by using the imposition of fines to persuade their leaders to cooperate with the employers and so police the rank and file on behalf of the bosses and government. The aim was a phased attack with mild legal impositions first, followed by more radical measures. The gradual approach should increase further the demoralisation among workers, which had already gone very far indeed under the 1974-79 Labour government.

It was not a walkover for the government. In 1984 a miners' strike broke out and they fought bravely for a whole year. Alas, the long period of the downturn, of declining militancy, led to the final defeat of the strike. Unlike the 1972 and 1974 strikes, in which there was not one miner scabbing, and hence no need for picketing any pit, now the situation was completely different.

The sectionalism which had been encouraged by the Labour government's incentive scheme of 1977 tore the miners apart and isolated them from other workers. In 1984-85 at most 10 percent of the miners were active on picket duty, and, in contrast to 1972, they had to spend much of their time picketing out other miners.

This time there was little industrial solidarity from other workers. The damage had been done. For example, in 1972 power workers had been organised in a rank and file combine throughout the industry; they were involved in a pay campaign of their own, so all power stations strongly supported the miners. Within a couple of weeks 12 power stations had been closed completely, and 1,400,000 workers had to be laid off in industry. In 1984-85, on the other hand:

> No meetings were organised by the TGWU and GMBATU between shop stewards in the power stations and miners' representatives. The first meeting between Arthur Scargill and shop stewards in the power stations in Yorkshire did not take place until the strike had been going for ten and a half months—on 16 January 1985![10]

And on 11 April 1984 the unions in the power industry signed a 13 month agreement for a 5.2 percent wage increase. Not one worker was laid off for lack of electricity in the 12 months of the miners' strike.

In all these disputes SWP members threw themselves into the fray. However, the damage done to rank and file confidence meant that the trade union bureaucracy controlled throughout, and it was not prepared to take the action necessary to win. This does not mean the members simply accepted the limitations. One story illustrates the situation. At the start of the 1984-85 miners' strike the NUM did not picket coal supplies to steel works as it had done in previous disputes. In Scotland, for example, the union said that the steel works at Ravenscraig could not be picketed because it would damage 'Scotland's industry'. As a result, the miners' strike was having little visible effect. Comrades active in the Lothian coalfield near Edinburgh drew up and circulated an open letter to Mick McGahey, the Scottish NUM leader, demanding that he call for pickets of coal supplies to Ravenscraig. It was very hard to get signatures as people were nervous about the strong hold that McGahey and the Communist Party still had in the union. In the end 18 miners signed. McGahey was sufficiently embarrassed by the letter to start mass pickets at Ravenscraig. However, our comrades were in no position to influence the extent or development of the picketing after that and so the initiative did not lead on to bigger and better tactics for the strike. Despite our efforts, the SWP's role ended up mainly as one of fundraising for the miners. This was essential to keep the strike going, but clearly not enough to win it.

The Orgreave coke depot near Sheffield should have been the Saltley of the 1980s, but miners' leader Arthur Scargill's call to repeat the 1972 victory here was not heeded. In 1972 Birmingham engineering workers had come to the aid of the miners. But in 1984 the engineering workers of Sheffield (which is much nearer to the coalfields than Birmingham) did not. At Saltley in 1972 the engineers joined the picket line en masse on its fifth day. At Orgreave picketing started on Thursday 24 May 1984 with about 1,000 miners. The nation's television screens showed several thousand miners on the picket line being hammered by the police on 27 May, 29 May, 31 May and 18 June. On 30 May Scargill was arrested, and on 18 June he was wounded and had to be taken to hospital.[11] But there was still no sign of the Sheffield engineers turning up to picket. Why? To answer this one must look at the state of the Sheffield engineers. The *Department of Employment Gazette* reported that in Sheffield there had been no major stoppages in 1981, one in 1982 (against redundancies), and again only one in 1983 (over redundancies).[12]

The defeat of Orgreave was not, however, just a consequence of the weakness of the Sheffield engineers. It also came about through the role of the NUM area leaders—above all Jack Taylor in Yorkshire—in blocking what Scargill and the activists wanted to do. Unlike in 1972 and 1974, no solidarity strike action took place. The strikes of the 1970s were brilliant. I remember in 1972 some miners stayed with us in Hackney. They went to picket the local power station, and straight away the workers in the station blacked coal and oil supplies, so the station came to a full stop. Another example: in 1972 a banner strung across a bridge over the railway line, saying 'NUM official picket', caused the train drivers to stop in their tracks and not cross it. Dockers and lorry drivers at that time refused to move coal.

Workers who lack the confidence to stand up to their own bosses cannot be relied upon to come out in support of other workers. This was the basic cause of the Orgreave tragedy.

The lack of success of the miners' strike after months of struggle had an effect on party members. During the first few months there was a hope that, even though the strike was not solid, nonetheless victory over Thatcher was not too distant. At this time our members were very active with the miners in the obvious political task of building support for organising mass pickets. But after eight or so months and no victory yet in sight, the clarity of the way forward became blurred. The question of plain survival for the miners' families—in the main through food—was beginning to raise its head.

For some of our eager young comrades this was a distraction from the main political thrust. They poured scorn on collections for food. Tins of beans, in their view, were for hurling at policemen. Some comrades, particularly older and more experienced ones, were becoming uneasy over the exclusive stress on mass pickets and saw the need for more straightforward financial and material support for miners and their families. A feud developed between the 'Young Turks' and older comrades. The former were not clear that a revolutionary party has to be sensitive to what workers need.

In this area Chanie was very quick and sharp. She had been closely involved with miners in Kent and Yorkshire since the start of the strike. A number stayed in our house for long periods. She became abruptly aware of the change in the type of support needed one day at a Yorkshire miner's house. He sat down to the evening meal with his young son and his wife brought in a plate of peas for each. When he said, 'OK, now what's for supper?' she said, 'That was supper.' Chanie was shocked and realised that to keep the strike going the need was to help miners to survive. In other words collections needed to be taken, not for mass picketing, but for food.

A few months later, at Christmas, some of SWP's fiercest upholders of emphasis on mass pickets were collecting teddy bears and other toys for the miners' kids, and food parcels for their families. This was a remarkable sight, showing how the right line, cutting with the grain of workers' requirements, can change even the most hidebound people. Some comrades forget that, while the party has to teach the workers, it has above all to listen to them, to learn from them.

The SWP response to Bennism

The situation was so complicated that it raised a whole number of questions. There were points of reference in the past that helped us think about it. The Independent Labour Party, for example, was founded in 1893, after the defeat of important New Unionism strikes (such as the Manningham Mills strike in Bradford). We knew that those movements were like the ripples that continue long after the stone has dropped in the water. Once you knew that these were ripples rather than the stone itself you were less impressed. One example of our relationship to the Bennite movement was the misnamed 'Debate of the Decade' which took place in Central Hall Westminster and which, though dominated by the Bennites, had an SWP speaker. Tariq Ali argued there that if the next Labour government did not advance towards socialism then there would be a need for an independent socialist party. Duncan Hallas, from the floor, spoke to say, 'What "if" is there about it? We have already had five Labour governments and none of them have advanced towards socialism!'

For us the key problem was saying what had to be done, and then explaining what were the impediments to this happening. The impediments were Labourism, the trade union bureaucracy and the influence of these two on the workers. It required a high level of argument and of theory. We concentrated on the three Rs—routine (of intervention), recruitment and retention.

This was in sharp contrast to the sort of things we had been doing in the 1960s and early 1970s. Now we did not have high expectations, yet neither did we think nothing could be done. We managed to retain the cadres and improve their quality—to operate in this difficult situation they had to know more and have confidence in putting difficult arguments. One example of the change was in the relative weights of intra-branch and extra-branch life. During the upturn our branch meetings had been mainly opportunities to get together to organise activities going on outside the meeting. Theoretical discussion, while never absent, was often in the second half of the meeting, after the key interventions had been sorted out. Now meetings began with a weightier political introduction and activities were discussed in the second half. The latter tended to be much briefer and concentrated on the branch routine of selling papers and so on. Indeed the geographical branch meeting became far more important than it had been to the life of the party.

Chapter 10

Looking ahead

Neither upturn nor downturn

After the 1987 general election there was a modest rise in industrial activity fuelled by the Lawson boom and a general feeling of prosperity. For example, Ford workers showed a level of militancy in 1988 that had not been seen for years. The next year public sector workers were out. In the engineering industry a successful campaign for shorter working hours was conducted. Industrial struggle in the 1990s has been at a historically low level. Yet, as Lindsey German has argued:

> At the same time it is clear that at least sections of workers are not on the defensive in the way that they were a few years ago. And even those in the public sector, much more under pressure from wage restraint and cuts in services, are very resilient, as in the case of the ambulance workers or local government workers.[1]

Today the industrial scene is very mixed indeed. It looks like a mosaic of contradictory colours. To illustrate this: recently two strikes took place in London with extremely different results, the Jubilee Line electricians and the Lufthansa catering workers. The electricians won their strike, achieving a hefty wage rise, notwithstanding the readiness of the employers to spend millions on beating them. The catering workers got the sack en masse and were replaced by scab labour. The victory of the former was rooted in the tightened labour market in their area of work; one cannot easily find highly skilled electricians to lay the cables in the underground. There is no difficulty in finding workers able to make sandwiches. The different outcomes of the two strikes did not depend on the leadership of the unions to which the workers belonged: the electricians belonged to the AEEU whose president is the extreme right winger and Blairite Ken Jackson, while the catering workers belonged to the TGWU, whose general secretary is the left wing Bill Morris. Alas, there was no osmosis between the Jubilee Line strike and the Lufthansa strike: the victory of the one did not bring any salvation to the other. And the picture of a mosaic with contradictory colours is bound to continue until a real massive upheaval in the class struggle takes place.

In general one can say that the level of workers' activity is not commensurate with the level of bitterness in the class. Under such conditions the anger and frustration are bound to arise, and this must lead to an explosion. The molecular process of change in the working class goes on and on. It is difficult to gauge it and to know when the violent outbreaks will take place. The last couple of decades in Britain remind one very much of the situation in France in the years before the biggest strike in world history took place there.

In 1968 ten million French workers went on strike, and occupied the factories. The event was totally unexpected, because the general strike did not follow on a growing wave of strikes. It was not like 1905 in Russia, where there were warning signs, or in Britain in 1972 and 1974. No—1968 was a break in the continuity: there were right wing governments for many years and the workers were on the retreat. The unions were very weak, but then enough was enough. Because of the brutality of the riot police in Paris, the whole thing exploded. It is quite interesting that, a couple of months before the May events, a French Marxist, André Gorz, wrote an essay in which he argued that no mass strikes are possible in advanced industrial society.

Following the French events, I wrote:

For decades Marxists used to infer the state of mass consciousness from a few institutional barometers—membership of organisations, readership of papers, etc. The deep alienation of workers from traditional organisations eroded all such barometers. This is why there was no way of detecting the imminence of the upheaval in May 1968. And also, more important, it explains the extreme, explosive nature of the events. If the workers in France had been accustomed to participate in a branch of the trade unions or the Communist Party, these institutions would have served both as an aid and as ballast, preventing the rapid uncontrolled spread of the strike movement. The concept of apathy or privatisation is not a static concept. At a certain stage of development—when the path of individual reforms is being narrowed, or closed—apathy can transform into its opposite, swift mass action. However, this new turn comes as an outgrowth of the previous stage; the epilogue and the prologue combine. Workers who have lost their loyalty to the traditional organisations, which have shown themselves to be paralysed over the years, are forced into extreme, explosive struggles on their own.

Traditional barometers are missing. The policies of the bosses and the state, as well as those of the trade union bureaucrats, are much less sure, much more vacillating, than before. Their reaction, even to marginal challenges, may be unexpected, brutal and seemingly irrational.[2]

Ideological agitators

If, at present, industrial action gives little immediate scope for our activity, the same certainly does not apply to the battle for ideas. We have referred earlier to the contrast Plekhanov drew between agitation and propaganda. Propaganda brings forward a number of ideas to a small number of people; agitation brings one or a couple of ideas to many people, leading to action. However, history shows that there is no Chinese wall between the two. As a matter of fact the battle of ideas can involve masses of people.

This consideration applies to the collapse of the Stalinist regime in Russia and Eastern Europe and the disappearance of Thatcher from the political scene in Britain. In regard to the first, from the beginning of our group the definition of Russia and Eastern Europe as state capitalist countries has been crucial.

As for the second issue, the battle of ideas has also been spurred on by the end of Thatcher which marked the end of the downturn. After winning the 1987 general election, Margaret Thatcher introduced the poll tax, christening it 'the flagship of the Conservative government'. Only an arrogant person out of touch with the ordinary people could believe that a tax that took the same amount from the duke and the dustman would be popular. Yet the current Labour leaders, Neil Kinnock and Roy Hattersley, condemned poll tax nonpayers. At the same time Margaret Hodge, leader of Islington council, who had declared in her earlier Bennite period that Islington was a citadel of socialism, now sent bailiffs to collect the poll tax. Despite all of this pressure, 11 million people evaded paying. Nobody could save the poll tax. And once it had gone nobody could save Thatcher.

The collapse of Thatcher signified, not an upturn in the industrial struggle, but the end of government confidence to go on the offensive against workers. Since then, while we are not in an upturn we are not still in a downturn.

In this general crisis of ideas the situation demands that we produce ideological agitators, a very apt term coined by Sean Venell while Manchester organiser of the SWP.

The circumstances of the 1990s made this a necessary turn for the party. The Tories' poll tax debacle was a symptom of a deeper process. In the 1990s the Tories' government was unable to continue to carry out the Ridley Plan of 'salami tactics' which had been so successful in the 1980s in attacking one group of workers at a time. And so, with the deepening economic crisis, the Tories opened up a wide front against practically everyone at one and the same time. The last years of the Tory government saw a sea change among workers in Britain. Not only the poll tax, but the Gulf War, and the pit closures programme of 1992 were a watershed that was followed by a series of mass demonstrations against the Nazis and the Criminal Justice Bill. This helped to create a sense of common cause and unity against the Tories among different groups of workers both young and old.

It was during this period that the SWP managed to break out of its previously necessary stress on propaganda characteristic of the 1980s. Now we were campaigning around the estates while setting up anti poll tax groups, building a united front against the Nazis, and campaigning within the unions and on the streets, shouting, 'Sack Major, not the miners!' We came out of these campaigns having deepened our influence and earned greater respect within the working class, and enjoying the biggest ever growth in membership, doubling it from 5,000 to 10,000 and doubling the number of branches to about 300.

Since the landslide victory of Labour in 1997 the shift to the left has continued. Now the anger is directed against Blair, not the Tories, and the sense of bitterness and betrayal is deepening all the time. This has led to a significant widening of the audience for our ideas.

It is in this context that we have learned to be 'ideological agitators'—a phrase which straddles a period of low level of generalised resistance with a leftward moving and politicised working class. When Engels argued that the class struggle takes place in three arenas— the economic, the ideological and the political—this did not mean that the three were completely separate from each other, nor that they were synchronised, or even went in the same direction. Two examples demonstrate this.

The British trade unions came into being long before the Russian ones, but the ideology dominating them was far more conservative than that dominating the Russian unions. Thus the Amalgamated Society of Engineers, which was founded in 1852, only organised male workers. It took 91 years and two world wars, with hundreds of thousands of women entering engineering, for the union to change its mind. Only in 1943 were women allowed into the engineering union, but even then there was discrimination against women; they were not allowed into the main branches, but were recruited into a special section, Section 5! Economic struggle preceded ideological struggle in Britain. But in Russia women and men were organised together from the beginning!

An example of workers moving massively forward ideologically while they lagged behind on the industrial front was France in the years 1934-35. The coming to power of Hitler in 1933 and the heroic but brutally suppressed resistance of Viennese workers to fascism affected the mood of workers in Paris. In the same month that the Viennese workers rose there was a bloody confrontation between socialists and communists on the one hand and a band of fascists on the other. A massive anti-fascist movement rose. As a consequence of this, in May 1936, the Popular Front government of Leon Blum was elected on a wave of left wing support. It was only now, several years after the rise in the level of ideological struggle that the economic movement made a giant stride forward with a mass occupation of the factories.

Of course a dogmatic Marxist would have said to Russian or French workers, 'Tut, tut. You are wrong to act like this. You should have begun with wage demand and only then moved on to the ideological struggle.'

Ideological agitation tries to connect the struggle for reforms here and now, however small, with general socialist ideas. Over the last few years we managed to increase our influence in the working class, firstly through being the best 'fighters for reform', knowing that any one of us makes a difference: fighting the privatisation of housing estates, stopping a refugee from being deported, defending a worker from being victimised. All these small, localised issues, in which the party is continuously involved, quite often successfully, have deepened the respect and influence of our organisation within the working class.

We managed to root ourselves ideologically by agitating over ideas, and not just campaigning around issues—through public debates ranging from economics and the Labour Party to postmodernism.

Through the *Socialist Worker* May Day rallies the party was the organisation that was able to re-establish the internationalist tradition. We managed to get significant trade union sponsors for these events, thus reflecting the move to the left of the class, and the inability of a left-reformist organisation to match up to it at present. The May Day rallies were also important for the party, because they managed to pull all the different aspects of the period and the party work within them together. The rallies acted as a cement between the ideological nature of the period and the agitational opportunities which on the night reflect the continuing growth of the SWP locally both in quantitative and qualitative terms.

One important demonstration of our success of combining our general politics with ideological agitation were the three successful lobbies of the Labour Party conference in 1997, 1998 and 1999.

Campaigning as ideological agitators is preparing the SWP to face the coming upturn in the struggle when all-round agitation is required.

A further impetus to the ideological struggle has been given by the coming to office of Tony Blair. Blair is by far the most ideological leader of the Labour Party ever. Where previous leaders sought to fudge the contradiction between the interest of workers and capitalism, Blair is the most enthusiastic proponent of the free market, of more privatisation, of enthusiasm for the 'wealth creators' (a pseudonym for the fat cats). He has been an enthusiastic warrior involving Britain in bombing Iraq and Yugoslavia in his short tenure of office. Lindsey German writes:

> All those who most identified with Labour's aspirations—for greater equality and fairness, for a curbing of the bosses' worst excesses, for ending the worst poverty in generations—now find themselves disappointed at the lack of change. Those traditionally most hostile to Labour—big business, the press, the champions of free enterprise— are pleasantly surprised that their wealth and power have been left untouched and that New Labour will do anything to appease 'enterprise' and the 'free market'.[3]

Evidence of the depth of disillusion with new Labour and of the opportunities opening up for the revolutionary left was furnished by the lobbies of the last two Labour Party conferences. In September

1997, some four months after the general election, 8,000 people came to lobby the Labour Party conference, meeting in Brighton; a year later a lobby of 12,000 encircled the Labour Party conference in Blackpool. Looking at the scene, I commented, 'A sea of revolutionaries surround an island of reformism.'

Labour voters are so far to the left of the government that a large space is created for real socialists. The weakness of the left of the Labour Party and the practical disappearance of revolutionary organisations that existed thirty years ago with the exception of the SWP, leaves the field wide open to us.

Building the IS tendency internationally

One aspect of my life not covered so far is international work. Of course I wanted to build our tendency not only in Britain, but also in other countries. My most important contribution was the writing and publishing of *State Capitalism in Russia*. It is encouraging that the book has been translated into a number of languages besides English: German, French, Russian, Polish, Spanish, Italian, Greek, Turkish, Farsi (in Iran), Arabic, Japanese, Korean, Bengali.

As an aside, the odyssey of the Russian edition is interesting. The English edition came out in 1955. In 1956 the KGB, of all bodies, got the book translated into Russian and printed. It was kept in a sealed section of the library, and one could not get hold of the book without a special permit. I found all this out when, under Gorbachev, a student photocopied the book with a camera hidden in the palm of his hand. The couple of hundred photographs reached me. In 1991, when the comrades were going to publish the book in the normal way, we found that the KGB edition was a very good translation, so there was no need for a new one. I still wonder why the hell the KGB made the original translation!

Some others of my writings were also translated into foreign languages. Thus, in 1975, after the Portuguese Revolution, I wrote a thick pamphlet, specially shaped for the Portuguese Revolutionaries, entitled *Portugal at the Crossroads*. The pamphlet was published in Portuguese, Spanish, French, Greek, Italian, German and English. Recently I wrote a special pamphlet for Indonesian comrades, entitled *Revolution and Counter-Revolution: Lessons for Indonesia*. We produced it in pamphlet form in English; it has now been produced in Indonesian.[4]

Again and again I wrote articles for our German, French and Turkish comrades. But the literary activities did not fully satisfy me.

Nazism and Stalinism so devastated the revolutionary working class movement that we had to start practically from scratch. In the desert it was necessary to nurture every seedling carefully, and for a long time. I would have liked to do in other countries what I did in Britain in the long days, months, years of the 1950s. I would have liked to go and stay for a few months in France and then in other countries. But this I could not do, as, since 1961, I have had no passport and so cannot travel abroad. Hence my participation in building our tendency internationally was very restricted, and mostly telephonic.

However, it is possible to draw up a balance sheet for our efforts to build the IS Tendency internationally. Alex Callinicos, SWP International Secretary, has done this:

Initially an organisation as tiny as the Socialist Review Group could not hope for significant contacts abroad, particularly since it rejected the pretensions of the 'Fourth International'. In the late 1960s the emergence of the International Socialists in the United States did offer the British IS a sister organisation. The two groups, however, had developed quite independently. The American IS came out of the Shachtmanite tradition, which viewed the Stalinist societies as examples of a new form of class society, bureaucratic collectivism. It had developed from the wing of Shachtman's group that had rejected his growing accommodation with American imperialism, participating in the student struggles of the 1960s, supporting the anti-war movement, and seeking to find a way of relating to the working class.

The upturn of the late 1960s and early 1970s dramatically changed the situation. May 1968 in France, the Italian hot autumn of 1969, the Portuguese Revolution of 1974-75, and the struggles that marked the end of Francoism in Spain created favourable circumstances for the rapid development of far-left organisations each of which, like the British IS by the early 1970s, could claim thousands of members and which began to win a hearing from a growing minority of working-class militants. In some cases these organisations came out of the orthodox Trotskyist tradition—for example, the Fourth International groups in France and Spain, and the French group Lutte Ouvrière. The biggest organisations, however, in Italy and the Iberian peninsula were influenced to a greater or lesser extent by Maoism, which appeared, particularly as a result of the

Cultural Revolution of the late 1960s, to represent a revolutionary alternative to both the official Communist Parties and social democracy.

The international work of the IS developed in two strands during the 1970s. In the first place, the very existence of the IS as a dynamic and growing revolutionary organisation encouraged the formation of groups elsewhere—notably in Ireland, West Germany, Australia and Canada. This was an unplanned process usually resulting from the initiative of individuals who had spent some time in Britain (or, in the case of Australia, a supporter of the American IS). The emergence of what later came to be known as the IS Tendency was largely confined to the English-speaking world in the 1970s and did not, at this stage, lead to the development of groups of any size or influence.

Secondly, the IS leadership pursued a conscious policy of developing political dialogue with some of the big European far left organisations. This approach was guided by the search for groups which, irrespective of their formal politics, seemed to pursue in practice a serious orientation to the working class and in particular towards rank and file struggles. This more or less ruled out the organisations affiliated to the United Secretariat of the Fourth International, then in any case preoccupied with a bitter factional struggle between its American and European sections. An effort to develop a relationship with Lutte Ouvrière proved abortive despite this group's extremely serious approach to factory work. Its theoretical conservatism (it remained wedded to the post-war Fourth International's view of the USSR as a workers' state and Eastern Europe as capitalist) and organisational sectarianism made it an impossible partner.

In the mid-1970s, therefore, the IS devoted its main efforts to seeking to win over organisations from non-Trotskyist traditions. These included so called 'soft Maoist' organisations which seemed more open minded than the hard Marxist-Leninist sects and which were making serious efforts to build a working class base—notably Avanguardia Operaia (AO) in Italy and Révolution in France as well as the PRP-BR (Party of the Revolutionary Proletariat-Revolutionary Brigades) in Portugal. This latter had a Guevarist past but seemed to be serious in its insistence that only the working class could emancipate itself.

Alas, these efforts proved to be wholly unsuccessful. Two main factors were involved. First and most important, we gravely underestimated the power of political tradition. The politics in which the cadres of the PRP and AO were formed ultimately stemmed from Stalinism.

Despite the subjectively sincere efforts to break with this, they remained deeply under its influence, particularly in pursuing the politics of substitutionism—looking, in other words, towards an agency other than the working class to achieve change. For example, AO, having been enthusiasts for building rank and file 'base committees' outside the unions at the height of the factory militancy of the early 1970s, began, as the tide receded, to put their hopes in electoral politics and in a left government led by the Communist Party of Italy which they believed the far left could influence.

Our roots in the revolutionary Marxist tradition allowed us to see the flaws in these attempted short cuts. In text after text translated into Portuguese (and in some cases other European languages) we insisted that there was no substitute for the tough work of building a base within the working class from which revolutionaries could begin to challenge the reformists for the ear of the majority. But we had not simply underestimated the strength of tradition. What authority could our arguments claim? When the Bolsheviks launched the Third International, their claim to lead was based on having led a successful socialist revolution. With our three or four thousand members in the mid-1970s we were smaller than the biggest Italian far left organisations, which at this time had between them 30,000 members and three daily papers. We were also operating in a country which, despite the strikes under the Heath government, seemed a lot less revolutionary than southern Europe. When Chris Harman met the leaders of the Spanish and Maoist organisation MC they asked him whether he really thought there could be a revolution in Britain and laughed when he said, 'Yes'.

The failure of our orientation on the continental far left did not mean that we were mistaken to have attempted it. Faced with the very rapid development of big revolutionary organisations, we had no alternative but to attempt to influence them. No doubt we were naive in our belief that this attempt could achieve results, particularly in the very fast moving situation of the mid-1970s, and no doubt we made various specific mistakes, but we were right to have tried. The most important thing was to learn the lessons of the experience. These were twofold: first, large organisations with long established traditions are very hard to influence; secondly, the only sure basis on which to build a group on the basis of our politics is to win individuals who fully understand this politics and are willing to work on its basis (and even then there are many pitfalls).

The real price for the substitutionist politics of the PRP and the soft Maoists was paid by the far left throughout the continent. In country after country the reformist bureaucracy was able to contain workers' struggles. As downturn succeeded upturn, the European revolutionary left went into profound crisis. Without exception, the soft Maoist organisations fell apart. The orthodox Trotskyist groups proved more resilient, but most experienced a severe decline in size and influence.

Despite our own internal crisis in the late 1970s, the SWP was able to hold together—thanks to the intrinsic strength of our tradition and the development of an analysis which identified and explained the downturn. However, we now found ourselves in a very different context, one in which we were now one of the largest surviving far left organisations in Europe.

Our international work reflected this changed situation. We began to focus much more on the IS Tendency. The experience of the 1970s encouraged a 'bottom up' approach starting from individuals or groups already committed to our politics. The Tendency itself was developing. In practice, the different groups moved, to a large extent independently, towards the kind of propaganda approach we evolved in the early 1980s.

Particularly important here was the ISO in the US, formed in 1977 from a split from the American IS (which in the mid-1970s developed its own form of substitutionism based on a policy of 'industrialisation'— building a working class base by sending students to work in factories). After an internal dispute in 1983 which reflected, in part, the influence of the British SWP, the ISO developed an approach of building on the basis of independent socialist propaganda and organisation which set it apart from the rest of the American left, which was rapidly disappearing into the Democratic Party, the union bureaucracy, and the academy.

From 1984 onwards the IS Tendency began to hold annual meetings in London. This reflected both the convergence of the different groups on a similar propaganda perspective and closer contacts arising in particular from more frequent speaking tours abroad by leading members of the SWP. The discussions at these meetings concentrated on the clarification of particular political issues and on problems of building. If there was a unifying slogan it was Trotsky's formula 'the primitive accumulation of cadres': with the class struggle at a low ebb in the advanced capitalist countries, the main task was to create in as many countries as possible an organised nucleus of revolutionaries rooted in our tradition and capable of relating to new workers' battles as they developed.

Collectively we were strong enough to weather the impact of the collapse of Stalinism and to respond very strongly to the outbreak of the Second Gulf War in 1991. Our organisations consistently played an active role in the mass anti-war movements which briefly emerged. This marked the beginning of a period in which we sought as a tendency to push outwards to seize the opportunities offered by a period in which the worst of the upturn was over, even though plainly there was no real downturn in workers' struggles. This changed situation was reflected particularly in the process of intense class polarisation that developed in continental Europe and to some extent in Ontario in Canada in the mid-1990s.

This emphasis on the Tendency did not mean that we ignored opportunities to relate to other far left groups where they presented themselves. Our greatest success came in Greece. The Socialist Revolution Organisation (OSE), now SEK, had its origins in a group of Greek students in London in the late 1960s. Here they were influenced by us. But, particularly after they returned to Greece with the fall of the dictatorship in 1974, they were also drawn towards the soft Maoist politics of AO in neighbouring Italy. After SWP supporters precipitated a misguided split, we lost contact with OSE during the first half of the 1980s.

In 1985 Panos Garganas and Maria Styllou visited Britain and resumed contact with us. They had just succeeded in reuniting OSE, but it was a tiny group of 40 facing big competition from the autonomists and the surviving Maoists in a political environment dominated by the reformist organisations—the Communist Party and PASOK. Remarkably, the OSE comrades succeeded in taking advantage of the situation in Greece, where workers' struggles have been more intense than elsewhere in Western Europe since the mid-1980s, to see off its rivals and build a substantial revolutionary organisation. SEK, with about 1,500 members, is now the second largest organisation in the Tendency.

The decisive factor was not, however, the objective situation, but rather the existence of a strong political leadership with the capacity to seize the opportunities offered by circumstances—first student struggles, then later the crisis in the Communist Party, the right wing ND government of the early 1990s, and more recently the evolution of PASOK in a Blairite modernising direction. This process has been accompanied by a political drawing together of OSE and the IS Tendency—though initially there were fierce disagreements, for example, over the SWP's line of supporting Iran against Iraq in the final stages of the first Gulf War in 1987-88. The OSE comrades discovered in practice that the politics and the experience of the SWP in particular were relevant to their own situation. After attending our international meetings for several years, they formally joined the Tendency at the end of the 1980s. Their contributions to discussions within the Tendency have consistently been of great importance, as has the practical example of their success.

A very important breakthrough beyond the advanced capitalist countries came at the end of the 1980s when we came into contact with South Korean socialists. Accident played a large role here—the fact that a Korean student studying theology in California during the early 1980s happened on some Bookmarks publications. The collapse of the Stalinist regimes threw the South Korean left, hitherto largely wedded to the Kim Il-sung regime in the North, into profound crisis. The failed Moscow coup of August 1991 played a decisive role in winning some outstanding individuals to building a group based on the theory of state capitalism. They have sustained the International Socialists of South Korea through successive waves of repression that have seen many comrades serving jail sentences.

Yet for successes like those in Greece and South Korea, there have been several failures. Our prolonged dialogue with Sosyalist Isci in Turkey, for example, failed ultimately because we were unable to break the hold of the Turkish left's Stalinist traditions on key individuals who, while subjectively wishing to reject Stalinism, still showed the influence of these traditions in their practice. And there are many other cases of groups which have failed to develop beyond small discussion circles or which, after seeming to break through beyond this stage, have subsequently slipped back. Primitive accumulation is an uncertain process: some small firms develop into huge multinationals, but most stay small or go bust.

The explanation of these failures is not objective—the ISSK in South Korea has been able to build in desperately difficult circumstances. Nor do they stem primarily from mistakes made by the IS Tendency collectively or by the SWP as the leading group in the Tendency

—though we have made plenty of mistakes. Our own experience in Britain and that of organisations such as SEK shows that everything depends on the existence of a hard core of individuals rooted in the revolutionary tradition and having the determination, energy, capacity, and commitment to build an organisation, however long it takes and however tough the situation. Where this core exists, there is a reasonable chance of success. Where it does not—and there is no simple or artificial way of creating it—then, however promising the context, the group will not flourish.

Alex's argument shows that to build the vital core needs a lot of moral courage and, most particularly, perseverance. I have no doubt that if I could have travelled, I could have helped the process more. To a great extent this makes me a passive onlooker, a spectator—in juxtaposition to Lenin's concept of active, hands-on leadership. To get a letter or a phone call from comrades abroad is not the same as spending time with them face to face.

I feel frustrated at not being able to do more. I became especially green with envy when Chanie, Donny and tens of other comrades went to Portugal in 1975, after the overthrow of the fascist regime.

Failure to convince the Portuguese PRP

The 44 year old fascist regime in Portugal was overthrown by the armed forces on 25 April 1974. This came about because the army had faced a very prolonged war against the people of the Portuguese colonies—Angola, Mozambique, and the smaller Guinea-Bissau. The army could not win the war, and the cost was prohibitive. Half the budget of the country was spent on the colonial war. The 25 April armed forces uprising was followed by the mass of workers entering the arena: a wave of massive strikes followed the collapse of the fascist regime.

Among the Portuguese organisations, the one nearest to us was the PRP. Tens of our comrades went to Portugal and tried to influence the PRP. Alas, we found it very difficult. The organisation was a very closed, conspiratorial group.

It is true it declared itself for the dictatorship of the proletariat, for workers' self activity. But it was a Guevarist organisation. Armed action by a small group was central to its activities. For a number of years the PRP-BR had carried out armed actions against the fascists and the colonial apparatus, including the blowing up of a NATO base, destroying trucks destined for the colonial wars, and trying to blow up power lines on May Day 1973.

The PRP's healthy emphasis on self activity by the proletariat was accompanied by a lack of clarity about the relations between the revolutionary party and the proletariat.

Armed struggle of a tiny organisation of a few tens or hundreds has nothing to do with the self emancipation of the working class with arms in hand. Trotsky led the Red Army of millions, but he never led a terrorist group. The Guevarists have far more in common with Blanquists than with Marxists. Blanqui, the 19th century French revolutionary, did not trust the rank and file workers and thought that they, the minority, would have to act for the majority: 'We will do the job of emancipating the working class.' A classic example of Blanquism took place on 12 May 1839, when Blanqui led his 1,200 or so armed followers in Paris into the streets to overthrow the monarchy. His 'Provisional Government' proclamation read:

> To arms, Citizens!
>
> The fatal hour has sounded for the oppressors...
>
> The Provisional Government has chosen the military to direct the struggle.
>
> These people have come from your ranks; follow them—they will lead you to victory.
>
> Forward! Long live the Republic!

This coup was quite successful at first. It had been very well prepared, in a technical sense. Key government buildings were occupied. But the whole operation had been prepared in the utmost secrecy. No political preparations had been carried out. The great mass of the working population of Paris knew nothing of Blanqui's plan. They were completely ignorant, not just of the technical plan, which had to be secret, but also of the political and social aims of the movement. They remained inactive. The government rallied, brought in reliable troops and the rising was crushed. It was not that the Paris workers of that time were incapable of revolutionary action. Far from it. In 1830 and again in 1848 they overthrew the regime. But in both cases a political ferment among them preceded the insurrection.

Because in April 1974 the revolutionary influence in the armed forces was greater than among the workers, the PRP looked to a group of 400 middle ranking officers who were organised in the Armed

Forces Movement for action. As the PRP fraternal delegate to the IS Annual conference in June 1975 said, 'Some officers are supporting these slogans...for autonomous revolutionary councils...the councils will open up the way to the dictatorship of the proletariat'.[5]

This statement is analogous to the views of left reformists regarding the trade union bureaucracy. Of course there is a difference between right wing trade union leaders and left wing ones. Hugh Scanlon, the left wing president of the AEU in the 1960s and 1970s was different to his successor, the right winger Terry Duffy. But revolutionary socialists do not rely on any bureaucrat to lead the working class in its struggle for emancipation. The rank and file in the Portuguese armed forces had far less control over the officers than members of trade unions have over their officials. The belief that army officers can bring about socialism is an elitist fantasy even more incredible than the belief that bureaucrats and MPs can advance socialism.

Focusing on the armed forces while neglecting the building of a mass revolutionary party among workers created a great danger for the Portuguese Revolution. As I wrote in October 1975:

> The great weakness of the revolutionary movement is the unevenness of the soldiers and the workers. The workers lag behind the soldiers... The conservative influence of the Communist Party is incomparably greater among the workers than among the soldiers. The unevenness cannot go on forever. If the workers will not rise to the level of the revolutionary soldiers, there is a great danger the soldiers' level of consciousness will sag down to the lower level of the workers... The soldiers will be wary of marching forward on their own to seize state power. An insurrection not supported by the mass of workers will not appeal to them.[6]

Relying on progressive middle ranking officers was a great mistake. A mass revolutionary party is tested daily in the struggle. The members of the party and the party as a whole can be judged and steeled. Lenin, who was destined to lead the only successful mass proletarian insurrection, explained how the organisation of the revolutionary party dovetails with preparations for an armed insurrection. He wrote in 1902:

> Picture to yourselves a popular uprising. Probably everyone will now agree that we must think of this and prepare for it. But how? Surely the Central Committee cannot appoint agents to all localities for the purpose

of preparing the uprising! Even if we had a Central Committee it could achieve absolutely nothing by such appointments under present day Russian conditions. But a network of agents that would form in the course of establishing and distributing the common newspaper would not have to 'sit about and wait' for the call for an uprising, but could carry on the regular activity that would strengthen our contacts with the broadest strata of the working masses and with all social strata that are discontented with the autocracy, which is of such importance for an uprising. Precisely such activity would serve to cultivate the ability to estimate correctly the general political situation, and consequently, the ability to select the proper moment for an uprising. Precisely such activity would train all local organisations to respond simultaneously to the same political question, incidents and events that agitate the whole of Russia and to react to such 'incidents' in the most vigorous, uniform and expedient manner possible; for an uprising is in essence the most vigorous, most uniform and most expedient answer of the entire people to the government. Lastly, it is precisely such activity that would train all revolutionary organisations throughout Russia to maintain the most continuous, and at the same time most secret, contacts with one another, thus creating real party unity; for without such contacts it will be impossible collectively to discuss the plan for the uprising and to take the necessary preparatory measures on its eve, measures that must be kept in the strictest secrecy.[7]

The writings of Lenin on the subject of the revolutionary party and the insurrection should have been a field book for the PRP. Instead, the PRP relied on COPCON, a special detachment of the armed forces regularly used for internal security purposes, the most radicalised section of the army. The commander of COPCON was General Otelo Carvalho. The PRP had great illusions in Otelo, notwithstanding the fact that he had broken into tears five years earlier at the funeral of the fascist dictator Salazar.

Chris Harman writes:

The PRP stressed the technical, armed preparation for socialist revolution far more than the political mobilisation of the masses. Its members became increasingly concerned with arms training, while its paper was neglected in 1975 to such an extent that it came out only roughly every three weeks—when events were changing by the day, if not the hour—and was written in a style remote from most worker activists. The party's leaders put more effort into trying to influence leftward-moving army officers than trying to win workers away from the Communist and Socialist parties.[8]

The PRP hardly grew between April 1974 and November 1975. It remained an organisation of a couple of hundred. Compare this to Lenin's effort to build a mass party during the revolutions of 1905 and 1917. At the Third Congress, in the spring of 1905, Lenin proposed a resolution urging the party to open its gates wide to workers:

> ...who should be brought forward to take a leading role in it, to make every effort to strengthen the ties between the party and the masses of the working class by raising still wider the sections of proletarians and semi-proletarians to full [revolutionary socialist] consciousness, by developing their revolutionary...activity, by seeing to it that the greatest possible number of workers capable of leading the movement and the party organisations be advanced from among the mass of the working class to membership on the local centres and on the all-party centre through the creation of a maximum number of working-class organisations adhering to our party, by seeing to it that working-class organisations unwilling or unable to enter the party should at least be associated with it.[9]

And the Bolshevik Party expanded massively. By 1907 it had 46,143 members. During the 1917 Revolution the membership expanded even more swiftly. Thus, for instance, in Saratov, at the beginning of March there were 60 party members, at the end of July 3,000; in Kiev the corresponding figures were 200 and 4,000; in Ekaterinburg 40 and 2,800; in Moscow 600 and 15,000; in Petrograd 2,000 and 36,000.

The revolutionary paper played a crucial role in building the organisation and increasing its influence in the class. On 4 April 1912 the Lena massacre took place, to be followed by a massive rise in working class struggle. On 22 April the Bolsheviks launched their daily paper, *Pravda*. Prior to the publication of this paper the Bolsheviks had a weekly paper called *Zvezda*, although quite often it appeared twice or three times a week. When the First World War broke out the tsarist authorities proscribed the paper. With the February Revolution, the Bolsheviks revived *Pravda*, and in addition started a new paper for the armed forces, *Soldatskaya Pravda*. Compare this with the cavalier attitude of the PRP to their paper, *Revolucao*. Formally it was a weekly paper, but as noted above, appeared much less often, and this in the midst of a revolution.

The Portuguese Revolution ended in defeat. On 24 November 1975 Otelo de Carvalho was removed from the leadership of the Lisbon military region, an obvious blow against the left. On 25 November the paras seized control of five barracks in the Lisbon area, while other troops loyal to the government took control of the radio and TV stations. This attack from the right did not meet with any serious resistance.

A Portuguese revolutionary explained two days later why there was so little resistance:

> There was no coordination, no real coordination... One of the military police told me these soldiers were prepared and organised for an insurrection, for socialist revolution. As soon as the two commanders disappeared, they did not know what to do. There wasn't anyone to give orders. Although the soldiers were refusing military discipline they did not know how to operate in any other way.
>
> At the light artillery barracks the soldiers wanted to do something, but they lacked military direction—their commander had surrendered.
>
> The so-called revolutionary officers are finished.[10]

Chris Harman writes:

> The revolutionary left did want to resist the right, but did not know how to do so effectively...their obsession with the purely military aspect of things meant they did not know how to react... The left wing units were disarmed on 25 November because the workers looked to the armed forces to act for them, and inside the armed forces the rank and file looked to the progressive officers for a lead.[11]

Sadly we in IS did not manage to influence the PRP. I am told that the delegate of the PRP to our conference was convinced by our arguments. Alas, he was removed from the leadership when he returned to Portugal. We had no core of Portuguese comrades in agreement with us.

Although disappointed by our failure, I was not really surprised. Chanie, on returning from Portugal, told me, 'The PRP have more in common with the IRA than with us.' Being very sensitive to people's moods, she impressed me with her judgment.

Linksruck—a success story

If Portugal was a failure in terms of SWP efforts to exert influence internationally, Germany is an example of some success. At the beginning of the 1990s great possibilities were opened for revolutionaries in Germany. Massive demonstrations took place against the Gulf War. Under increasing economic pressure in 1992 Kohl attacked the mighty ÖTV public sector union and provoked a two week general strike of 400,000 workers. In order to defeat the social unrest the political right pushed ahead with a nasty campaign against asylum seekers. A terrible wave of Nazi murders and the rise of the fascist Republikaner Party were the effects. The shock again provoked a determined response, especially by the youth. Several millions took to the streets to protest against racist terror and fascism.

For the German IS group, the Sozialistische Arbeitergruppe (SAG), a phase of enormous possibilities opened up. For the first time in decades revolutionaries could break through the wall isolating themselves and their ideas from the rest of society. Unfortunately the subjective factor was not able to rise to the objective opportunities. Since the early 1970s the SAG had been a tiny group. During the long downturn it almost disintegrated. Towards the end of the 1980s it rebuilt itself to some 100 members, mainly by stressing theoretical propaganda. The SAG was a small, passive, sectarian group.

At the beginning of the 1990s it became clear that massive changes were necessary to match the unfolding situation. A new generation were taking to the streets and some looked for a fighting socialist alternative. The SAG actually managed to recruit a number of individuals out of these movements. But the more youngsters joined the organisation, the more it became obvious that many of the old guard were a brake on the development of a new layer of cadres. On a local level they saw the new comrades as a threat to their old habits of the downturn years, while they were opposed to any kind of determined leadership on a national level. Unfortunately the national leadership itself was not prepared to take sides. Instead of forcing the old cadre either to adapt to the new mood of activism or to leave, it vacillated, hesitated and tried to moderate the developing conflicts.

The collapse of the Stalinist regimes in Eastern Europe, including East Germany, made me follow what was happening in Germany more intensively. When 30,000 people left the SPD in response to the party's agreement to a racist asylum bill, I decided to take the initiative.

I tried to convince the SAG leadership that it had to break from the isolation of the group and build a bridge to the socialist youth. I wrote a letter to the founder and then leader of the SAG, Volkhard Mosler, whom I had know since 1966. I stressed the splits that had occurred inside reformism and told the story of the early IS years in Britain. But apart from a half-hearted and quickly aborted attempt to send some comrades into the SPD's youth organisation—Jungsozialisten (Jusos) in Munich, the leadership showed no initiative.

It was clear to me that the passivity of the SAG had led to its isolation and the isolation increased the passivity. To break the vicious circle, it was necessary to take a decisive step to involve the comrades with the youth. I chose Marxism 1993 (our annual week of discussion and debate in London) to go on the offensive.

Having lost all faith in the old SAG leadership, I sought an alternative and found it in Ahmed Shah, who had joined the SWP in the early 1980s and moved to Hamburg in 1988. As he had recently become a member of the SAG's national leadership I saw the chance to build up a new leadership around him. Ahmed and another four young SAG members joined the Jusos in the summer of 1993 and started to set up an organisational structure independent of the SAG.

I was in very close contact with Ahmed. He is hard, but not rigid, observant of changes in the situation without being empiricist, adaptable without being opportunist. He is really an excellent young leader. Of course he commits mistakes, but he is very quick to correct them, without fuss. Talking to him, I found I was able to grasp the situation in Germany, and the strengths and weaknesses of the new young group. Being a non-German, so to say an outsider, encouraged Ahmed to grasp the essentials. The more complicated the situation, the more vital it is to see the key link in the chain of events, and Ahmed does that very well indeed.

Florian Kirner, editor of the *Linksruck* newspaper, describes some developments since these early beginnings:

> From now on we had to stand on our own feet, outside SAG and inside a totally new environment. The reformist camp! Overcoming the sectarian isolation, characteristic not only of the SAG, but the great bulk of the revolutionary left in Germany, was now a question of sheer existence. This was especially so as our initial five members

had to work in an organisation with—counting all SPD members below the age of 35 as Jusos—135,000 official and something like 8,000-10,000 active members.

In order to pull people around us, we launched a paper called *Linksruck* [*Leftwards*]. Formally, the first editions of the paper were not very impressive. The number of wrongly-spelled words was appalling, and the layout totally dilettante. Far from being disappointed, the dilettantism seemed to satisfy Cliff. It was a break with the passive routinism of recent years, and created an atmosphere around the paper as a platform for young activist rebels. And that was not just fiction! Everybody could write for the paper. A number of 'real' Jusos were invited to do so and the printed articles regularly included political ideas much closer to the SPD than the IS line. Real debates developed round the paper and our activities. And the Jusos-entrists had for the first time to defend their politics against experienced reformist critics, while convincing those young elements who had confused left wing ideas. The connection between Cliff and Ahmed was the crucial factor in the game.

As a first operational base inside Jusos we found 'Arbeitskreise gegen Rechts' [Anti Far Right Workers' Circles] in Hamburg, Munich and Berlin. By various activities against the Nazis, we developed a reputation as good and devoted activists. But there was a permanent effort to extend the number of areas of activity: from anti-fascism to anti-militarism, to the question of the cuts in social services, international issues, etc.

We started to pull a layer of activists around us and Volkhard was persuaded to send another 25 comrades from SAG into the Linksruck Project, making the start of Linksruck branches possible in places like Frankfurt and Cologne.

A routine developed in our branches around selling the paper, and this trained a new cadre in order to force the newly founded branch committees to cling to a disciplined routine.

After successfully having developed Ahmed, Cliff started to search for more contact with the people around Ahmed in order to create a collective leadership.

From that time on it is difficult to point exactly to Cliff's contribution. He was so much part of the leadership, took so close an interest in every detail of our work, and threw himself with such energy into our debates, that his frequent joke of 'being a secret member of the

Bundeskoordination leadership' came very close to reality. To understand why this strong intervention from the outside did not develop a feeling of dependence among the young German leadership, it is important to see how Cliff intervened. We never had the feeling of being pushed to a decision. It was getting told the right story at the right time. But it was always our organisation, our decisions and our experiences that Cliff seemed to modify, sharpen or interpret. He channelled our experience, analysis and ideas into the right direction. It was never like Cliff teaching and we learning. His determination to learn from us and our experience was always apparent. Of course Cliff's role was absolutely crucial; but it was crucial within a dialectical, two-sided relationship, not in a command-and-follow sense.

The emergence of a real national leadership during 1996-97 happened against a background of growing social and political tensions. The final battle against the Kohl government began.

After an electoral victory of the conservatives in Hesse, the bosses pressed for a sharp offensive against the unions. Kohl introduced the 'Sparpaket', a package of severe cuts in the welfare system. It was the beginning of the end of Kohl's rule. It also created a tide that brought a real rise of Linksruck.

Already in May 1996 the trade unions had organised a number of demonstrations. When the decision about the 'Sparpaket' drew closer, a national demonstration took place in Bonn on 15 June. When the national demonstration took place Linksruck had already started to grow. On 15 June itself we fought our first battle as a national organisation.

While 350,000 workers took to the streets of Bonn, Linksruck managed to mobilise 450 members and sympathisers. In an exhausting operation reaching a logistics level unknown to that point, we sold 2,000 papers calling for mass strikes against the cuts package on our front page.

We had started to get into contact with workers. What we had experienced before the Bonn demonstration led to big debates at all levels of the organisation, about the character of the current situation.

The intensifying class struggle, the crisis of reformist politics, and the development of a new generation of activists were now rooted in the organisation's approach.

While all this happened, we still were seen or saw ourselves as Jusos, now calling ourselves the 'revolutionary current inside Jusos'. But with every successful step in the outside world we put more weight on our independent leg as Linksruck and less on the Juso-leg.

This was also forced from the other side, as the Juso bureaucracy felt increasingly unhappy about Linksruck. The fact that Jusos had a national decision that banned Linksruck from student branches made it necessary to set up Linksruck structures there. In financial terms Linksruck had always been independent from Jusos.

After the crisis over summer 1996 Linksruck started to experience a real rise. The 'Sparpaket', which could not be stopped in parliament, provoked massive social unrest in October, as the employers tried to reduce sick pay. After a three day strike by IG Metall in the Daimler factories in Stuttgart, the employers' offensive was repulsed.

From that time on the Kohl government was paralysed. It was too weak to push through any substantial cuts. Every right wing offensive was met by confident and angry resistance. Steel workers, construction workers and miners took strike action in the course of 1997. A Nazi demonstration in Munich on 1 March was stopped by 25,000 blocking the road; tens of thousands tried to stop nuclear transport.

Linksruck was part of every struggle we could reach. The introduction of Linksruck placards on every demonstration made us the most visible left wing organisation. But learning from our inability to retain of the summer campaign of 1996, we had a much closer look at the working of our branches. A series of national rallies marking the 80th anniversary of the October Revolution in late 1997 made the branches fit for the influx of new members. We published John Rees's *In Defence of October* in German and sold 500 copies.

Growth was shown by the fact that the print order of the paper soared, from an initial 300 to 3,500. The membership reached some 500 after the October rallies in November 1997. New opportunities came soon after. In the winter term 1997-98 the biggest student strike in German history erupted. Beginning in the small town of Giessen, the movement spread within weeks across Germany. Tens of thousands of students demonstrated.

Linksruck was not especially strong in the universities. But we had a centralised organisation, mainly school students still, that we could throw into the universities, and at least the beginnings of student work.

What followed within the next half year was a real rise of Linksruck. The student strikes made us by far the most visible revolutionary organisation. In a number of places comrades could play a crucial role in the strikes. And when several thousand students stormed the 'banned mile' around the Bonn Bundestag at a national demonstration in early 1998, they carried a forest of Linksruck placards.

We raised the slogan 'Millionäre besteuern' ('Tax the millionaires') and developed a profile of being oriented on the social question and the working class. We recruited some 85 during the strikes. Another series of rallies followed the end of the strike, on 'Is Marxism still Relevant?' which pulled 750 people nationally. Linksruck continued to grow when the 'Rosa-Luxemburg Tage' (Rosa Luxemburg Day—similar to the SWP's Marxism school) came closer and we managed to get 940 people to the event in Frankfurt, recruiting 100 within the four days of the congress. After the Rosa-Luxemburg-Tage 98 Linksruck had 800 members, the print order of the paper reached 5,000, and the cadre on a local level got much more confident.

To sum up, when the Linksruck Project started there were five members of Linksruck and on paper 200 in the SAG. Five years later, in May 1999, Linksruck reached 1,075 members. The circulation of the paper rose from 300 in 1994 to 6,000 in 1999. The national leadership grew from one man leadership in the person of Ahmed Shah to a centre with 15 people in it, a number of them working full time. The publishing house is able to publish mammoth works like Chris Harman's 400 pager, *The Lost Revolution: Germany 1918-23*.

A look at the list of branches reveals more about the real changes. The SAG never had more than one branch in one town. Linksruck today has five branches in each of Hamburg, Munich and Frankfurt, four in Berlin and two in Freiburg and Cologne—not including the university branches. This alone demonstrates the development of a confident national cadre. The social composition of the organisation is also transformed. Being a school students only group in the beginning, among the delegates to our 1999 conference were 44 percent students and 14 percent workers.

In a way the success of Linksruck made me even more frustrated for not having a passport. If I had one I could have gone, for example, to Paris for a couple of days every month. Over a period of five or six months I might have been able to help our French comrades; the cost of travelling between London and Paris is more or less the same as between London and Glasgow.

I have to control myself to avoid turning into a cantankerous old man.

'Neither Washington nor Moscow but international socialism'

That was the slogan that summed up our organisational position throughout our existence from its beginning in 1950. For a long time it served to guide activity mainly in Britain for the SWP. But now it can come into its own more generally.

The year 1989 witnessed the most massive earthquake of the social and political order in Eastern Europe. It was on a scale reminiscent of 1848 and 1917.

Practically everybody saw in the collapse of the Stalinist regime the end of socialism. The capitalist press always identified Russia with socialism, with communism. In parallel, the whole left did the same. It was not only the Stalinist parties, but the Labour left in Britain. Even 'orthodox' Trotskyists saw Stalinism as a transitional formation between capitalism and socialism.

In August 1989 the celebrated Francis Fukuyama, adviser to the US State Department, declared that the fall of the Soviet bloc meant 'the end of history' and 'the unabashed victory of economic and political liberalism'. At last the American dream was being realised. Alas, before the ink on Fukuyama's article was dry, history showed itself alive and kicking.

First of all, US and British imperialism and their allies and satellites started bombing Iraq. Saddam Hussein, the tyrant created by US and British imperialism, was now their target. In 1963 Saddam Hussein's Ba'ath Party carried out a coup against Abdul Kassim, the man who, in 1958, got rid of the monarchy imposed by the British. The coup led to the massacre of some 30,000 Communists. In 1974 Saddam Hussein launched a war on the Kurds in the north of the country, a war that continues to this day. When he turned his chemical weapons on Kurdish villages, the Western press largely ignored this. In February 1977 his army massacred Shi'ite Muslims in the south of the country. In 1980 Saddam Hussein sent his army over the Iranian border and launched the Gulf War. Through eight years of this war the US and Britain backed Saddam.

In 1990 the Frankenstein they had created started acting in a way that threatened the interests of the master: he sent his army to occupy Kuwait and thus threaten Western oil interests. A massive US-led attack on Iraq followed. It seems neither Saddam Hussein, nor the president of the US, nor the prime minister of Britain, had read Francis Fukuyama.

Fukuyama promised us not only a world free of war, but also free of economic crises. Sadly the movers and shakers of world capitalism did not read this part of Fukuyama's essay either. A long world recession started shortly after it was published. And of course, since August 1998 even worse has happened: the collapse of the Asian economic tigers, so admired and praised two years before by Tony Blair and Peter Mandelson; the collapse of the Russian economy, and the long recession in the second biggest economy in the world—Japan.

But Fukuyama and other spokesmen of world capitalism were not the only ones declaring that 1989 was the end of socialism and communism. In February 1990 Eric Hobsbawm, the guru of the British Communist Party for decades, was questioned: 'In the Soviet Union it looks as though the workers are overthrowing the workers' state.' Hobsbawm replied, 'It obviously wasn't a workers' state, nobody in the Soviet Union ever believed it was a workers' state, and the workers knew it wasn't a workers' state'.[12] Why didn't Hobsbawm tell us this 50 or even 20 years ago?

Nina Temple, general secretary of the British Communist Party, said around the same time, 'I think the SWP was right, the Trotskyists were right that it was not socialism in Eastern Europe. And I think we should have said so long ago.' Reading Nina Temple's statement, one can only wonder what would have happened if the pope declared that god does not exist? How would the Catholic church survive?

Now, I do not know if the pope really believes in god, but we know for a fact that the leader of the largest Communist Party in the West—Massimo d'Alema, prime minister of Italy and general secretary of the the Communist Party of Italy, now calling itself the Party of the Democratic Left (PDS)—is full of admiration for the pope. On 8 January 1999 he had an audience with the pope in Vatican City. Reuters reported, 'He addressed the pope as "Holy Father", and bowed respectfully before the leader of the world's one billion Catholics... D'Alema, who is accustomed to leading some of the largest rallies in Europe, later acknowledged that he had felt small and nervous in front of the pope. "I must admit that I felt a great emotion. I arrived feeling extremely tense but this tension melted right away thanks to the Holy Father's extraordinary capacity to engage in direct, human

221

contact," D'Alema told reporters'.[13] And this is said about Pope John Paul, who covered up the collaboration of the Catholic church with Nazi Germany during the war when the extermination of the Jews took place! Massimo D'Alema's behaviour and the words of Hobsbawm and Temple are a clear demonstration of the complete collapse of the ideology of Stalinism.

Throughout the world social democratic parties were also shattered by the events in Eastern Europe. Along with them, the left centrists as well as the orthodox Trotskyists, saw Russia as communist, socialist, or at least having some elements of these systems.

In contrast to all these currents, those of us who declared Russia to be state capitalist long before the collapse of the Stalinist regime established a bridgehead to the future and preserved the authentic tradition of Marxism, of socialism from below.

Of course, it would have been easier to go with the stream. The prevailing ideas are influenced by capitalism, and only in a revolutionary crisis do our ideas gain mass backing. But only by building and organising the minority who understand capitalism and who want to fight it, can a successful outcome to that revolutionary crisis be achieved. We have seen many times (for example in Spain 1936-39, Chile 1973, or Portugal 1974) that without a revolutionary party capitalism recovers from a revolutionary crisis and reimposes its regime of exploitation.

In conclusion

Political biographies achieve success to the extent that they show the continuity and change between the beginning of the story and its end. There is huge dissimilarity, but at the same time a continuity between my rebellion at the age of 14 against the fact that Arab kids were not in my class, and my attitude to national and social oppression in the 1990s.

Only with death does change stop. Of course, an individual group can die intellectually while physically still existing. This is the fate of all dogmatic sects whose point of honour is what distinguishes them from others. In contrast, as Marx put it, the communist emphasises what is common between him and the mass movement. The other side of the coin to sectarianism is opportunism, adapting to the level of the movement, without in any way helping it to step forward.

The real difficulty for a political biography is to know where to stop. When I wrote my biographies of Lenin and Trotsky, it was obvious where to stop—with their deaths. Although Lenin never dreamt of writing an autobiography, his *Collected Works* are a summing up of the actions and thoughts of his entire political life. But an autobiography cannot end with the death of the author. Again, if the biography is part of a polemic to defend an individual against slander, there is also a natural point where the biography can stop. Trotsky was forced to write his autobiography, *My Life*, because of the massive slander campaign of the Stalinists.

This autobiography is not motivated by the same considerations. It tries to show the continuity and change over six decades of revolutionary activity, which involved me in a massive variety of situations, even in terms of the different countries in which I was active.

When I became a Trotskyist, Trotskyism was a tiny fringe group while Stalinism looked omnipotent. Today the space for us is wide open, and Stalinism is in the process of disintegration, if not death. Had I ended the book in 1974, when the curve of struggle was rising sharply, the whole book would have had a clear climax: UCS and 200 factory occupations, the Pentonville Five freed by a national strike of dockers, Fleet Street and engineers, the miners' national strike breaking the Incomes Policy and bringing down the Tory government. Had I ended the book in 1985, straight after the catastrophic defeat of the miners, the picture would again have been clear.

Alas, at present we are in a very complicated situation. Lenin's most important writings were located during times of the ebb and flow of class struggle, and that was also our main theme: (1) describe and analyse the objective situation; (2) what is to be done by the class facing this situation; (3) what the revolutionaries should do when for them the object is not only the economic, social and political conditions at the time, but also the consciousness and organisation of the workers of the time.

If you read our writings, let us say in 1972, they were largely about what was to be done. To repeat the same in 1985 would not have been good enough. At that time there were different needs. Of course it was necessary to explain what action was necessary to win victory for the miners in 1984-85. But no less important was to answer the question why that action did not take place. Putting the right slogan is not enough. It frustrates the revolutionaries, because they say, 'We did everything correctly. We analysed the situation correctly. We put forward the right slogans.' But one must never forget that it is not only important what the slogans are but whether they are acted upon. The number of times the Workers Revolutionary Party and its predecessors called for a general strike is astonishing. But it never managed to relate to actual strikes which are much smaller in scale and under the influence of the trade union bureaucracy.

This same need for understanding reality in all its complexity rather than as a dry abstraction applies to the relationship between the rank and file of the unions and the union bureaucracy. Even here there is not a clear cut abyss. There is a difference, but there is also a bridge between them.

What about the full time factory convenor? Of course he is much closer to the rank and file than the general secretary of the union, whose job is guaranteed for life. But he is still a transmission belt between the bureaucracy and the rank and file. Many shop stewards who work on the job are still quite often influenced by a bureaucratic attitude—substitution for the rank and file, mistrust of the rank and file. Their experience seems to indicate to them that the majority of workers are passive. I have heard the same refrain thousands of times: 'You don't know my workers. They are so apathetic. They are so selfish.' I have never heard anyone saying to me, 'You don't know me. I am so apathetic. I am so selfish.' Apathy is widespread. But its meaning is not without ambiguity. It can be the result of workers being so happy with their lot that they say to themselves, 'I'm alright, Jack.' Apathy can also be the result of exactly the opposite—a feeling of powerlessness. 'I'm so powerless that nothing can be done about it.' For while Lord Acton wrote, 'Power corrupts, and absolute power corrupts absolutely,' I believe a more correct statement would be, 'Power corrupts, but lack of power corrupts absolutely. I can do nothing to change my circumstances, so I capitulate to apathy.'

Because we are not in the glorious days of the 1970s, nor are we under the hammer-blows of Thatcherism, the situation is much more complicated, and how it will turn out no one can now predict. We need an analysis of the objective situation internationally and nationally. We have to put forward correct slogans, that fit the situation. At the same time we have to explain again and again the role of the trade union bureaucracy and the Labour leadership in preventing the action. This by itself is not enough, because it can become an excuse for passivity. We also need to propose the different levels of activity that are possible connected with the general slogans we put forward. After looking at the big picture of the economic basis of society, one has to look at the superstructure—the political relations, and finally the ideological situation.

The Blair government has created a wide space for us. Blair is so far to the right of Labour supporters as to make millions of them very critical and angry with his kowtowing to the fat cats, his attacks on single mothers, the disabled and students, and his measly minimum wage for low paid workers. There are great opportunities to recruit to the SWP, and the reports we get on recruitment at present are very encouraging indeed. What is needed is to carry on the ideological battle against the market, against capitalism, to sharpen the arguments in defence of revolutionary change as against the failure of the reformists who capitulate to capitalism at every turn. But we have to walk on both legs, projecting the big picture in the ideological battle, and to relate to every workers' struggle, however small.

The contradiction in the economic basis of society reflects itself in contradictions in the ideas of working people. Under 'normal' conditions, workers' thinking is full of contradictions. Workers take it as 'common sense' that profits are necessary; if there is no profit there are no jobs. Side by side with this conflict there is another one. 'Yes, of course profits are alright, but my boss is a greedy pig. His profits are too high, and our wages are too low. It is common sense that the boss has the right to hire and fire, but the insecurity in our workplace really makes me angry.' Workers can, at one and the same time, accept capitalism and reject the workings of the system in practice.

If one simply argues against capitalism without relating to workers who resist the bosses but accept the system as 'common sense' one is bound to be abstentionist and irrelevant.

If one relates to the workers' resistance to the bosses without making a basic criticism of capitalism, one is trapped in 'economism' and opportunism. There is a very thin line between the two deviations. A revolutionary should not say, 'We must choose between action and argument.' On the contrary, we need to combine action and argument. In the final analysis the contradictions in the grey matter, in the worker's brain, are subordinate to the contradictions in the material world.

After looking at every aspect of society, at the big picture, one cannot stop there, because that can lead to complete passivity, making us simply commentators on events. One has to locate every struggle in the big picture, but to relate to every struggle.

I have been a Marxist, Leninist, Trotskyist, for the last 66 years. Marxism did not stop developing with the death of Marx in 1883, or the death of Rosa Luxemburg in 1919, or the death of Lenin in 1924, or the death of Trotsky in 1940. Marxism generalised from the historical and international experience of the working class, and this experience is cumulative.

In approaching any issue as a Marxist one has to combine a general theory that is the summing up of experience hitherto with the immediate problem we face. Throughout my political life I tried to be consistent about this. I mentioned that the first serious essay I wrote in 1935 was on the agrarian question in Egypt. During the work on this essay, I had on my table a lot of data about the actual situation in the countryside in Egypt at the time and all the writings of Lenin on the agrarian question in tsarist Russia. Had I looked at only one of these two things, I would have been in trouble. The data itself can lead to eclecticism and impressionism. Reading Lenin on the agrarian question by itself is not enough to understand what happened in Egypt. When Lenin wrote his *Development of Capitalism in Russia* in the 1890s, tsarist Russia was very different to Egypt in the 1930s. The combination of the empirical data with the general theory made it possible to criticise myself and find out where any mistakes I may have committed lay.

Another chapter in my political development was the theory of state capitalism. Here again I used the same method. I collected a great amount of factual material about the state of the Russia economy, society and politics, together with the Marxist classics on the nature of the workers' state, the laws of motion of socialist economy vis-à-vis those of capitalist economy, etc. It was not enough to simply read the classics alone, although this was absolutely vital. It was not only amassing statistics, which was also vital. The first would have led to completely abstract Marxism, the second to being lost in a welter of detail. When one navigates the way through a thick forest, one needs not only a good compass and map but good eyesight to see around. Without a compass and a map one will be lost in the forest. But compass and map by themselves do not carry you through to the other side of the forest.

Again, when it came to the theory of the deflected permanent revolution, although the pamphlet is a very short one (38 pages), it took me some four years to develop it. I spent 40 to 50 hours a week reading translations from the Chinese daily press, at the same time as reading and re-reading Trotsky's writings on the permanent revolution, his writings on China during the 1925-27 revolution and his subsequent writings in the 1930s, plus the marvellous book of Harold Isaacs, *The Tragedy of the Chinese Revolution*. The result of my four years of research was my voluminous book *Mao's China*, published in 1957, of which the pamphlet is a distillation.

It is a caricature of Marxism to think that it develops with simply an interpretation and reinterpretation of the Marxist classics. I remember a short story by Heinrich Heine entitled *The Dream of Professor Marx*. Heine did not refer to Karl Marx, because at the time he wrote this story Karl was still at kindergarten. What is the dream of Professor Marx? He sees a garden, but in the garden it was not flowers that were growing, but quotations. And what a joy it was to take quotations from one bed in the garden and plant them in another bed in the garden! This is not the real meaning of Marxism.

I believe that in the various chapters of my political activity I have tried to be consistent in using the Marxist method. Of course I made mistakes, but it is better to be right in principle, even if mistakes are made in the specific, than the other way round. A blind hen sometimes picks up a piece of grain. A sighted hen will make mistakes and pick up a small stone, but there is no doubt the second will flourish compared with the first. If you make tactical mistakes but your general approach is right, you can correct the mistakes. On the other hand, if you are right on specific tactics, but your general approach is wrong, you are bound to get into a greater and greater mess.

Looking back at my activities since I came to Britain, I have quite some satisfaction with the outcome. This sounds arrogant, but I have to tell things as I believe they are. Marx wrote, 'Communists never tell lies to the class.'

If in the 1950s I, or Chanie, were run over by the proverbial bus, our group would probably have ceased to exist. Now, with thousands of members in the SWP, the party will survive even if a catastrophe took place in the outside world and we suffered. Let us look back at the history of the Bolshevik Party.

The total number of Bolsheviks in 1907 was 46,143.[14] In the

Moscow district, in mid-May 1906, there were 5,320 Bolsheviks. Alas, the bloody reaction decimated the party. By mid-1908 the Moscow membership had dropped to 250, and six months later it was 150. In 1910 the organisation ceased to exist, when the district secretary's job fell into the hands of one Kukushkin, an agent of the Okhrana, the secret police.

In May 1911 Lenin wrote:

> At present the real position of the party is such that almost everywhere in the localities there are informal, extremely small and tiny party workers' groups and nuclei that meet regularly. They are not connected with each other. Very rarely do they see any literature.[15]

But Bolshevism still survived, and after the massacre of gold miners in Lena on 4 April 1912 there was a massive revival of the labour movement. Six thousand miners were on strike in the Lena goldfields, which were situated in a region of taiga forests almost 2,000 kilometres from the Siberian railway. An officer of the gendarmerie ordered the unarmed crowd to be fired on, and 500 people were either killed or wounded. In August 1913 Lenin estimated party membership as something between 30,000 and 50,000.[16] However, this was probably an exaggeration.

Even if we face a catastrophe as terrible as the Russian workers faced in 1906, the SWP will survive. Not only is our number far greater than in the first decade of our existence, but the quality of the cadres, steeled and tried, is far superior to those we had when we started.

The story of our past is quite important for British revolutionaries, but even more so for revolutionaries abroad in groups that are quite small. If they face reality, if they persevere, and never deceive themselves or anyone else, they are bound to succeed, because we do live in the age of revolutions.

If the reader of the present book learns something about the Marxist method, and it encourages the reader to face new problems, then I am more than satisfied.

Studying Marxist theory and developing it is motivated by the urge to change society. There is a dialectical unity between the theory and practice of building a Marxist revolutionary party. James Connolly, the great Irish revolutionary socialist, said that the only prophets today were those who shape the future. And the future does not start in the next century, in the next decade or the next year. It starts here and now.

Socialism or barbarism

I became a revolutionary in my early teens. Now, nearly 70 years later, my condition has not changed except that my convictions have deepened and strengthened. We live in a world afflicted by famines and wars. Terrible poverty in the midst of plenty. Hell on earth, while Paradise on earth is potentially possible. The three richest individuals in the world own as much wealth as the annual income of 600 million people, or the 43 poorest countries. Twenty million children, it is estimated, die annually because of lack of clean water. The profits of Bill Gates in one year would be enough to establish pipes and wells to guarantee a supply of clean water for everybody in the world.

When I became a socialist I was convinced that the arguments for socialism were so obvious, so compelling, that it would take a very short time to convince the overwhelming majority of humanity to become socialists. And if the millions of us spat together at the tiny minority of parasites we would flood them away. Over the years, by studying history, it became clear to me that the story is not as simple as that. The transition from one society to another is very difficult and moves along a rough road.

Reading a book about the transition from feudalism to capitalism could take half an hour or an hour; in actuality it took many centuries. There were centuries between the Renaissance and the French Revolution. History does not just go forward. The ideological advance of the Reformation was followed by the massively destructive Thirty Years War (1618-48). Humanity takes two steps forward and one step back, and sometimes one step forward and two steps back. Germany at the time of Luther and Münzer was more advanced than after the Thirty Years War when nearly half the population perished. And the Spain of the 11th century was more advanced than the Spain of half a millennium later.

We live in a century of wars and revolutions. In the present century the US alone has engaged in nearly 100 wars, large and small.

During the time I have been writing this book a typical example has occurred. NATO, led by US imperialism, launched a war against Yugoslavia. To justify this attack Slobodan Milosevic was described as a present day Adolf Hitler, forgetting some small differences. Through the last few years massive demonstrations took place against Milosevic in Yugoslavia, even during the weeks of the war itself. I do not remember anything similar in Nazi Germany. Hitler headed Germany, the second greatest industrial power in the world, and a massive military force that occupied practically the whole of Europe. Milosevich could not impose his will even on the small nations of Yugoslavia that rebelled against Serbia—Croatia, Slovenia, Bosnia and Macedonia. The military budget of Serbia is equal to only 1 percent of that of the US, or half of 1 percent of the 19 NATO allies. And here we see the shark of US led imperialism declaring, 'Look at that sardine. He threatens me!'

The excuse for the war on Serbia was the latter's persecution of the Albanians in Kosovo. This persecution was abominable. However, it pales besides the persecution of the Kurds in Turkey, and of the Palestinians by Israel. And in these cases the US, Britain and the rest of NATO have not lifted a finger in support of the persecuted. Some 400 to 500 Albanian villages in Kosovo, inhabited by 800,000 Albanians, were destroyed. As against this 4,000 Kurdish villages in south east Turkey have been razed to the ground and four million of its population made into refugees. A few hundred Albanians in Kosovo were murdered by the Serbs. More than 30,000 Kurds were murdered by the Turkish army. The number of Palestinian refugees surpasses three million. Neither Kurdish nor Palestinian refugees ever appear on British or American television. The Kurds and the Palestinians are invisible people. No crime committed by allies (or should we say lackeys) of the US is mentioned. Fifteen years ago the mass removal of the Kurds from south east Turkey took place, and 50 years ago a similar fate was suffered by the Palestinians. The world media have not yet managed to catch up with these events.

In addition to wars in which the imperialist powers play a direct role, there are innumerable local wars in the Third World in which imperialism does not play a direct role. These are wars between countries, or between tribes in countries, or civil wars which are a combination of these. To mention just a few: the war between Tutsis and Hutus in Rwanda; the war in and around the Democratic Republic of Congo; the long civil war in Sudan between the Muslims in the north and the Christians of the south; the 25 year civil war in Angola between the MPLA and Unita; the war of Morocco with the Polisarios; the civil war in Sierra Leone; the war between Ethiopia and Eritrea, as well as the numerous battles between India and Pakistan in Kashmir. The fact that imperialist armies are not directly involved in these wars does not mean that imperialism does not play a crucial role in them. The crisis of world capitalism, the activities of the multinational companies as well as the international financial institutions like the IMF and the World Bank, increase the burden on the countries of the Third World, deepening the economic, social and political crises in these countries, pushing them into sharp conflicts with their neighbours, as well as within individual countries, leading to national and tribal conflicts. Arms are produced in the advanced countries and supplied to the Third World for a price. Side by side with modern machine guns, the old methods of warfare continue. And so we see the mass expansion of the use of machetes. Victims of machine guns join with many amputees.

The only alternative to capitalist barbarism is the socialist revolution. The 20th century has witnessed many revolutions. Alas, the overwhelming majority of them did not culminate in victory. Of all the revolutions in the 20th century only that in Russia was victorious. Proletarian revolutions do not break free from the shackles of the past at one go. Side by side with the new, representing the future, the old still survives. To use Marx's words: 'The tradition of the dead generations' still hangs over the living.'

The February 1917 Revolution in Russia created an exciting new situation: the Tsar abdicated; centuries of the monarchy ended. The police were disbanded. In every factory workers' committees were established. In many army units soldiers' committees came into being. Soviets of workers and soldiers arose everywhere.

But after the revolution in February, parallel to the soviets, the old institutions continued. In the factories the old owners and managers continued to hold their positions. In the army the generals were still in command; the Commander in Chief of the army was General Kornilov who was appointed by the Tsar. Parallel to soviet power was a bourgeois government headed by a liberal politician from tsarist times. This situation, which Lenin and Trotsky called 'dual power', was full of contradictions.

Notwithstanding the nature of the soviet, its leaders begged the bourgeoisie to retain power. The majority of the Petrograd soviet delegates were right wing socialists—Mensheviks and Social Revolutionaries.

Out of 1,500 to 1,600 delegates only 40 were Bolsheviks. This was not an accident. It was the inevitable outcome of a situation in which millions of people moved to the left but still carried a lot of the ideological baggage of a tsarist past. For millions who had hitherto supported the Tsar and the war, a move to the left did not mean straight away joining the most extreme of the parties—the Bolsheviks. The strong man of the Mensheviks, J G Tseretelli, who became Minister of the Interior in the bourgeois Provisional Government, explained the necessity of compromise with the bourgeoisie: 'There can be no other road for the revolution. It's true that we have all the power, and that the government would go if we lifted a finger, but that would mean disaster for the revolution.'

It was only after days, weeks and months of stormy events that the Bolsheviks managed to win over the majority of workers. On 9 September the Petrograd soviet went over to Bolshevism and Trotsky was elected as its president. On the same day the Bolsheviks won the majority of the Moscow soviet. From this point it was only a small stride towards the attainment of workers' power on 7 November 1917.

In contrast to the Russian Revolution of 1917 the German Revolution of 1918 got stuck midway. In November 1918 the revolution in Germany got rid of the Kaiser and brought the First World War to an end. Alas, big employers like Krupps and Thyssen remained along with the generals and the reactionary army officers who set up right wing units called Freikorps. As in Russia, dual power prevailed in Germany, for side by side with parliament were the workers' councils. Under the umbrella of the German social democratic government, Freikorps officers murdered the revolutionary leaders Rosa Luxemburg and Karl Liebknecht. The revolutionary events continued with ups and downs until 1923, but they ended with the victory of capitalism. The Nazi movement was born in 1919. Although its 1923 coup in Bavaria failed, the fact that the workers had missed opportunities in the revolution meant they would pay dearly when Hitler came to power in 1933.

The events in Germany after 1918 completely confirm the prophetic words of St Just, a leader of the French Revolution of 1789: 'Those who half make a revolution dig their own grave.'

Another example of a missed opportunity was seen in France in the 1930s and has been alluded to above. Here there was a massive rise of working class struggle which started in February 1934 and culminated in 1936 in a decisive victory for the Popular Front—an alliance of the Communist Party, the Socialist Party and the Liberals (who were mistakenly called Radical Socialists—they were neither radical nor socialist). Millions of workers said to themselves, 'Now we own the government, let's take over the factories.' And in June 1936 a wave of factory occupations took place. The leaders of the Communist Party and Socialist Party, however, led a retreat following a compromise with the employers. After this the Communist Party was thrown out of the Popular Front. It was the Radical Socialist, Daladier, who signed the Munich agreement with Hitler in 1938. It was the same parliament elected in the great Popular Front victory of 1936 which voted support for Marshal Pétain, head of the Vichy regime which collaborated with the Nazis from 1940 onwards.

There are other examples to learn from. When Indonesia won its independence from the Dutch in 1949 the country was led by the bourgeois nationalist Ahmed Sukarno. His ideology was based on the principles of Pancasila whose main planks were belief in god and national unity. Tragically the Indonesian Communist Party did not challenge Sukarno, but, on the contrary, agreed with him completely on the need for national unity. The result was that St Just's words came true. The Communist Party of Indonesia had far more members than the Bolshevik Party had at the time of the 1917 Revolution: three million as against a quarter of a million. The working class of Indonesia as well as the peasantry were more numerous than in Russia. In 1965 a general appointed by Sukarno, one Suharto, organised a coup with the backing of the US, the British Labour government and Australia. Somewhere between half a million and a million people were slaughtered.

The Middle East is another area which has seen great upheavals which shook the establishment but failed to win a fundamental breakthrough. In Iraq, King Feisal was overthrown in 1951 by a mass movement. The Communist Party of Iraq was a very strong party, indeed the strongest CP in the Arab world. It entered into an alliance with the bourgeois nationalist party, the Ba'ath Party. The Communist Party, under Stalinist control, believed that the coming revolution would be a democratic one, which demanded an alliance between the working class and the bourgeois parties. Such an alliance means in practice the subordination of the former to the latter. The Communist Party members and workers paid heavily for this alliance. The

Ba'ath Party, headed by General Saddam Hussein, with the aid of the CIA, carried out a mass slaughter of Communists.

In Iran a general strike led to the overthrow of the Shah in 1979. Shoras (workers' councils) mushroomed throughout the country. Tragically the leadership of these shoras, largely the pro-Moscow Tudeh Party and the Fedayeen, saw the way forward as a bourgeois democratic revolution instead of a proletarian one, and so gave support to the establishment of the Islamic republic. Ayatollah Khomeini came to power without showing any gratitude to the Tudeh or Fedayeen, and the left was subjected to bloody repression. One could mention other failed revolutions, such as Hungary in 1919 and 1956, Germany 1923, China 1925-27, Spain 1936 and Portugal 1974-75.

The working class, not the party, makes the revolution, but the party guides the working class. As Trotsky aptly wrote, 'Without a guiding organisation the energy of the masses would dissipate like steam not enclosed in a piston box. But nevertheless what moves things is not the piston or the box, but the steam'.[17]

The difference between success and failure, between Russia in October 1917 and the other workers' revolutions, was that in the former case there was a mass revolutionary party providing effective leadership. While socialists cannot determine the moment when the revolutionary crisis breaks, they do determine the eventual outcome by the degree to which they build a strong revolutionary party.

Cato the Elder, a member of the Roman Senate, used to end all his speeches with the following words: 'Cartago delenda est'—Carthage must be destroyed. And finally Rome did destroy Carthage. We have to end with the words, 'The revolutionary party must be built.'

Notes

Chapter One

1   V I Lenin, *Collected Works*, vol 11 (Moscow), pp334-335.
2   *Jewish Labour*, a collection of articles and speeches published by the Histadrut in Hebrew (Tel Aviv, 1935), p53.
3   *From We and Our Neighbours, Speeches and Essays* (Tel Aviv, 1931), in Hebrew.
4   Ibid.
5   Ibid.
6   Ibid.
7   *The War Front of the Jewish People*, in Hebrew.
8   *The Guardian*, 26 March 1999.
9   *A Liwa*, 1 June 1936.
10   Yu Haikal, *The Palestine Problem* (Jaffa), in Arabic, pp215-216, 219.
11   M Magannan, *The Arab Woman and the Palestine Problem* (1937), in Arabic, pp217-218.
12   See, for instance, *Falastin*, 4 February 1937.
13   T Cliff, *Lenin*, vol 4 (London, 1979), pp10-11.
14   *Kol Ha'am* (Hebrew organ of the Palestine Communist Party), June 1940.
15   *Kol Ha'am*, December 1942.
16   *Kol Ha'am*, July 1940.
17   *Al-Ittihad* (organ of the Arab Stalinists in Palestine), 3 September 1944.
18   F Engels, *The Origin of the Family, Private Property and the State* (Peking, 1978), p190.
19   A Cohen, *The Contemporary Arab World* (Tel Aviv, 1960), in Hebrew, pp168-169.
20   The following is a list of key struggles in Egypt in the 1980s and 1990s:

    1984: Most of the 26,000 workers at Misr Fine Spinning and Weaving Company in Kafr al-Dawwar occupy for democratisation of the (state-run) union. Massive local solidarity and three-day 'uprising'. Riot police stormed the factory— three dead, 220 arrested.

    1986: Mahalla al Kubra strike: 25,000 workers on strike. They led mass demonstrations through the city. Hundreds were arrested.

    1986: Railway strike: major national dispute paralysing the whole network for three days, in which 10,000 workers participated. Hundreds were arrested for leading an illegal strike.

    1986: All 17,000 at Esco textile mill in Shubra al-Khayma (north Cairo), of whom one third are women, occupy in pay struggle. Riot police storm the factory but most demands are met.

    1989: 27,000 workers at Helwan steel works occupy the plant for two weeks over pay and union democratisation. Senior management taken hostage. Riot police storm plant: one killed, 700 arrested.

1994: 25,000 workers in strike and occupation of Kafr al-Dawwar mill. Mass demonstrations in city surround the mill. Four killed, hundreds arrested.

1998: 5,000 workers of Gianaclis winery and fruit processing plant (in the Delta) strike and occupy in opposition to privatisation. Owner taken hostage and only freed after massive police intervention. Hundreds arrested.

1998: 15,000 silk textile workers in Helwan occupied the factory and led major demonstrations. The government shut the factory for 30 days.

(Thanks to Phil Marfleet for this information.)

Chapter two

1   *Fourth International*, April 1946.
2   *Fourth International*, June 1946.
3   This statement was made in November 1945. See J P Cannon, *The Struggle for Socialism in the 'American Century'* (New York, 1977), p200.
4   W Reisner (ed), *Documents of the Fourth International* (New York, 1973), p183.
5   *Fourth International*, June 1946.
6   Ibid.
7   *International Socialism* 1:12, Spring 1963.
8   T Cliff, 'Perspectives for the Permanent War Economy', *Socialist Review*, March 1957, reprinted in T Cliff, *Neither Washington Nor Moscow* (London, 1982), pp101-107.
9   T Cliff, 'Fifty Years a Revolutionary', *Socialist Review* 100, 1987, pp14-19.
10 A Crosland, *The Future of Socialism* (London, 1956), pp520-522.

Chapter three

1   K Marx, 'Thesis on Feuerbach', in K Marx and F Engels, *Collected Works*, vol 5 (Moscow), p5.
2   *British Industry Week*, 3 October 1967.
3   A very good history of our group up to 1979 was written by Ian Birchall and called *The Smallest Mass Party in the World*. The title is a quote of mine from the 1970s referring to the group. It was made up of three articles, two written in 1975 and published in *International Socialism* 1:76 and 1:77 the same year. The third, which took the story up to 1979, was written in 1981. In the introduction to the pamphlet Birchall commented, 'Readers may...notice certain discrepancies of style and perspective between the first two articles and the third.' He was right. The first two had a long gestation period, reflecting on the events years after they happened, while the third did not have this advantage, and hence suffered, I believe, from impressionism.
4   I Birchall, ibid, p5.
5   Ibid, p6.
6   V I Lenin, *Collected Works*, vol 5 (Moscow), pp22-23.
7   K Marx and F Engels, *The Communist Manifesto*.
8   *International Socialism*, Autumn 1960.
9   T Cliff, *State Capitalism in Russia* (London, 1988), p276.

10   I Deutscher, *Heretics and Renegades* (London, 1955), pp204-205.
11   I Deutscher, *The Prophet Outcast* (London, 1963), p419.
12   I Deutscher, *Russia After Stalin* (London, 1953), p173.
13   I Deutscher, *Stalin* (Oxford, 1949), p294.
14   Ibid, pp360-361.
15   *Universities and Left Review*, vol 1, no 1, p10.
16   I Deutscher, *The Prophet Unarmed* (Oxford, 1959), p462.
17   I Deutscher, *Heretics and Renegades*, op cit, p20.
18   Reprinted in T Cliff, *Neither Washington Nor Moscow*, op cit, pp166-191.

Chapter four

1   T Cliff and D Gluckstein, *The Labour Party: A Marxist History* (London, 1988), p279.
2   *The Observer*, 7 March 1966.
3   *The Economist*, 3 October 1964.
4   S Brittan, *The Treasury under the Tories 1951-1964* (London, 1965), p276.
5   M Stewart and R Winsbury, *An Incomes Policy for Labour*, Fabian Tract 350 (October 1963), p18.
6   *The Economist*, 5 June 1965.
7   *The Economist*, 4 September 1965.
8   See T Cliff and C Barker, *Incomes Policy, Legislation and Shop Stewards* (London, 1966), pp59-62.
9   Ibid, p136.
10   I Birchall, op cit, p10. Since long before Labour came to power, IS had taken a firm position of unconditional opposition to all incomes policy under capitalism. This position left it almost completely isolated from the rest of the left. For example, at a conference organised by the Institute for Workers' Control in April 1964, the two IS members present were the only people to take a position of all out opposition to incomes policy. Ibid, p9.
11   Ibid, p12.
12   L Trotsky, *The Intelligentsia and Socialism* (London, 1966), p12.
13   T Cliff and I Birchall, *France: The Struggle Goes On* (London, 1968), pp11-13.
14   C Harman, D Clark, A Sayers, R Kuper, M Shaw, *Education, Capitalism and the Student Revolt* (London, 1968), pp48-49.
15   D Widgery, *The Left in Britain, 1956-1968* (London, 1976), p310.
16   Ibid, p311.
17   Ibid, p313.
18   Ibid, p315.
19   I Birchall, op cit, p15.
20   D Widgery, op cit, p349. This leaflet was consistent with the publication by the SLL a couple of years earlier of the pamphlet by Trotsky we have referred to, *The Intelligentsia and Socialism*, op cit.
21   A Callinicos and S Turner, 'The Student Movement Today', *International Socialism* 1:75, p15.
22   I Birchall, op cit, p16.
23   Ibid, p15.

24   E McCann, *War and an Irish Town* (London, 1993), p32.
25   Ibid, p46.
26   Ibid, pp99-100.
27   Ibid, p106.
28   Ibid, p297
29   Ibid, p311.
30   Ibid, p312.
31   Ibid.
32   Ibid, preface.
33   T Cliff, *Neither Washington Nor Moscow*, op cit, p215.
34   T Cliff, *Lenin*, vol 1, op cit, p269.

Chapter five

1   A Callinicos, 'The Rank and File Movement Today', *International Socialism* 2:17 (Autumn 1982), pp20-21.
2   L Trotsky, *The History of the Russian Revolution* (London, 1977), p1130.
3   *Socialist Worker*, 5 August 1972.
4   *Socialist Worker*, 17 November 1973.
5   International Socialism, Internal Bulletin, p26.
6   Ibid, p13.
7   I Birchall, op cit, pp22-23, notes that a breakdown of the delegating bodies shows that there were 37 TGWU bodies. Eight of these were from bus garages, six of them in London and the direct result of the London Transport Platform. One year before we would not have received any of them. The work of *Hospital Worker* resulted in delegates from ten NUPE, four ASTMS, four COHSE, one GMWU and two TGWU branches.

Applications came in from 22 ATTI bodies, including two divisions; from 28 NALGO branches; 12 NUT bodies plus two EIS, including one district; and nine CPSA branches—all of them connected to the work of the white collar rank and file papers. Other white collar applications came from ASTMS, 23 including two divisional committees; from TASS, 17 including two divisions; and from four NUJ bodies—all unions in which our fractions were active.

Our growth of membership in engineering and motors and the sale of 9,000 copies of the 1973 engineering pay claim pamphlet was reflected in the splendid total of 51 applications, including two district committees, from the Engineering Section (AUEW). *Car Worker* would have had something to do with the 11 TGWU and 13 AUEW branches and the 12 shop stewards committees in the motor industry that applied. Indeed, in four of the 12 motor factories where shop stewards committees did apply for credentials we don't have any members. Another 23 factory shop stewards committees also applied for credentials, as did the Strachans occupation committee, and this total of 36 SSCs is, as modestly described by comrade Nagliatti in April, 'success indeed'!

In addition to the above, we received applications from six NUM bodies, seven UCATT and 12 bona fide print bodies. Nineteen trades councils also sent in for credentials.
8   *Socialist Worker*, 8 April 1972.

9   *Socialist Worker*, 5 August 1972.

10 *Socialist Worker*, 2 December 1972.

11 International Socialism, Internal Bulletin, Pre-Conference Issue, 1974, p14

12 Ibid, pp28-29.

13 Ibid, p51.

14 Ibid, pp54-55.

15 Ibid, p56.

16 Ibid, pp56-57.

17 Ibid, p16.

18 Ibid, p27.

19 Quoted in T Cliff, *The Employers' Offensive: Productivity Deals and How to Fight Them* (London, 1970), p45.

20 Quoted ibid, pp51-52.

21 Quoted ibid, pp51-52.

22 Ibid, p58.

23 Ibid, pp99-112.

24 Ibid, p205.

25 Ibid, p13.

Chapter six

1   See T Cliff and D Gluckstein, op cit, pp328-331.

2   T Cliff, 'The Balance of Class Forces Today', *International Socialism* 2:2, p5.

3   Ibid, p33.

4   T Cliff and D Gluckstein, op cit, p332.

5   T Cliff, 'The Balance of Class Forces Today', op cit, p12.

6   T Cliff, 'Patterns of Mass Strike', *International Socialism* 2:29, p48.

7   T Cliff, 'Patterns of Mass Strike', op cit, p14.

8   Ibid, p22.

9   V I Lenin, *Collected Works*, vol 11 (Moscow), p17.

10 Ibid, p130.

11 International Socialism, Internal Bulletin, Pre-Conference Issue, 1974, p49.

12 *Socialist Worker*, 3 December 1977.

13 SWP Internal Bulletin, January 1978, pp2-3.

14 SWP Internal Bulletin, May 1977, p3.

15 *Socialist Worker*, 6 March 1976.

16 *Socialist Worker*, 10 September 1977.

17 *Socialist Worker*, 17 June 1978.

18 *Socialist Worker*, 13 October 1979.

19 V I Lenin, *Collected Works*, vol 16 (Moscow), p32.

20 SWP Internal Bulletin, September 1976, p5.

21 V I Lenin, *Collected Works*, vol 31 (Moscow), p38.

22 SWP Conference 1984 Discussion Bulletin, no 1, p5.

23 T Cliff and D Gluckstein, op cit, p365.

24 A Bobroff, *The Bolsheviks and Working Women 1905-20*, Soviet Studies, October 1974.

25 A Balabanoff, *My Life as a Rebel* (Bloomington, 1973), pp132-133.

26   Ibid, p144.
27   *International Socialism* 2:13 (Summer 1981).
28   *International Socialism* 2:14 (Winter 1981).

Chapter seven

1   T Cliff, *Lenin*, vol 1, op cit, p353.
2   T Cliff, *Lenin*, vol 1, op cit, p238.
3   *Socialist Worker*, 8 February 1975.
4   *Socialist Worker*, 24 September 1977.
5   'Where Do We Go From Here?', April 1978.
6   I Getzer, *Martov* (London, 1967), p110.
7   L Trotsky, *My Life*, p182.
8   Quoted in T Cliff and D Gluckstein, op cit, p313.
9   T Cliff and D Gluckstein, op cit, pp332-333.
10   C Rosenberg, 'Labour and the Fight against Fascism', *International Socialism* 2:39, p72.
11   Ibid, pp73-74.
12   Ibid, pp74-75.
13   Ibid, p75.
14   Ibid, pp75-76.
15   *Labour Party Annual Report 1977*, pp310-311.
16   Ibid, p314.
17   *Socialist Worker*, 4 October 1986.
18   *The Times*, 17 August 1977.
19   *Morning Star*, 17 August 1977.
20   C Rosenberg, op cit, pp77-78.
21   C Rosenberg, op cit, pp80-81.
22   *Socialist Worker*, 24 April 1979.
23   *Pravda*, Vienna, no 1, quoted in I Deutscher, *The Prophet Armed*, op cit, p193.
24   Much later, in 1984, Chris Harman, in an article, 'The Revolutionary Press', *International Socialism* 2:24 (Summer 1984), dealt in depth with the 1978 dispute on *Socialist Worker*, and concluded, rightly, that we were all wrong.
25   V I Lenin, *Collected Works*, vol 18 (Moscow), pp181-182.

Chapter eight

1   T Cliff, *Lenin*, vol 1, op cit, p256.
2   Ibid, pp66-68.
3   Ibid, p179.
4   Ibid, p170.
5   Ibid, pp255-256.
6   Ibid, p357.
7   Ibid, p358.
8   Ibid, p358.
9   T Cliff, *Trotsky*, vol 4 (London), p11.
10   L Trotsky, *Trotsky's Diary in Exile* (London, 1958), p66.

11   T Cliff, *Trotsky*, vol 4, op cit, pp215-216.
12   Ibid, p155.
13   Ibid, p223.
14   Ibid, p286.
15   Ibid, pp379-381.
16   Clyde Workers' Committee leaflet in the Beveridge Collection, British Library of Political and Economic Science, section 3, item 5.
17   L Trotsky, *Writings on Britain*, vol 2 (London, 1974), p191.
18   T Cliff and D Gluckstein, op cit, p2.

Chapter nine

1   *Tribune*, 30 January 1981.
2   *Militant*, 30 January 1981.
3   *Socialist Challenge*, 29 January 1981.
4   *Morning Star*, 26 January 1981.
5   T Cliff and D Gluckstein, op cit, pp372-373.
6   *The Guardian*, 23 June 1983.
7   *Socialist Worker*, 25 September 1982.
8   *Socialist Worker*, 8 October 1983.
9   *Militant*, 12 October 1985.
10   A Callinicos and M Simons, *The Great Strike* (London, 1985), p156.
11   Ibid, ch 4.
12   *Department of Employment Gazette*, July 1982, July 1983 and July 1984.

Chapter ten

1   L German, 'The Last Days of Thatcher?', *International Socialism* 2:48, Autumn 1990, pp21-22, 36.
2   T Cliff, *Neither Washington Nor Moscow*, op cit, p234.
3   L German, 'The Blair Project Cracks', *International Socialism* 2:82, p3.
4   It appeared in *International Socialism* 2:80, Autumn 1998.
5   *Socialist Worker*, 14 June 1975.
6   T Cliff, 'Portugal: The Great Danger', *Socialist Worker*, 18 October 1975.
7   V I Lenin, *Collected Works*, vol 5 (Moscow), pp525-526.
8   C Harman, *The Fire Last Time: 1968 and After* (London, 1998), p286.
9   V I Lenin, *Collected Works*, vol 8 (Moscow), pp409-410.
10   Quoted in T Cliff and C Harman, *Portugal: The Lessons of 25 November* (London, 1975). This pamphlet was published in Portuguese a couple of weeks before it was published in English.
11   C Harman, *The Fire Last Time*, op cit, pp302-303.
12   *Independent on Sunday*, 6 February 1990.
13   Reuters, 9 January 1999.
14   T Cliff, *Lenin*, vol 1, op cit, p179.
15   V I Lenin, *Collected Works*, vol 17 (Moscow), p202.
16   V I Lenin, *Collected Works*, vol 19 (Moscow), p406.
17   L Trotsky, *History of the Russian Revolution*, op cit, p19.

Index